DATE DUE			

Academic Libraries
by the Year 2000

Academic Libraries by the Year 2000

Essays Honoring Jerrold Orne

EDITED BY HERBERT POOLE

R. R. BOWKER COMPANY   New York & London, 1977

Published by R. R. Bowker Company
1180 Avenue of the Americas, New York, N.Y. 10036
Copyright © 1977 by Xerox Corporation
Printed and bound in the United States of America

Library of Congress Cataloging in Publication Data
Main entry under title:

Academic libraries by the year 2000.

  Includes index.
  CONTENTS: Poole, H. Jerrold Orne, a biography.—
Holley, E. G. What lies ahead for academic libraries?
—Hickey, D. D. The impact of instructional technology
on the future of academic librarianship.—Marshall,
A. P. This teaching/learning thing. [etc.]
  1. Libraries, university and college—Addresses,
essays, lectures. 2. Orne, Jerrold, 1911–
I. Orne, Jerrold, 1911–   II. Poole, Herbert,
1937–
Z675.U5A333   027.7   77-81880
ISBN 0-8352-0993-8

CONTENTS

PREFACE

This volume stems from a chance meeting that occurred in the early autumn of 1961 when I found myself refugeeing from the position of a scrub-nurse trainee in the university hospital in Chapel Hill, North Carolina to the catalog department of the Louis Round Wilson Library. As a graduate of an army interpreters' school where I had been trained as a linguist, it fell my task in this new position to catalog descriptively all additions to the collection printed in Russian and German.

Chapel Hill is at most seasons of the year a lovely place. In the autumn, however, it is simply a magic place. I shall always remember the beauty and fragrance of dying summer in that village. It remains for me truly the "southern part of heaven," described so lovingly by William Meade Prince in his book of the same title.

I have often wondered why it is that my memories of Chapel Hill and the several years I spent there stand out so vividly. I have concluded that this is true simply because it was such an adventuresome and formative time in my life. Whatever the case, I remember quite clearly one morning in the autumn of 1961 when a well-dressed man in his late forties approached me at my desk.

I can see him clearly still—of medium height, neatly trimmed mustache, smiling as he moved in my direction. He stopped, did not introduce himself, but said that he had heard that I was a Russian and German linguist (talents that were rare in those days for a student assistant), and that he was a linguist himself and hoped that I would enjoy working my way through the backlog of materials that now awaited me. I assured him that I would.

Following his departure, both my supervisor and the chief of the catalog department came to inquire if something were wrong. Their questions puzzled me, and so I asked if something was supposed to be wrong. "No," they said, but they had seen Dr. Orne talking to me and wondered what was on his mind. Continuing in my puzzled state, I asked who Dr. Orne was, at which point I was informed that he was my ultimate boss, the university librarian. I am glad to this day that I did not know who he was; otherwise I would probably have been too intimidated to converse with him.

During the course of the next several months, Jerrold Orne would stop periodically at my desk and inquire how things were going. We came to know each other a little better and discovered that we had a mutual interest in numismatics. Eventually, he encouraged me to consider taking a full-time clerical position elsewhere in the library after my graduation the next summer.

I had been in the library's full-time employ a little over a year, undecided about a career, when one morning Jerry appeared in my office, inquired how I was doing in German graduate school, and asked me why I did not get off my backside and enter the university's library school. I told him that it was out of the question because I had no money except what my wife and I earned or received occasionally from my parents and that I had a family to support. He then posed a question that changed my life: "What if I made it possible for you to attend library school on a work/study basis?" The next sixteen years are now history, but for the most part they have been good years in which Jerry Orne has always served as a willing guide when asked, but never has he pushed.

My experience with Jerry has, I am sure, been a common one for countless other librarians who have known him. In one very real sense, this volume is my way of saying thank you on behalf of hundreds of individuals whose lives have been touched and changed by the loving, professional watchfulness of one of the notable men in the history of American libraries. For the contributors to this volume, it is a way of expressing their appreciation for the man's other numerous contributions to our profession.

We find it particularly significant that this *Festschrift* honors Jerrold Orne by addressing what may be the greatest problem that has faced our educational system and hence academic libraries in this century. If he were to have a second career, I feel certain that he would like nothing better than to confront head-on the issues discussed here. Problem solving, pointing the way, and looking far into the future have always been his major interests.

As academic institutions in America enter the last quarter of this century, they are confronted by an era of growing uncertainty unlike any other in their experience. Not only do they face a period of diminishing federal support and of continuing rapidly increasing costs for goods and services, but for the first time a national decline in enrollments or at best a steady-state condition of no enrollment growth appears to be a certainty. According to the Carnegie Foundation for the Advancement of Teaching in its 1975 report entitled *More Than Survival*, "Higher education in the United States is undergoing the greatest overall and long-run rate of decline in its growth patterns in all of its history."

The effect of this decline will be felt throughout the structure of our educational system. Most vividly, it will manifest itself in the form of stable or declining budgets. At a time when the rate of international publication continues to be high and when humankind is on the threshold of so many intellectual and technological breakthroughs, the results for academic libraries could be troublesome to say the least.

The purpose of this volume, then, in addition to honoring Jerrold Orne, is to confront this problem and to explore its implications for academic libraries. Those who have contributed to it have tried to suggest what the climate for our libraries will be between now and this century's end and to suggest ways in which we might appropriately contend with the change that seems to be the only constant in our lives. The nature of professional response to this period of change will determine the future quality of academic libraries and, consequently, of higher education in America.

We have not given all the answers simply because we do not know all the questions. Even if we did, it would make no difference because we could probably not address them all. On the other hand, one might easily say that the questions themselves are more valuable than the answers; and it is with this thought that the contributors hope the following text will be of practical value to our profession as we move rapidly, ever so rapidly, toward the end of the twentieth century.

Writing in the June 1975 issue of *Change Magazine*, Kenneth Boulding noted with concern the ignorance of administrators in higher education regarding appropriate measures for the management of decline. To date few monographs have attempted to treat this topic within the context of higher education, and fewer still have dealt with it in the area of academic librarianship. It is hoped that this volume will respond to a genuine need of the educator, serve as a "thought piece" for the library profession, and be used as a text in professional schools of librarianship.

It has been a great privilege for me, as the editor of this volume, to cooperate with twelve other contributors whose names are among some of the most well-known of contemporary American librarianship. On behalf of myself and those who will read the pages that follow, I thank them most sincerely for their long hours of working under pressure from me, for meeting dreaded deadlines, and for joining in this effort to explore the future while honoring a respected fellow traveler. I am indebted to Judy Garodnick and Nada Glick at R. R. Bowker Company for their support of the proposal that has now finally culminated in this volume. I am especially grateful to Mrs. Glick, who has served as a pleasant, supportive, and understanding sponsoring editor; to production editor Iris Topel; and to Dr. Rose Simon of Guilford Library's staff for her careful technical assistance. Finally, I am most grateful to my soulmate, Jo, who waited patiently and kept my dinners warm on many winter evenings while the work of writing, assembling, and editing went on.

H. P.

JERROLD ORNE: A BIOGRAPHY

by Herbert Poole

We never quite seem able to adjust or accustom ourselves to change even though it is such a part of our lives. Thus, the feelings of sadness and loss that many of us felt upon hearing the news that Jerrold Orne was retiring, or was even old enough to retire, evoked for some the feeling that an era of American librarianship might be nearing a close.

The realization that we live out our lives with our colleagues and never really know them other than in a highly impersonal, professional way prompted those contributing to this volume to resolve that, despite some reluctance on his part, we would set down for the record some detail about the man whom we now honor. Those who consult this volume in the future have a right to know something more than the name of the honoree and to be able to read firsthand the facts of a life that has been significant in the world of librarianship and higher education during the mid-years of the twentieth century.

To the end of creating this record, a correspondence was opened with Jerrold Orne in the autumn of 1976. Although we had spent many hours together in the sixteen years of our acquaintance that should have been partially sufficient for the purpose of writing his biography, our exchange of letters revealed much about the man that does not appear in any biographical source. No attempt to analyze him or to piece together the causal chain of his life and his professional record will be made. The facts themselves seem interesting enough.

Jerrold Orne spent the first ten years of his life near downtown St. Paul, Minnesota. His first introduction to libraries came during this time, when he was permitted to spend many hours in the children's room of the central public library. According to one letter from him, he read his way around the children's collection "at least three times" before he was old enough to "invade" the adult section.

When he was ten years old, his family moved away from the central part of the city, and he was enrolled in a new grade school where he was placed in an accelerated class. He was able to enter high school by age twelve. At the time,

1

according to his own account, he was "wholly immature and unpredictable." As a consequence, he became the despair of his high school teachers, taking four full years plus three summer sessions to graduate at the age of sixteen.

Jerry's family numbered seven, the parents and five children. His father and mother had been born in Romania and arrived in the United States with the wave of European immigrants that reached this country just prior to World War I. Their economic situation required that just as soon as they were old enough to hire themselves out each child had to work. Jerry's parents had only a limited education themselves, common for immigrants of that time, but according to him they took great pride in the education of their children even though they were unable to support it beyond the high school level. Jerry's first job at age twelve was as a clerk in a grocery store where he worked for fourteen cents an hour. He held this job for four years until he entered the employ of the public library.

While still sixteen, he sat for the city civil service examination for library page and entered the employ of the St. Paul Public Library. Still continuing his work in the public library, first as a page and then as a clerk in the reference department as well, he entered the University of Minnesota and elected to major in modern languages, because Spanish had been his "only successful subject in school." Jerry describes these years as "a joyous time." The library, he wrote, "opened up the whole world of learning," and his work in college went well as a consequence. In 1928 he graduated from the university with a Bachelor of Arts degree *cum laude* with a major in French and a minor in comparative literature.

During his work in the public library, Jerry came under the influence of Katharine Dame, head of the reference department. He has described her as a "brilliant woman . . . one of the earliest graduates of the first library school at Albany, N.Y. . . . old but sharp." It was she, he observes, who brought him to the early realization that women were great professional librarians. He has said that he "had no real understanding of librarianship as a possible field of life work at that time." For him, it was primarily a way of making it through the Depression, paying his tuition and room and board at home, and being able "even to have a date now and then."

He continued to work in the public library through 1933, attended graduate school, and received a Master of Arts in French and Italian in 1933. By 1934 he had saved enough money to pay for a year at the Sorbonne in Paris. Completing a diploma and a certificate from the University of Paris in 1935, he returned to the United States and his old job. During the next year, he saved enough to enter the Ph.D. program in modern languages at the University of Chicago, which he did in 1936. Obtaining a series of working assistantships and tuition scholarships, he continued there until completing his degree in 1939.

Two significant occurrences took place in Jerrold Orne's life during this three-year period. In 1938 he met Catherine Bowen, a Radcliffe graduate with a Master of Arts degree in languages, who was also a candidate for an advanced degree. She later became his wife. He also met Louis Round Wilson. At that time Wilson was Dean of the Graduate Library School at the University of Chicago.

Dean Wilson was aware that Jerry had worked as an assistant to the noted Italian literary giant Guiseppe Antonio Borgese and that for two years Jerry had supervised language examinations that Orne's department gave in French, Spanish, Italian, and Portuguese. The job market for new Ph.D.'s was still poor with only one instructor's position having been announced that year and three new doctorates available for it. Dean Wilson was also aware of Jerry's library experience and began to urge him to consider entering the library profession rather than teaching languages.

With a new degree, a new wife, and no job, Jerry finally decided to enter library school in the fall of 1939. He graduated with a Bachelor of Science degree *cum laude* in 1940. Before Jerry had completed this fourth degree, Dean Wilson offered him an assistantship on the staff of the *Library Quarterly*. Jerry returned to Chicago, planning to take the position and to pursue more course work in the Graduate Library School. As fate would have it, however, Archibald MacLeish had just been appointed the Librarian of Congress and had announced "a new program of working fellowships for academic bibliographers." Dean Wilson had submitted Jerry's name along with others, and Jerry was selected to receive one of the fellowships. Prior to departing for Washington in October 1940, Jerry spent the summer session at the Graduate Library School. He observed recently that he was in great company that summer in Wilson's seminars on university library management. Among his fellow students were Ralph Shaw, Maurice Tauber, Jesse Shera, and others.

At the Library of Congress, Jerry worked directly with Archibald MacLeish and his principals who were to become the leaders of American librarianship. Among his associates were Verner Clapp, David Mearns, Luther Evans, Quincy Mumford, and Herman Henkle. Jerry was usually on special assignment at the Library of Congress, and he formed many lifelong friendships while there. For about six years following 1940–1941, he was listed as a titular fellow of the Library of Congress and returned twice for short summer assignments during that period.

By the close of his year as resident Fellow in Librarianship and Italian Bibliography, Jerry felt that he was really a member of the American library profession. He had attended his first conference of the American Library Association, published his first paper (jointly with Archibald MacLeish) in the *ALA Bulletin*, and obtained his first professional library position at Knox College in Galesburg, Illinois. He remained there for two years from September 1941 to September 1943 as librarian and professor of languages. Jerry describes these as two very happy years that came to a close with his induction into the navy in September 1943.

According to his own account his navy career was not illustrious: boot camp, personnel work, and a six-month convalescence in several navy hospitals in an attempt to recover from rheumatic fever. Within a short while after his release from the hospital, he was ordered to San Francisco for the United Nations Conference on International Organization (UNCIO). This was the conference during which the United Nations was established. Jerry's assignment, which was requested of the navy by Luther Evans, then Librarian of Congress, was to establish, serve, and disestablish the UNCIO Reference Library. Leaving that assignment in August 1944, he moved to the Office of Research and Inventions at the Department of the Navy in Washington. He was mustered out of the navy in February 1945. He then served as the director of the Office of Technical Services in the Library Division of the U.S. Department of Commerce for six months, intending to return to the position that had been held for him at Knox College.

Before he could return to Galesburg, however, he received offers from both Washington University in St. Louis, Missouri, and the University of Florida in Gainesville. He chose to go to Washington University as Director of Libraries, a position which he held for five years until 1951. Following that position, he made a five-year commitment to the position of Director of the Library at the Air University Library on Maxwell Air Force Base in Montgomery, Alabama. In 1957 he completed his sixth year with the Air University Library and moved to Chapel Hill where he would serve as the University Librarian at the University of North Carolina until 1975.

In 1975 Jerry made a major career change, giving up his position as University Librarian and returning to his first love—teaching. He ended an illustrious career as a professor of library science in the University of North Carolina School of Library Science. He wrote not too long ago saying, "I think I was more alive when I was teaching than at any other time and I will miss that kind of involvement more than anything else for all of my remaining years." If one looks back at Jerrold Orne's career, teaching in the classroom was always a part of his life, except for his time in the university library in Chapel Hill. At the Library of Congress, he taught Italian; at Knox College, he taught French and comparative literature; he was an instructor in the navy; at Washington University, he organized an undergraduate program in library science; at the Air University and in the Louis Round Wilson Library at Chapel Hill, he taught many of his staff, including me.

That Jerry was a success as a teacher was attested to by Ed Holley in a recent conversation. Ed noted that Jerry was an excellent teacher in every respect. His insistence on high standards, his conscientious approach toward his work, and his tremendous productivity earned for him the approval of his students. More important, it earned for him their deep respect. His colleagues felt it unfortunate that he had waited until he was near retirement to return to full-time teaching. By any standard, he seems to have left his mark wherever he has gone.

These biographical facts portray only a part of the man. The reality of the man stretches far beyond my ability to describe him. The record of his publications alone requires no fewer than ten single-spaced typewritten pages, and although a bibliography of his published works appears elsewhere in this volume, it seems only appropriate to note those several for which he is best known. His *Language of the Foreign Book Trade*, which appeared in a third edition in 1976, is a monumental and highly valued tool of the profession. Of the same ilk is *Education and Libraries: Selected Papers of Louis Round Wilson*, a book that he edited along with Maurice Tauber to honor his mentor Wilson. Likewise, *Research Li-*

brarianship, his *Festschrift* honoring his respected colleague Robert B. Downs, is a model to be emulated. By 1975 his list of publications numbered twenty-one monographs or parts of monographs and over a hundred articles or reviews. This is a formidable record by any measure. His work on academic library buildings may well be the articles for which he is best known.

It cannot be within the scope of this biography to describe the myriad improvements that he has left behind him over the years. The Robert B. House Undergraduate Library and the excellence of the University of North Carolina's numerous collections are only selected examples typical of the works left in his wake.

His professional affiliations are also far too numerous to describe in detail. He has been an active member of the American Library Association, the Association of Research Libraries, the Special Libraries Association, the Southeastern Library Association, the North Carolina Library Association, and the Association of University Professors. From 1947 to 1951 he served as editor of the *Missouri Library Association Quarterly*. From 1949 to 1951 he edited the *Washington University Library Studies*. From 1953 to 1957 he served as the associate editor of *American Documentation*. From 1962 to 1964 he worked as an editorial consultant for the *Library Journal*. In 1966 he served as issue editor for one number of *Library Trends*. From 1966 to 1972 he edited the *Southeastern Librarian*. Finally, one of his most notable services has been that of chairing Standards Committee Z39 of the American National Standards Institute where he directed the activities of more than two dozen subcommittees developing standards in the areas of library work, documentation, and related publishing practices.

How then, in closing, does one evaluate the contributions that an American librarian like Jerrold Orne has made to our profession in the more than thirty-five years that he has devoted to it? It would be a difficult task, indeed, because the aftereffects of his work will continue for as long as there are libraries. We know intuitively that this is so. An outstanding evaluative statement was made in 1974 when Jerry was recognized for his work in the profession by being chosen to receive the J. W. Lippincott Award sponsored by the American Library Association. As the citation reads:

> Jerrold Orne was one of the first to recognize the urgent need for libraries to provide specialized services to scientists, research workers, and technicians and he has worked unstintingly to meet this need.
>
> As chairman of the U.S.A. Standards Committee Z-39, he expanded its program by adding eight subcommittees and under his leadership several new or revised U.S.A. Standards were completed.
>
> He has edited and published extensively and skillfully. To his credit are over a score of monographs and more than 100 articles of significance.
>
> He is a librarian-scholar with broad interests in the humanities. Always at the forefront of the library profession, he is a distinguished practitioner and we are proud to present the 1974 J. W. Lippincott Award to Jerrold Orne.

Jerry's friends who have contributed to this volume hope that their work expresses in part the depth of the appreciation that they feel for him and for the lifelong contributions that he has made. They hope, too, that no one will conclude that this man's life seems worth no more than a modest *Festschrift*, because their gratitude and respect for him go far beyond.

WHAT LIES AHEAD FOR ACADEMIC LIBRARIES?

by Edward G. Holley

In the past decade, we have been flooded with literature dealing with the future. The popularity of works both of the optimists and the Cassandras indicates that speculation about the future is a major pastime for many people. At the same time, in no area has the proliferation of literature reached a more overwhelming flood stage than in higher education. Articles, books, papers, and pamphlets have poured from the presses in a steady stream as higher education moved from phenomenal growth to stabilization and now to prospective decline. Indicative of the concern, as well as the lack of easy answers, are the essays by distinguished educators in the fall 1974 and winter 1975 issues of *Daedalus, Journal of the American Academy of Arts and Sciences*. Ominous, too, is the title given to these two volumes, which run to over 700 pages: "American Higher Education: Toward an Uncertain Future."[1] If one wanted an overview of the topics currently of concern to higher education, he or she could scarcely do better than to read the titles of the articles and ponder some of these very literate presentations. Significantly, not one of them deals with libraries as such, though almost all contain recommendations about higher education's future that have some bearing on how academic libraries can operate, whether one is talking about purpose, elites, humanities, skilling versus learning, professionalism, research, the place of women, political activism, faculty, and so on.

In this paper, I have been asked to look at the climate in which higher education will operate during the next twenty-five years and to try to determine what impact that climate will have on libraries. As Jerrold Orne, whom these essays honor, knows very well, that climate has everything to do with the ability of academic libraries to perform their function, because the purpose, mission, and scope of an academic library are derivative. Academic libraries do not exist in isolation; they draw their meaning and function from the nature of the parent institution. Although their central goal of supporting teaching and research, with an occasional nod at public service, remains fairly constant, the type of institution, the size, and the ways in which the library carries out its goals have changed decidedly in the past twenty-five years. Very likely most institutions will change even more significantly in the next two decades.

As is true in academic libraries, no less than in higher education generally, prophecy about the future has a way of being fulfilled far differently from one's projections. A good healthy skepticism toward gazes into one's crystal ball is, therefore, in order. I recently discussed with an architect of a multimillion-dollar university library building the usefulness of that magnificent structure and the assumptions that guided its planning. Somewhat ruefully the architect noted that almost every assumption they made as an architectural firm, as well as the projections made by the university, turned out to be wrong. The site, which appeared to meet all criteria for centrality of location, is on the periphery of the campus. University plans to erect further buildings beyond it have come to a halt because of environmental considerations and a concern to preserve a historic part of the city. The role of the library in its region, so promising at the time, has been eliminated. The nature of the university's enrollment has not changed in the direction anticipated. Was this multimillion-dollar library a mistake and who is culpable if it was? No one yet knows if it was a mistake, and one cannot fault a distinguished firm and leading university administrators for engaging in the most rigorous and systematic planning of which they were capable. Indeed, given the same set of assumptions, carefully examined, any reasonably competent architect, librarian, or university official would likely have come to the same conclusions. There is no need to seek a "devil theory" here. As frail human beings, we can merely act upon the knowledge we have and try to correct that knowledge when events beyond our control indicate that it is no longer valid.

The point being made here at the beginning is that the knowledge upon which we make our plans and the assumptions we use for planning purposes often turn out to be incorrect. On the other hand, predictions often have a way of becoming self-fulfilling, sometimes in a negative sense, but often because our "educated guesses" prove remarkably accurate.[2] Nowhere has this been more true than in higher education. Thus, one should approach carefully any predictions about higher education's future and even more carefully predictions about the academic library in that future. With this warning at the beginning, let us look at the past fifteen years in higher education before making an assessment about its next two decades.

HIGHER EDUCATION SINCE THE EARLY 1960s

According to *Change* magazine, Clark Kerr headed the list of most influential persons in higher education in 1975.[3] Architect of various California master plans for higher education that strongly influenced other such plans across the country, Kerr's impact on the thinking of public officials and of his fellow university administrators has been profound. Chancellor of the University of California at Berkeley between 1952 and 1958 and President of the University of California System from 1958 until his abrupt firing in 1967, Kerr articulated exciting prospects for the future of higher education in a manner matched by no other university president. His advocacy of higher education's role in society came at a propitious time.

In the aftermath of Sputnik in 1957 and with the advent of President Lyndon Johnson's Great Society programs in the early 1960s, higher education became a favored vehicle for increasing the economic base of society and achieving technological competence, while solving the problems of poverty and extending the good life to all. In the ferment of that glorious period, no voice was more persuasive than was Clark Kerr's. When Kerr delivered the Godkin Lectures at Harvard, subsequently published as *The Uses of the University* (1963),[4] he saw the knowledge industry, a product of the research university, as doing for society in the second half of the twentieth century what the automobile had done in the first half of the century and what railroads had done in the last half of the nineteenth century. Many states, especially those without strong public systems of higher education, such as New York, some of the states of the Old South, and New England, began proliferating public institutions across the landscape to take care of enrollments that had never ceased their upward spiral since the implementation of the GI Bill after World War II.

Increased Enrollment and Period of Optimism

Just to cite figures for the three decades: higher education's degree-credit enrollments rose from 2,281,000 in 1950 to 3,583,000 in 1960 and 7,920,000 in 1970.[5] As the late Allan Cartter has pointed out: "Between 1957 and 1967, higher education enrollments grew at the average of 7¾ percent annually, while research funding grew nearly 10 percent annually in real (constant dollar) terms."[6] In the rhetoric of the period, higher education was the key to a prosperous and happy future; many expected higher education to save the world. The focus on ever-expanding enrollments, financial resources, and demand for technically trained individuals seemed insatiable. Libraries shared in the cornucopia of support that followed this enthusiasm for higher education's products. Operating expenditures for colleges and universities increased tenfold from $2.2 billion in 1950 to $21.0 billion in 1970.[7] Figures on total library expenditures can be seen in Table 1, where they are compared with the traditional percentages of educational and general (E & G) expenditures.[8] The libraries' piece of the pie was not as impressive in 1950 and 1960 as one might have expected, but libraries did see their expenditures rise at roughly a twelve-fold rate between 1950 and 1970, while total expenditures for institutions of higher education experienced a tenfold increase, and the total E & G increase was a little less than tenfold.

A building boom, only now diminishing, saw the construction of 647 academic library building projects at a cost of $1.9 billion between 1967 and 1975.[9] Many of these projects had partial funding supplied from federal funds under the Higher Education Facilities Act of 1963 (up to one-third of the cost) until 1969, when

TABLE 1

Year	Educational and General Expenditures ($ millions)	Libraries ($ millions)	% for Libraries
1970	$ 15,789	$ 653	4.1
1960	4,513	135	3.0
1950	1,706	56	3.3
1940	522	19	3.6

Source: Historical Statistics of the United States (Washington, D.C.: U.S. Government Printing Office, 1975).

appropriations began to decline. Although total figures for federal funding are unknown, there seems little doubt that William S. Dix was correct in asserting that "a majority of the college and university libraries have been rehoused since World War II . . . and the stimulus provided by federal aid undoubtedly boosted the library building boom which had already begun in response to the needs built up by the enforced moratorium of the Depression and the war."[10] Since 1967, Jerrold Orne has annually chronicled this building boom in a December issue of *Library Journal* and now has underway a ten-year review of academic library buildings.

Disenchantment

By the late 1960s, when the attitude toward higher education changed drastically, with riots in the cities and on campus, the question was not whether higher education could save the world but whether some of the oldest and most prestigious universities could themselves survive. Inflation, added to declining federal support and disenchantment of society as a whole, was finally capped by energy bills that threatened the continued existence of many institutions, especially those in the northeast. Those institutions whose future had been built on the expectation of limitless expansion were suddenly confronted with a fact to which few had paid much attention: declining birthrates and the prospect of a decline in college enrollment. Despite some early papers by Allan Cartter warning that supply of doctorates might exceed the demand,[11] as late as 1971 he met with "surprise and initial disbelief" when he presented a paper before the American Association of Higher Education documenting the fact that graduate expansionist policies of the 1960s would lead to a surplus of doctorates in the 1970s.[12] Some even criticized his theory and interpretation of statistical data. Thus, it was not until almost the depression of 1973–1975 that higher education began to take seriously its changed circumstances.

Carnegie Commission Studies

Meanwhile, recognizing that higher education had become big business and that it warranted serious study of its needs and organization, the Carnegie Corporation joined forces with the Carnegie Foundation for the Advancement of Teaching in establishing the Carnegie Commission on Higher Education to study the financing, structure, and functions of higher education.[13] Clark Kerr, originally scheduled to be chairman of the Carnegie Commission on a part-time service basis, suddenly had the opportunity to head the commission full time when the Board of Regents of the University of California dismissed him as president. The Carnegie Commission was fortunate in Kerr's leadership, and his dismissal at California inspired his famous quip that he entered the presidency fired with enthusiasm and left it the same way![14]

The Carnegie Commission sponsored a series of studies by many outstanding scholars, but unfortunately not one on libraries.[15] These studies were to have a significant impact on the public. By the time the commission completed its assignment in 1973 after six years of work, the expenditure of $6.3 million, and the publication of 400 recommendations in 22 of its own reports plus a vast number of other sponsored publications,[16] it had attracted national attention and had made a major impact upon legislators and the lay public. Along the way, its reports made popular some phrases like "invisible colleges," "forgotten Americans," which President Nixon used to identify those voters who, he believed, constituted a majority of the electorate, "new depression," "stopouts," "doctor of arts," and others. Six of the reports sold more than 10,000 copies each.[17] The Carnegie Commission has been criticized for being conventional in its thinking, for spending money foolishly, and for employing more rhetoric than reality in its recommendations.[18] Whatever the substance of the criticisms, the commission unquestionably gained national attention for its work. The editor of this volume has asked each contributor to read the publication of the Carnegie Foundation for the Advancement of Teaching, *More Than Survival: Prospects for Higher Education in a Period of Uncertainty* (1975), a project of the Carnegie Council on Policy Studies in Higher Education, really a successor group to the Carnegie Commission.[19]

Warnings of Future Trouble

The warning that the future might be grim for higher education came with the publication of Earl Cheit's first book, *The New Depression in Higher Education*, in 1971. Cheit's work received considerable publicity in newspapers across the country and called attention to the fact that 71 percent of the forty-one institutions he studied were either in financial trouble or headed in that direction.[20] Two years later, his dire warnings that some institutions were in serious trouble were mitigated by the knowledge that these institutions had helped themselves to reduce their deficits by deferring maintenance, decreasing salary increments, and doing other things that could not solve their problems, only postpone them.[21] Librarians, dealing with financial problems in an atmosphere of near panic in some colleges, faced stabilized finances and actual reductions in book budgets, which often appeared to be the easiest place to cut expenditures quickly. *More Than Survival* highlighted some of the other problems that had been emerging as institutions recognized the fact that the halcyon days of the 1960s would not soon return. Equally significant, from my point of view, is the late Allan M. Cartter's *Ph.D.'s and the Academic Labor Market*, which appeared in 1976 and contains massive quantities of data on enrollments, degrees, future needs for faculty, and alternate sources for jobs for those having doctorates. Cartter's conclusions are especially a matter of concern for the humanities. Given the current rate of output, American graduate schools are likely producing at least one-third more doctorates than are needed at present and in the 1980s may well overproduce by 50 percent.[22] Under these circumstances, Cartter states that it is imperative that universities inform students of the likely demand, tighten admissions standards, and take some leadership in curtailing doctoral output lest their legislatures do it for them.[23]

In the twelve years between the publication of Kerr's *Uses of the University* and *More Than Survival*, higher education has gone from a period of unbelievable optimism to deep despair. Only now are the administrators and boards of most institutions taking an objective look at the path ahead to see what can be done to assure survival or "more than survival" for social institutions that will enroll 10.8 million students, or about 5 percent of the population, in 1990 under even the most pessimistic enrollment projections.[24]

Having already noted the enormous proliferation of literature on higher education during the past twenty years, what does it say about libraries and their future? Very little directly but much indirectly. As one who has either read or scanned much of the literature, the observations that follow seem reasonable at this moment for consideration by library faculty and their teaching faculty colleagues whose decisions will be so necessary if we are to attain "more than survival" for libraries during the rest of the century.

The first point to be made is that academic librarians, like their teaching faculty colleagues, are often woefully ignorant of most of the higher education literature. Like their teaching faculty counterparts, whose perquisites they so often seek, librarians are more isolated from the outside world than they would like to admit. True, most college library administrators are becoming painfully aware of pinched budgets for materials and stabilization or reduction in staff. However, their overview, achieved through interaction at the top, rarely is shared by the librarian or the supportive staff members who do the library's day-to-day work. If librarians expect to have their voices heard and become a positive factor in their institution's survival, then they are going to have to be conscious of reports, documents, plans, and the like that normally collect dust on library shelves. Moreover, because librarians frequently are in a better position to assess the overall contribution of faculty and educational programs to the mission of the university, they have much to offer in any reexamination of the university's purposes.

FUTURE PROBLEMS

Size and Type of Student Body

One of the problems facing all higher education is the sheer size of institutions. In 1974, thirty-seven campuses had more than 30,000 students enrolled, and in that same year over half the students in higher education were attending institutions with more than 10,000 students.[25] Such enrollments, which number in the hundreds of thousands, take enormous quantities of money, even when the teacher-pupil ratio may be relatively high. Allan Cartter says that this ratio is likely to increase from the traditional one faculty member for ten graduate and professional students and one faculty member for seventeen undergraduate students in the near future.[26] Despite our humanistic background and the tremendous influence of colleges of arts and sciences in major universities, we cannot ignore these statistics or make them go away by talking about improving the quality of higher education through a reduced faculty-student ratio. Every state system has some way of connecting financing with enrollments and programs, even if it may be only a general understanding and even though there may be a good deal of flexibility as to how this formula is applied on campus. This faculty-student ratio, allied to costs, affects not only public education but also private education, whose dependence on the state treasury has been increasing during the last half-dozen years. It is safe to predict that any private institution (and the line drawn between public and private is increasingly blurred) that receives substantial sums of public money will have to conform to some guidelines for accountability for that money. That has certainly been clear from the federal government's categorical and research grants just as the opponents of federal aid a quarter of a century ago assured us it would be. In that reassessment, how one spends money for faculty, the most expensive component in any educational institution, will not escape serious attention.

That enrollments have a substantial impact on library support is clear to many librarians, but what is often not so clear is that the largest institutions have the greatest amount of dollar expenditures while the smaller institutions have a greater per full-time equivalent (FTE) dollar amount spent for library purposes. A recent American Council on Education publication on the differences between public and private higher education highlights this fact. Library expenditures of more than $100 per FTE student in 1972–1973 were reported by only 20 percent of the public institutions but by 50 percent of the private institutions, with very high proportions at private liberal arts colleges (82.3 percent) and private doctoral institutions (77.3 percent).[27] What is clear from looking at statistics on enrollment and the percent of institutions spending more than $100 FTE on libraries is that the large institutions are chiefly public institutions whereas the small institutions are chiefly private.[28] Obviously, it costs more per student for basic library operations in colleges with fewer than 2,500 students (most of the private colleges) than it does in colleges with more than 2,500 students (about one-half of the public institutions). Librarians may argue that this is a denial of quality in the public institutions (and in some cases it clearly is), but the statistical data are undeniable: the smaller the college the higher per capita cost for libraries and most other operations. There is something to this business of economy of scale.

In our concern for the amount of money likely to be available from tax dollars and for the decline in enrollments predicted to begin about 1980, perhaps it is good to remind the body politic that the lowest figure anyone has yet mentioned for total enrollments during that period is 10.8 million students. This means, as noted earlier, that roughly 5 percent of the country's population will be directly concerned with higher education, plus another sizable group of husbands, wives, parents, and children.

What does all this mean for the academic librarian and his or her library? The answer to that question lies partially in what kind of institution one is talking about. In broad terms the following institutions will be our major concern:

1. *Private liberal arts colleges.* These institutions have traditionally been an important part of higher education, from the founding of Harvard in 1636. They have been a steadily declining part of the total enrollment picture,[29] and many of them are in serious financial difficulty. In the case of most liberal arts colleges, enrollments have stabilized in the last two decades, though many still regard their programs as the best undergraduate training one can secure. Their chief problem will be to convince parents that they should go to the additional expense of sending a child to their college because said child will receive a superior education, or one that is religiously based, or is special for some other reason. *More Than Survival* gives some credence to this "conventional view."[30] The superiority of the typical liberal arts colleges, though, is unquestionably harder to maintain these days, when public education has been competing successfully for the best faculty and has built laboratories and libraries to signal their rising concern for excellence. As Cartter has noted, the myth that the quality of teaching has eroded over the last two decades cannot be sustained, at least so far as the credentials of college teachers are concerned.[31] Nonetheless, the private liberal arts college will continue to push both for its superior or special educational programs as well as for additional tax dollars to subsidize in-state students. New York's Bundy Plan pours substantial state dollars into private education in New York, as does the Pennsylvania plan for subsidizing certain private universities, the North Carolina plan for private colleges, and the Texas tuition-grant plan.[32] Programs of state aid to students in all types of colleges have been increasing, but the lag in educational statistical reporting makes any analysis difficult. Elaine El-Khawas, writing in *Public and Private Higher Education*, reported that 23.4 percent of liberal arts colleges in her Category I and 12.1 percent of liberal arts colleges in her Category II indicated receipt of some form of state appropriations for their educational and general revenue in 1972–1973.[33]

2. *The state colleges and universities.* This is where the bulk of the enrollment growth took place in the 1960s, with some of it having been drained off recently by the community colleges. Size of some of these state universities is certainly a factor in the achievement of mass education. As previously indicated, about one-half of all students are in institutions with enrollments of more than 10,000 each.[34] Most of the enrollment increase from 1950 to 1975 took place in these colleges and universities. Private education, which accounted for approximately 50 percent of the total enrollment in 1940, accounted for only about 20 percent in 1974. Because funding of state colleges and universities is usually derived from some form of faculty-student ratio, they can surely be counted upon to

fight for their share of students during the period of stabilization and decline. Few state universities adopted ceilings for their enrollments or fought the battle for "less is more" educationally. With the exception of a few prestigious private universities, state universities enroll most of the graduate and professional students and have the broadest curricular programs. As numerous critics have pointed out, the question for them is how to make their undergraduate education as good as their graduate and professional education. In other words, how does one combine mass education and quality successfully? Many of them would argue that it is a part of the mythology of higher education that their undergraduate programs are qualitatively poorer than similar programs of most liberal arts colleges. Even in the debate on state aid for private colleges, the view rarely surfaces that public higher education is qualitatively poorer at the undergraduate level.

3. *The community colleges and technical institutes.* This segment of higher education also grew enormously during the past decade. For example, FTE enrollment in two-year colleges tripled from 1962 to 1972,[35] and 90 percent of non-degree students in higher education (11.5 percent of all enrollments in 1973) are in two-year colleges.[36] Their growth has been accompanied by the rhetoric reminiscent of that surrounding the land-grant universities in the late nineteenth century. Some states operated on the principle that a two-year college should be within driving distance of every person in the state. The future for them seems open-ended if they can match their rhetoric with reality—that is, if they can become true community centers, offer technical and vocational education, prepare students for university entrance, assume responsibility for adult education, and provide strong continuing education programs. I share Cartter's skepticism about their continued growth, or at least the rate of increase in growth.[37] Their enrollments still constitute only about 20 percent of the FTE undergraduate enrollment in higher education, though about two out of every five students entering college today matriculate at a two-year college.[38] Competition for students from colleges and universities in El-Khawas' Categories I and II will undoubtedly become much more serious as total enrollments decline, whatever may be the two-year college's proposed solution to the problem of "the management of decline."

Aside from these broad generalizations perhaps one should add that colleges and universities come in a variety of shapes and sizes, though the diversity that has often been touted as one of the glories of American higher education seems also to be declining. Some believe that most colleges have tried too successfully to model themselves after the research university pattern, and this has led to an increasing homogeneity of approach. Nonetheless, programs are still diverse, geography makes a difference, and any college's relationship to the body politic, especially that segment called "state boards of higher education," will have a large part to play in its future viability.

Enough, though, by way of general background. Higher education has moved from the halcyon days of the 1960s into the cautious and even pessimistic 1970s. What will it be like in the 1980s and 1990s and how will libraries adjust to that future? Perhaps at this point it will be useful to repeat the recommendations from *More Than Survival* about an institution's future viability as it relates to enrollment. Summarizing those recommendations,[39] a college or university will be better off to:

1. Attract all ages rather than only 18- to 21-year olds.
2. Provide for part-time rather than only full-time students.
3. Be less, rather than more, dependent on teacher education.
4. Have public state support than not have it.
5. Be of an effective size rather than forgo the economies of scale.
6. Be located in an urban rather than in a rural location.
7. Have comparatively low tuition and few local competitors.
8. Have a national reputation or a devoted specialized constituency rather than neither.
9. Be older rather than younger as an institution.
10. To have made wise expansion commitments in the 1960s rather than to have become overcommitted.
11. Have a stabilized undergraduate enrollment rather than a volatile graduate enrollment.
12. Be related to the health professions rather than not.
13. Be in a sound financial condition rather than not.
14. Be closely related to reality rather than not.
15. Be located in the South or California or New York rather than in other parts of the country and particularly than in the North Plains and Mountain States.

Some of these suggestions are obviously no longer as applicable as they were just two years ago. The health professions have come in for serious public concern as the cost of health care has risen, and there is now some expectation that a surplus of M.D.'s will develop in the 1980s. Both California and New York have financial problems and the Sunbelt states, although their promise for the future may be bright, have seen state budgets for all social services either stabilize or decline due to the recent depression. That may be temporary, but nonetheless it should warn us that no region is immune from the general economic pause that affects the entire country, and we had better target our resources carefully.

Admitting that these broad categories of institutions are only convenient designations, what lies ahead for each group in terms of the Carnegie Foundation's projections for those that will survive?

Private Liberal Arts Colleges

The private liberal arts colleges would seem to have the worst of it from any point of view. They are unlikely to attract students from all ages, their programs are not geared to part-time students, they have minimal state support, they are not generally of an effective size, they have high tuition and often neither a national reputation nor a devoted specialized constituency, they are rarely in a sound financial condition,[40] and the relevance of the liberal arts to life in a technologically sophisticated society seems obscure to many citizens. Many of the Catholic colleges have folded (though not as many numerically as it might appear) and only religiously fundamentalist or evangelical colleges still appear to have a strong support from their denominations.[41]

Libraries

Tough decisions lie ahead for these institutions, and cutting the library budget may be the most costly mistake they make. Funds in any academic institution are largely tied up in faculty salaries. To make real economies does not mean just cutting the travel budget or turning off lights in the stacks or cutting the lawn once a month instead of twice, though all these things may help. Many of these institutions already have minimal library staffs (five to seven individuals full time), their budgets for library materials will scarcely keep up with the best of the current output of the American book market, and reducing library services or hours is likely to hurt the institution's chief claim for attention from its constituents—that it pays more attention to its students as individuals than do other types of institutions.

Take a hypothetical college of 1,000 students with a book collection of 100,000 volumes, a staff of eight, and an annual budget of $140,000 out of the institution's $3 million for educational and general (E & G) expenditures. (This is probably very optimistic. Twelve four-year private colleges in North Carolina spent less than $100,000 on their libraries in 1974–1975.[42]) Even with computers (which are not cheap), commercial processing, large gifts of books and journals, and dedicated staff working at low salaries, it is difficult to see how modern management techniques, operations research, a new sense of mission, or whatever will do much to help such a library. Even if one reduced the library budget by 25 percent, the savings in real dollars would be relatively insignificant in a total college budget of $4–5 million (E & G plus the dormitories and auxiliary enterprises). What will doubtless happen in these institutions is serious library competition with other needs, including the teaching faculty, for scarce resources. There is no need for anyone to pretend that one can operate a college library or any other kind of library without minimal funding. The library itself can argue that it ought to be a much more vital part of the educational program, that the bibliographic training students receive is worth more than an occasional course in Latin or Italian, and that judicious pruning of the curriculum so that faculty dollars can be used for library purposes is in the college's best interest. That is not likely to win many friends on campus nor thrill the heart of the ambitious college administrator, but we are talking about survival and beyond. Otis Hall Robinson and Justin Winsor each opined a hundred years ago:

> A librarian should be much more than a keeper of books; he should be an educator. . . . the relation . . . ought especially to be established between a college librarian and the student readers. No such librarian is fit for his place unless he holds himself to some degree responsible for the library education

of his students. . . . Somehow I reproach myself if a student gets to the end of his course without learning how to use the library. All that is taught in college amounts to very little; but if we can send students out self-reliant in their investigations, we have accomplished very much.[43]

A collection of good books, with a soul to it in the shape of a good librarian, becomes a vitalized power among the impulses by which the world goes on to improvement. . . . the object of books is to be read—read much and often. . . . At the average college it is thought that if anybody gets any good from the library, perhaps it is a few professors; and if anybody gets any amusement, perhaps it is a few students, from the smooth worn volumes of Sterne and Fielding. What it is to investigate, a student rarely knows; what are the allurements of research, a student is rarely taught.[44]

If they were correct, colleges may well be more competitive with an excellent library than with some important but costly faculty positions. Bibliographic instruction periodically gets renewed attention in the library profession and has had recent support from the joint National Endowment for the Humanities-Council on Library Resources College Library Program.[45] If the liberal arts colleges would invest relatively small amounts of additional money in such library programs, the results might be substantial, and the library would come nearer achieving its goal of being a vital part of the educational enterprise. The same could certainly be true of a stronger emphasis upon nonprint media and connections to networks. They will be valuable adjuncts to traditional library services and are well within the scope of libraries as broadly conceived. But no administrator should expect such new services to cost less money. So far, all of the experiments in new learning patterns, use of nonprint and video instruction, computerization, and other innovations have added to the cost of library operations, and the opinion of those knowledgeable in this area, with no axes to grind, is that the cost will continue to increase, though not at the same rate as before. I do not intend to argue the pros and cons of cost/benefit ratios, but I do feel compelled to call attention to an editorial by Murray Martin on the necessity of being absolutely honest with college administrators concerning future cost projections.[46] Claiming that a computer or a videotape machine or whatever will save a college money after an initial investment of $30,000–40,000 and then being faced with a bill for $10,000–15,000 in continuing costs is not likely to warm any college administrator's heart. It would be far better to say we need this improvement in the future to make this college a first-rate educational institution with more potential for its ultimate survival than to promise what one cannot deliver.

Emerging networks at the local, state, and/or national level offer immense benefits for some research-oriented faculty and relatively few graduate students in the private liberal arts college. Their services will not be free, however, and any college library would be wise to budget for participation in such networks. Already some large university libraries are attempting to recover costs by imposing a fee for interlibrary loan service. These and similar actions are likely to increase in the future unless the federal government assumes responsibility for funding such programs. Because Title VIII, "Networks for Knowledge," was never funded and was dropped quietly from the Higher Education Act of 1965, there does not seem to be much optimism that the federal government will assume such responsibility in the near future. Of course no one can predict the success of the proposed national plan of NCLIS, the national periodicals bank, or other similar measures.[47] The point remains that, although such proposals have enormous potential for colleges trying to do more than survive, they will inevitably cost more money.

One additional comment on college libraries and their finances seems warranted. In the scramble for funds, libraries probably stand a better chance than most departments in colleges to raise money annually for some parts of their programs. Alumni and parents are not likely to respond to appeals for money to buy light bulbs or janitorial supplies, but they do respond to appeals to give a book or two a year or to purchase some other item that will improve the library. Few librarians are effective fund raisers. All librarians are likely to find fund raising more important in the future. What ought to be avoided are actions that will tie the librarian's hands subsequently. There are only so many rooms that can be named for a donor, and some gifts should be diplomatically but firmly refused. It is my impression that those prospective donors with a commitment to advancing the educational programs of a given institution want to be advised how to do this most effectively. The prescient librarian would do well to have a list of projects with various price tags for opportunities that present themselves and then be able to articulate how their accomplishment would advance the college's programs. In many ways that is easier to do in the private liberal arts college, whose mission and purposes are fairly well defined, than it is in a larger institution with less well defined purposes.

State Colleges and Universities

State colleges and universities face a host of problems that sometimes seem to defy solution. Their rapid growth in enrollments, collections, staff, faculty, and programs has created problems of organization and administration that clearly need to be addressed. The work of the ARL Office of Library Management Studies,[48] the recent Academic Library Development Project at UNC-Charlotte under a CLR grant,[49] and the various self-studies required by the regional accrediting associations have focused on these problems of organization and administration. With the opportunity for less expensive decentralization through computerized bibliographic systems, there will certainly be a renewed demand on many large campuses for splitting up collections and putting segments closer to their constituencies. An idea that has died a slow death in most large institutions is that it is better to buy one unique title rather than ten copies of the same book for which there is heavy demand. This idea is recurring with the spiraling costs of periodicals these days.[50] Is it really better to eliminate a second or third copy of *American Libraries* in a library science library as opposed to dropping the *Zeitschrift für*

Bibliothekswesen? (I cite this as a familiar example for library schools but draw your own conclusions for other disciplines.) The answer is probably "no," but the emphasis in most libraries will be to keep as many unique titles as possible. Can one truly justify such an approach on a campus with 10,000–15,000 undergraduates, many of whom want access to a discipline's most heavily used journal? It seems unlikely, though even those institutions with separate undergraduate libraries have been reluctant to supply a large number of duplicates of the most heavily used journals and monographs. The five-year review of the University of Pennsylvania's library director noted that the staff had recently attempted to identify and systematically purchase multiple copies of high-demand titles that are frequently unavailable in the library.[51] Such a policy not only appears sound educationally (remember Dewey's "the best books for the largest number at the least expense"?), but also promises to ensure "more than survival" for the academic library. Perhaps in this instance academic libraries, especially those serving large student populations, have learned too little from their public library colleagues.

Another factor that will influence many of the state colleges is the decline in the need for school teachers. A declining birthrate means a decline in the need for teachers, and one recent estimate suggested that there already is a surplus of 500,000 unemployed school teachers. *More Than Survival* indicates that teacher-education programs have traditionally enrolled 20–25 percent of all students in higher education.[52] In those former teachers' colleges that have become multipurpose institutions, the percentage is doubtless much higher. Several states are now taking a hard look at teacher-education programs, and it may be a time for all institutions to emphasize what Steven Muller calls "higher learning" versus "higher skilling."[53] The shift from teacher-education programs to a broader base will confront librarians with changes in acquisition policies and in services to support the newer programs and force them to try to figure out where the college is headed and why. Some observers of the higher education scene believe that reexamination of the mission of these institutions deserves their highest priority. The librarian needs to be a part of this reexamination. He or she often has a better view of the institution as a whole than does any other member of the faculty or administrative staff, not excluding the president. Many of these institutions have large enough budgets so that readjustments can be made over a five- or ten-year period without excessive trauma. That depends, of course, on the amount of flexibility within the institution. It will be particularly difficult in those institutions like SUNY or the California State University system where rigid budget categories handed down from superboards or the legislature itself make adjustment in personnel lines difficult. The danger of statewide coordinating and/or governing boards is that they may defeat the very purposes they were established to achieve: the best use of the state's dollars for higher education. While they push hard for each institution to define its objectives and make plans to fit fiscal reality, they must also leave the individual campus sufficient flexibility to avoid the bureaucratic inefficiency so characteristic of large systems. Although the outlook is not overly encouraging, I have worked with several coordinating board staffs and found them very sensitive to the problem. They, of course, are beset by many problems from a variety of political constituencies, and it is remarkable that executive directors manage to survive even for the short terms now so characteristic of such positions. Librarians will discover a need (if they have not already) to work with such staffs much more closely in the future, because many decisions affecting academic libraries will be made in Albany, Austin, or Sacramento.[54] When such relationships have been established, they have often been very successful, especially in the new areas such as networks. In Arkansas, for example, close work of academic librarians with state officials resulted in the initial funding for state colleges to become members of AMIGOS.

Libraries

Librarians should be cautious about their quite understandable tendency to demand that all library appropriations be specifically earmarked. Such earmarking does often result in immediate improvement but sometimes also works against long-term increments necessary for staff support and also decreases their institution's ability to respond to new directions, specifically allocating more resources to libraries and less to other university programs. In my opinion, administrative flexibility is absolutely essential in assuring "more than survival."[55]

Like the libraries of the private liberal arts colleges, libraries of the state colleges and universities will be competing with other departments in the institution for scarce resources. Over the past decade, gross figures indicate that 4–7 percent of most institutional budgets go for libraries, with somewhat more for smaller schools and somewhat less for the largest ones. Size and economies of scale, therefore, make a difference. Today, 4 or 5 percent of $1 million is no longer an adequate sum for an academic library; 4 or 5 percent of $100 million is another matter. Still, as the ARL group likes to remind us, their responsibilities as research universities have to be considered. Even $5 million may not be enough for Princeton, Chicago, Illinois, or Michigan (indeed it is not).[56] How does one recognize the excellent research universities and the national function they serve without inviting unintended invidious comparisons? "Flagship campuses" (a Carnegie Commission term, incidentally) are in trouble politically across the country as their aspirations compete with the aspirations of other state institutions and they receive a declining share of the higher education dollar. In an egalitarian society, how can one justify institutions that are frankly meritocratic and elitist by their very nature?[57] Someone is going to have to articulate for a public increasingly hostile to meritocratic ideas the necessity for these research universities to be regarded as national institutions. The Rousseauesque idealism of the late 1960s certainly had an impact on American thinking about this problem. It may well be that the future of those fifty universities that educate the bulk of the graduate and professional students will be determined by the federal government. There have already been numerous suggestions that they serve national functions and that they are poorly supported for their contributions to national goals. The new Title

II-C of the Higher Education Act of 1965 for federal library support of not more than 150 distinguished research libraries is unquestionably a step in this direction.[58] Whether the United States would fare better by adopting a University Grants System for those universities whose contributions extend beyond state boundaries may be debatable because it appears not to have worked so well in the United Kingdom.[59] Still one can understand the view of a state taxpayer that it is not his or her responsibility to support 10,000–12,000 out-of-state students per year, mostly in expensive graduate and professional programs. With the economic barriers to the out-of-state student moving ever higher, the problem demands serious national attention.

On the other hand, one could argue, as many do, that the largest and most prestigious universities can generate enough funds for improvement from their own resources. If an improvement fund of 1 to 3 percent is needed, a budget of $100–200 million should certainly have sufficient flexibility to provide that small amount.[60] What is often overlooked is that most of these institutions have been using their so-called "fat" or "flexibility" to achieve the economies and reductions necessary to keep their budgets balanced these past half-dozen years. As Martin Meyerson has noted: "Excellence might not always require more resources, but it can rarely be achieved with less."[61] Meanwhile, many institutions have been forced to absorb necessary salary increases through economies within the institution. In the face of increased fuel bills, inflation, and reductions in federal research funds, less is obviously not always more. Nonetheless, the libraries of the research university are going to have to get by with less. They are caught between the demand for a better-quality undergraduate program for the masses and sustaining the excellence of doctoral and research programs for the few. On most campuses, the political power, in terms of educational policy and library policy, lies with the latter group. Walter Metzger is probably right when he says the universities will terminate junior faculty, not fill senior positions, and will excise the "small, undistinguished department, but keep the monumental losers— the graduate school and the school of medicine—on which their scholarly reputation rests."[62] It is hard to see how they can do anything else and remain universities committed to the advancement and dissemination of knowledge.

In several incisive papers, Richard De Gennaro has recounted the problems and austere future of the research library.[63] His recent report from the University of Pennsylvania, "Toward a More Responsive Library: Five Years of Progress," and Douglas Bryant's "The Changing Research Library"[64] provides a succinct presentation of their problems. Both directors have been articulate voices raised in behalf of the research library community while at the same time seeking solutions that are forward-looking and will address the issues of bibliographic sharing, fiscal crises, new technology, staffing, and the like in a realistic manner. The difficulties that lie ahead for the research library are somewhat mitigated by the resources and support they are likely to command over the long haul. Nonetheless, it is no wonder that their numerous problems have made the task of replacing their directors with younger models particularly difficult.[65]

Community Colleges

As James O. Wallace has indicated in his article in *College and Research Librar-ies*, the two-year community college is a relatively new phenomenon in higher education.[66] Although there were junior colleges, mostly private, before 1945, the real development of the two-year college came in the post-World War II period. Their enrollments have grown from approximately 310,000 in 1950 to approxi-mately 2 million in 1974 and now comprise approximately 20 percent of higher education's total enrollment.[67] According to Cartter, approximately two out of every five students entering college today matriculate at a two-year college, as opposed to one out of four a decade ago.[68] Some observers believe that the two-year share of the market will soon grow to 50 percent for first-time enrollment, but I tend to believe the rate of growth of two-year college enrollments will stabilize, barring some as yet unforeseen thrust by these institutions. Like other public institutions, two-year colleges grew enormously during the past decade. They em-phasized open admissions, technical and vocational training, community in-volvement, and college preparatory work. Although they have often seemed as sensitive to criticism as the land-grant colleges were in their early days, the two-year colleges have enjoyed great community support and a strong financial base in many states. At least part of the criticism, as occurred with the land-grant col-leges, is sheer envy at their success in increasing their share of the state and local tax revenues. Nonetheless, there seems little doubt that the great period of build-ing and expansion is over for them as it is for other colleges and universities. A technical institute with an FTE enrollment of fewer than 1,000 students is no more economically viable than a liberal arts college with the same number.[69] If most of them do achieve economy of size, they are likely to be somewhat better off finan-cially than their counterparts in the other two categories. In the recent analysis of finances in *Change* magazine, 70 percent of the two-year colleges were judged to be financially healthy, or relatively so.[70] Not burdened by the problems of dormi-tories or living accommodations and expensive research laboratories and librar-ies, the two-year colleges should continue to fare well, especially if they can keep their community involvement through adult education programs. In this, as in other matters, they will compete with community institutions like the church, the school, and the public library, and so the future may not be without local battles for community support. Too, their role in continuing education is likely to be a bone of contention with four-year colleges and universities except for the strictly technical and vocational areas. One of the criticisms of the two-year colleges is that they have a lack of focus and that their sense of mission is too broad. Such criti-cisms are worth consideration, though the lack of careful targeting of institutional mission is scarcely limited to two-year colleges.

Libraries

Beginning with B. Lamar Johnson's *Vitalizing a College Library*,[71] an account of how Stephens College made a virtue out of necessity, the two-year college librarian has seen his or her role differently from that of other academic librarians. In general, such librarians see themselves as engaged in more active involvement in the educational program than their colleagues elsewhere. "Library" is their term for the traditional print-oriented establishment. "Learning resources" is the term for the expanded program of materials and services characteristic of the up-to-date two-year college.[72] How many of these colleges actually have integrated print and nonprint materials under a special librarian/director competent in both areas is difficult to judge. One recent study in North Carolina would indicate not as many as one might have assumed.[73] Even some very large community colleges have separate and distinct print and nonprint units whose contact with each other is minimal. Nonetheless, the generalization still holds: Two-year college librarians are far more sympathetic to, and involved with, nonprint materials than their counterparts in the rest of higher education. That seems likely to continue, especially with the emphasis upon open admissions and meeting the needs of the disadvantaged. It may well be that the two-year college by its very nature is the best place to achieve that combination of remedial work and college-preparatory work or vocational skill where success has so far eluded other higher education institutions. One word of caution seems necessary here. Two-year colleges would do well to tone down their rhetoric and not promise more than they can deliver. They should learn from the example of the research university and the four-year colleges' messianic dreams of the 1960s. More *is* sometimes less, and all one's piety and wit may not cancel out the memory of performance that did not meet expectations.

Program, Enrollment, and Funds

Three things will determine an academic library's future: the educational programs, enrollments at various levels, and the financial resources to support programs and enrollments. They are inextricably linked. Whatever foolishness has emerged about better management, smaller collections, networking, and so forth does not alter that fact. As Steven Muller and others writing in the two *Daedalus* issues (fall 1974 and winter 1975) titled "American Higher Education: Toward an Uncertain Future" have warned us, there is a confusion of purpose in most educational institutions today. That confusion is reflected in the academic library, trying to second-guess what programs will emerge, what enrollments will look like, and what financial resources will be available to do the job. Beset by faculty and students who always want more resources and services, but more aware of fiscal constraints and long-range projections than most of their teaching colleagues, the academic librarian appears constantly beleaguered to the point where a major problem today is finding sufficient candidates for major administrative vacancies. That problem seems unlikely to be resolved in the near future.

Library Books, Buildings, and Staff

By way of concluding this paper, it would seem useful to discuss briefly that triad so necessary for service in an academic library's operation: books, buildings, and staff. Within this volume, others will discuss some of these matters in more detail.

Books. Thanks to the surge of support during the 1960s, most academic libraries are far better off in terms of library materials than they were a decade ago.[74] The expenditures from gifts, grants, and appropriations strengthened basic collections, reference materials, and journal files. While the new ACRL Standards of 1975 provide a real challenge for many college libraries, the future is certainly brighter because of the capital investment in library materials in the sixties.

Unfortunately, the cost of keeping up has increased at a greater rate than other institutional costs.[75] Journals and indexes are a real problem for all colleges and universities. Few small colleges can even afford to subscribe to such a basic tool as *Chemical Abstracts* at $3,500 per year, even though they may have a complete file from 1907 to 1970. Networks hold some promise for reducing the serials cost, but a British-style National Lending Library for a country as large and diverse as the United States, and with a deteriorating postal service, seems likely to be less useful than many assume. There may have to be a new way to disseminate scholarly information, a solution for which may emerge from the massive ACLS study now under way.[76]

Meanwhile, other materials like books, films, equipment, and micro-technology are raising costs in a way that makes it especially difficult for small colleges that cannot achieve economies of scale. Certainly, the move toward national bibliographic control will be helpful in stabilizing and even reducing costs in processing, but a better system always entails higher initial costs, and the actual saving in dollars may be hard to document. Unfortunately, one of the first places colleges cut budgets is in the area of materials (the state of North Carolina suspended all purchases of books and journals for six months in 1976). Such panic behavior does not really solve financial problems even temporarily, and the long-range problem is usually made worse by such behavior. Panic reductions are no more defensible than panic buying to use up all the funds.

Buildings. As Jerrold Orne has documented, there has been unprecedented construction of academic library buildings during the past decade with 647 buildings having been erected at a cost of $1.9 billion.[77] One important stimulus was the provision for federal matching of one-third of the costs under the Higher Education Act of 1963. Fortunate indeed were the institutions that built libraries in the 1960s and early 1970s and could utilize federal matching funds.

Indicative of the future is a recent decision by the New York State Board of Regents to press SUNY and private colleges in New York to eliminate plans for the construction of additional facilities "in all but the most crucial cases."[78] Their judgment was that, except for CUNY, existing facilities could more than accommodate future enrollments. The only glimmer of hope for many institutions needing library buildings will be the gift of a generous donor or a public works program to stimulate the economy. Some institutions will still be fortunate, and certainly it will be easier to find money for smaller rather than larger buildings. Still, I feel that librarians have often been too apologetic about the cost of library buildings. On my own campus, a prospective research library building is scheduled to cost $23 million—an unusually large sum until one remembers that a laboratory-office building for the School of Medicine will be completed in 1978 at a cost of $18 million and that there is a request to the next legislature for over $7 million just to renovate the chemistry laboratories. A case can be made that a library building serving the humanities and the social sciences is a far better investment for the total educational programs of a college and university than is any other building, even if its total cost may be that of two or three other buildings.

Staff. What kind of staff will be needed for the next two decades? Academic library directors and library school deans wish they knew. One thing is clear from the economic constraints: There will not be enough staff to do everything the campus community wants done. Certainly, the older view that one needs a firm grounding in classification and cataloging will give way to a new approach to bibliographic records. One still hears talk about how students are graduating without "practical skills," but the most "practical skill" a student can learn these days is how to manipulate a computer even though she or he may not use that skill immediately in a small college in the hinterlands. Internship programs are highly desirable, as they have been for the past century, but there is likely to be more benefit from an internship geared to a sophisticated special library than fetching books from the stacks in a university library's circulation department.

Meanwhile, the shift from graduate study in the humanities and social sciences to library education programs reflects the reality of the market place.[79] However, some individuals are going to be disappointed when they discover that their freshly minted Ph.D. and library school sheepskins do not automatically lead to placement either as an English literature bibliographer in a research university or a faculty member in a library school. There are only a limited number of subject bibliographers needed, especially because enrollments in the discipline itself may decline.

Nonetheless, as indicated earlier, this is an opportunity for academic libraries to improve the quality of staffs and to relate more effectively to the educational programs. Bibliographic instruction is back with us again,[80] and the renewed emphasis upon teaching, independent study, and self-directed learning will create heavier demands on traditional as well as nontraditional library services. There should not be great debate over the matter of the doctorate in library science versus the subject doctorate. Each has its place, and, in any case, the number of doctorates now being produced by library schools (about 65 per year)[81] will not satisfy the demand of library schools themselves much less university demand for more highly skilled administrators. The anti-intellectualism implied in the downgrading of credentials like advanced degrees, which is now coming to the fore in public libraries, is unlikely to affect most campuses where the ingrained tradition of terminal degrees will remain strong for at least the next decade. In a choice between a candidate with a doctorate and a library science degree and one without the doctorate, the library will likely tip the scales in favor of the doctorate. I am bothered by that fact, for I believe that the profession may lose those bright and energetic youngsters just out of undergraduate school and full of ideas about the challenge of the profession. Will library schools be forced to develop a two-track system for those with and without advanced subject degrees?

Up to this point, this paper has not dealt with several problems, including unionization, the push for academic and/or faculty status, governance, affirmative-action programs, or other personnel problems facing academic libraries. That is not because they are unimportant but because they will be solved within the total context of the institution's mission, its legal status, and its financial support.

The librarian's push for academic and/or faculty status had some encouragement in the 1960s and culminated in the joint ACRL-AAUP Statement of 1973.[82] Joining with a large organization like AAUP is probably very much to an academic librarian's advantage. Certainly, it was easier to secure faculty status when funds were more plentiful and promotion and tenure regulations less strict. Now, when promotions are under heavy scrutiny, some librarians are even questioning the concept of faculty status if it means strict comparability with the teaching faculty. The move of Ph.D.'s into the library may help with faculty status, but it is also likely to create tensions among the staff. If academic librarians can use the increased capability of the staff to work with the faculty in improving the educational program, then the movement for faculty status is likely to succeed. On the other hand, library staffs have little experience in operating as a faculty, and there is some evidence that their fumbling attempts have set back the faculty-status movement. Complicating all of the personnel problems are the loss of flexibility for positions, the advent of collective bargaining, and the thrust toward affirmative-action programs for women and minorities. Unfortunately, the achievement of faculty status, the employment of more women and minorities, and increased salaries are likely to be the victims of increasingly bureaucratic structures that will hinder rather than help in the achievement of these goals.

In conclusion, I would urge academic librarians to be aware of the political, social, and economic problems of our time. The librarian is probably in a better position to assess the educational strengths and weaknesses of an institution than are most faculty. He or she should be aware of the major educational trends, the arguments about general versus specialized knowledge, higher learning versus higher skilling, undergraduate versus graduate/professional students, continuing versus adult education, centralization versus decentralization. The academic librarian may be in the center of controversies over such matters. That need not be a bad place to be so long as one keeps in mind the place of the library in the educational process and remembers Justin Winsor's hundred-year-old dictum:

A collection of good books, with a soul to it in the shape of a good librarian, becomes a vitalized power among the impulses by which the world goes on to improvement.[83]

NOTES

1. "American Higher Education: Toward an Uncertain Future," *Daedalus* 103 (Fall 1974) and 104 (Winter 1975).
2. A remarkable instance of this self-fulfilling prophecy can be found in Harvard University's estimate ten years ago that its collections would rise to ten mil-

lion volumes and its expenditures to $14.5 million in the next decade. Rene Kuhn Bryant, *Harvard University Library, 1638–1968* (Cambridge, Mass.: Harvard University Library, 1969), pp. 52–53. As Douglas W. Bryant notes in his Harvard University Library, *Annual Report, 1975–1976*, pp. 1–2, Harvard missed its projections on volumes by only about 5 percent but came within its projected expenditures by 0.3 percent. That Harvard would actually contemplate spending almost $15 million on its library system by 1976 astounded librarians a decade earlier. The planning document had called attention to financial support as the most pressing of the libraries' problems in 1966. That remained true in 1976, for despite these expenditures, the libraries had adopted economy measures to try to deal with the mounting costs, including a smaller staff than anticipated and lower book budgets than projected.

3. "Who's Who in Higher Education," *Change* 7 (February 1975): 24–31. Kerr received one-fourth of all the nominating votes in *Change*'s poll on leadership figures in higher education. Only Rev. Theodore M. Hesburgh, with 15 percent, came reasonably close to Kerr's popularity.

4. Clark Kerr, *The Uses of the University* (Cambridge, Mass.: Harvard University Press, 1963).

5. U.S. Department of Commerce, Bureau of the Census, *Historical Statistics of the United States: Colonial Times to 1970* (Washington, D.C.: U.S. Government Printing Office, 1975), pt. 1, p. 383.

6. Allan M. Cartter, *Ph.D.'s and the Academic Labor Market* (New York: McGraw-Hill, 1976), p. 1.

7. *Historical Statistics of the United States*, pt. 1, p. 384.

8. Ibid.

9. Jerrold Orne and Jean O. Gosling, "Academic Library Building in 1976," *Library Journal* 101 (December 1, 1976): 2345.

10. William S. Dix, "Cause and Effect on University Libraries," *American Libraries* 3 (July–August 1972): 727.

11. See, for example, Allan M. Cartter, "Future Faculty: Needs and Resources," in *Improving College Teaching*, ed. by Calvin B. T. Lee (Washington, D.C.: American Council on Education, 1967), pp. 113–135.

12. Cartter, *Ph.D.'s and the Academic Labor Market*, pp. 18–19.

13. Alan Pifer, "The Nature and Origins of the Carnegie Commission on Higher Education" (New York: Carnegie Foundation for the Advancement of Teaching, 1972).

14. Ibid., p. 4.

15. For a summary of all these studies up to 1973, see Lewis B. Mayhew, *The Carnegie Commission on Higher Education* (San Francisco: Jossey-Bass, 1973). Libraries formed a minor part of only one volume and that a fairly unsatisfactory one, *The Fourth Revolution: Instructional Technology in Higher Education* (New York: McGraw-Hill, 1972), pp. 29–35. However, Mayhew believes this volume may be a "sleeper" (p. 419).

16. Larry Van Dyne, "A Busy, Nostalgic Week Marks Windup of Carnegie Commission," *The Chronicle of Higher Education* 8 (October 23, 1973): 5.

17. Ibid.

18. A few of the comments and criticisms of the Carnegie Commission's work can be found in the following: Donald McDonald, "The Carnegie Commission

Study of Higher Education: A Six Million Dollar Misunderstanding," *The Center Magazine*, Center for the Study of Democratic Institutions (September–October, 1973); Wendell V. Harris, "The Carnegie Commission: To Date, Less than Satisfying," *The Chronicle of Higher Education* 7 (January 15, 1973): 12; David Mathews, "Carnegie and Newman: Higher Education in Transition," *SR/World*, February 8, 1976, pp. 63–64; George W. Bonham, "The Carnegie Commission," *Change* 5 (November 1973): 7–8.

19. Carnegie Foundation for the Advancement of Teaching, *More Than Survival: Prospects for Higher Education in a Period of Uncertainty* (San Francisco: Jossey-Bass, 1975).

20. Earl F. Cheit, *The New Depression in Higher Education: A Study of Financial Conditions at 41 Colleges and Universities* (New York: McGraw-Hill, 1971).

21. Earl F. Cheit, *The New Depression in Higher Education—Two Years Later* (Berkeley, Calif.: Carnegie Commission on Higher Education, 1973), pp. 51, 66–67, 71.

22. Cartter, *Ph.D.'s and the Academic Labor Market*, p. 238. See also Chapter 10, "An Overview of Projected Academic Labor Market Conditions."

23. Ibid., pp. 246–250.

24. Ibid., p. 94.

25. U.S. Office of Education, National Center for Education Statistics, *The Condition of Education* (Washington, D.C.: U.S. Government Printing Office, 1976), pp. 20, 24.

26. Cartter, *Ph.D.'s and the Academic Labor Market*, pp. 105–106, 222.

27. Elaine H. El-Khawas, *Public and Private Higher Education: Differences in Role, Character, and Clientele*, Policy Analysis Service Reports, vol. 2, no. 3, December 1976 (Washington, D.C.: American Council on Education, 1976), p. 20.

28. Ibid., pp. 55, 58.

29. *The Condition of Education*, p. 20, indicates that the private college enrollment grew only 100,000 from 1968 to 1974, while total enrollment in higher education increased by almost 4 million students. Most liberal arts colleges are private. See El-Khawas, *Public and Private Higher Education*, p. 55.

30. Carnegie Foundation for the Advancement of Teaching, *More Than Survival*, pp. 104–106.

31. Cartter, *Ph.D.'s and the Academic Labor Market*, pp. 16–17.

32. See Richard M. Millard, "State Aid to Nonpublic Higher Education," *Higher Education in the States* 4 (1974): 149–172, which gives the status of various plans as of 1974. A number of changes have been made during legislative sessions since then, and M. M. Chambers, *A Record of Progress: Four Years of State Tax Support of Higher Education, 1972–73 through 1975–76* (Danville, Ill.: Interstate Printers, 1976), provides complete state-by-state data on appropriations for higher education, including aid to private education. Another source is Howard R. Bowen and W. John Minter, *Private Higher Education: Second Annual Report on Financial and Educational Trends in the Private Sector of American Higher Education* (Washington, D.C.: Association of American Colleges, 1976). Carnegie Foundation for the Advancement

of Teaching, *More Than Survival*, p. 68, details rising state support for student financial-aid programs, $274.1 million of which went to private institutions in 1974–1975.

33. El-Khawas, *Public and Private Higher Education*, p. 57.
34. *The Condition of Education*, p. 24.
35. Cartter, *Ph.D.'s and the Academic Labor Market*, p. 89.
36. Ibid., p. 54.
37. Ibid., pp. 61–62.
38. Ibid., p. 68.
39. Carnegie Foundation for the Advancement of Teaching, *More Than Survival*, pp. 80–81.
40. For a recent report on finances in various types of institutions, see Andrew H. Lupton, John Augenblick, and Joseph Heyison, "The Financial State of Higher Education," *Change* 8 (September 1976): 21–26.
41. See C. Robert Pace, *Education and Evangelism* (New York: McGraw-Hill, 1972).
42. North Carolina State Library, *Statistics of North Carolina University and College Libraries, 1975*, p. 2.
43. Otis Hall Robinson, "Proceedings," *American Library Journal* 1 (November 30, 1876): 123–124.
44. Justin Winsor, "The College Library and the Classes," *Library Journal* 3 (March 1878): 5.
45. Unfortunately this program has not been described extensively in print, though some information is available in the Council on Library Resources *Annual Reports* and brochures from the National Endowment for the Humanities. See also Deborah H. Bodner, "A Descriptive Analysis of the Council on Library Resources' College Library Programs" (master's paper, School of Library Science, University of North Carolina at Chapel Hill, 1975).
46. Murray Martin, "Truth in Packaging, or How to Work with the Administration," *Journal of Library Automation* 9 (June 1976): 87–88.
47. National Commission on Libraries and Information Science, *Toward a National Program for Library and Information Services: Goals for Action* (Washington, D.C.: U.S. Government Printing Office, 1975).
48. Michael K. Buckland, ed., "The Management Review and Analysis Program: A Symposium," *Journal of Academic Librarianship* 1 (January 1976): 4–14.
49. P. Grady Morein, Joseph F. Boykin, Jr., H. Lea Wells, and Johnnie E. Givens, "The Academic Library Development Program," *College and Research Libraries* 38 (January 1977): 37–45.
50. Richard De Gennaro, "Escalating Journal Prices: Time to Fight Back," *American Libraries* 8 (February 1977): 69–74.
51. See the excellent article by Richard De Gennaro, "Toward a More Responsive Library: Five Years of Progress," *1975–76 Report of the Director*, University of Pennsylvania Libraries, *Almanac Supplement*, October 12, 1976, p. iv.
52. Carnegie Foundation for the Advancement of Teaching, *More Than Survival*, p. 6. There is a suggestion that teacher education now accounts for only 10 percent of total enrollment (p. 59), but that figure seems low to me.

53. Steven Muller, "Higher Education or Higher Skilling?" *Daedalus* 103 (Fall 1974): 148–158.
54. I. T. Littleton has recently completed a study of the relationships of library councils to state boards of higher education under a CLR Fellowship Grant. His findings should tell us much about this virtually unexplored area.
55. Texas offers a good example of the kind of formula that initially raised the library capability of all state-supported institutions, but the lag in revising the formula to account for inflation and the funding of the library formula at less than 100 percent has created problems for the larger institutions. Moreover, the library formula never did work very well for the major state university. Edward G. Holley, "Academic Libraries in the Sixties: Was the Future Bright?" *Texas Library Journal* 46 (Spring 1970): 10–16, 42–60; and "Academic Library Finance in the Seventies: The Picture Blurs," *Texas Library Journal* 48 (March 1972): 25–29, 38–45.
56. In the Association of Research Libraries, *ARL Statistics 1975–76*, p. 37, the median figure for total library operating expenditures was $3,525,042, but twenty-seven of the ninety-three institutions spent more than $5 million and three university libraries more than $10 million.
57. Daniel P. Moynihan discusses this problem and the Nixon Administration's attempt to deal with it in "The Politics of Higher Education," *Daedalus* 104 (Winter 1975): 128–147.
58. "Research Libraries," ALA Washington Office *Newsletter* 28 (November 2, 1976): 2; ALA Washington Office *Legislative Report*, July 1976–January 1977, p. 18; *Federal Register* 41 (November 22, 1976): 51550–51551.
59. Harold Perkin, "The Financial Crisis in British Universities, or How to Live with 29 Percent Inflation," *AAUP Bulletin* 61 (Winter 1975): 304–308.
60. Carnegie Foundation for the Advancement of Teaching, *More Than Survival* (p. 87) recognizes both the need and the complexity of the problem. Procedurally, colleges and universities are not well equipped for the kind of flexibility and reallocation of resources likely to be necessary. As Cheit's *The New Depression in Higher Education—Two Years Later* recognizes (pp. 64–65, 67–69), the central role of the administration becomes crucial in the management of the university's resources, but that will be a problem for many institutions where faculty control over educational policy is a dogma of academic faith.
61. Martin Meyerson, "After a Decade of the Levelers in Higher Education: Reinforcing Quality While Maintaining Mass Education," *Daedalus* 104 (Winter 1975): 312.
62. Walter P. Metzger, "The American Academic Profession in 'Hard Times'," *Daedalus* 104 (Winter 1975): 29.
63. See, for example, Richard De Gennaro, "Austerity, Technology, and Resource Sharing: Research Librarians Face the Future," *Library Journal* 100 (May 15, 1975): 917–923.
64. Douglas W. Bryant, "The Changing Research Library," *The Library Scene* 4 (September 1975): 2–4, 15.
65. A spate of articles have appeared subsequent to the widely read article of Robert B. Downs and Arthur M. McAnally, "The Changing Role of Directors of University Libraries," *College and Research Libraries* 34 (March 1973):

32   ACADEMIC LIBRARIES BY THE YEAR 2000

103–125. Some of the debate is summarized in Edward G. Holley, "The Magic of Library Administration," *Texas Library Journal* 52 (May 1976): 58–63.

66. James O. Wallace, "Newcomer to the Academic Scene: The Two-Year College Library/Learning Center," *College and Research Libraries* 37 (November 1976): 503–513.
67. U.S. Department of Commerce, Bureau of the Census, *Statistical Abstract of the United States, 1974* (Washington, D.C.: U.S. Government Printing Office, 1975), p. 136.
68. Cartter, *Ph.D.'s and the Academic Labor Market*, p. 68.
69. In South Carolina, eight of the technical institutes had fewer than 1,000 FTE students in 1975 and eighteen of the thirty-eight North Carolina technical institutes reporting in 1975 had fewer than 1,000 FTE students. South Carolina Commission on Higher Education, *Annual Report*, January 1976, p. 25, and North Carolina State Library, *Statistics of North Carolina University and College Libraries, 1975*, p. 6. A study, *Resources of South Carolina Libraries*, soon to be published by the South Carolina Commission on Higher Education, indicates that small enrollments in many institutions are a major problem in securing the financial assistance necessary to provide adequate library resources and services.
70. Lupton et al., "The Financial State of Higher Education," pp. 25–26.
71. B. Lamar Johnson, *Vitalizing a College Library* (Chicago: American Library Association, 1939).
72. Wallace, "Newcomer to the Academic Scene," p. 504.
73. John Wayne Modlin, "A Survey of the Relationship between the North Carolina Community College Libraries/Learning Resources Centers and the AAJC-ACRL Guidelines for Two-Year College Learning Resources Programs" (master's paper, School of Library Science, University of North Carolina at Chapel Hill, 1975).
74. Thedore Samore, "College and University Library Statistics," in *The Bowker Annual of Library and Book Trade Information, 1975*, pp. 227–229, reveals that not only did "total volumes held" almost double between 1964 and 1974, but the number of volumes per student increased from 45.3 in 1964 to 51.7 in 1974. Yet a similar report in *The Bowker Annual, 1976*, p. 236, indicated that a decline occurred in volumes per student. Library statistics are best utilized in gross terms, and so one probably should think more in terms of total growth and not volumes per student, which, in any case, is likely to vary greatly from institution to institution.
75. According to D. Kent Halstead, *Higher Education Prices and Price Indexes* (Washington, D.C.: U.S. Government Printing Office, 1975), pp. 32–33, only fringe benefits increased at a greater rate than did the cost of books and periodicals between 1961 and 1974. In the four years from 1970 to 1974, periodical prices averaged an increase of 14 percent annually. See also earlier references to De Gennaro articles. According to Hugh Atkinson, "Prices of U.S. and Foreign Published Materials," in *The Bowker Annual, 1976*, p. 202, in the first five years of this decade (1970–1975) the price of U.S. periodicals has more than doubled.
76. Chester Kerr, "A National Enquiry into the Production and Dissemination of Scholarly Knowledge," *Scholarly Publishing* 7 (October 1975): 3–13; "Booher: Toward the Enquiry," *Publishers Weekly* 210 (August 9, 1976): 34.

77. Orne and Gosling, "Academic Library Building in 1976," p. 2435.
78. "NY Regents Propose Four-Year State Plan," *Higher Education and National Affairs* 25 (August 20, 1976): 5.
79. Rush G. Miller, "The Influx of Ph.D.'s into Librarianship: Intrusion or Transfusion?" *College and Research Libraries* 37 (March 1976): 158–165.
80. At the midwinter meeting of the American Library Association in 1977, a new unit, Round Table on Library Instruction, was approved. This reflects increasing concern about this apparent neglect of this matter by other units of the ALA.
81. Charles H. Davis, comp., *Doctoral Dissertations in Library Science: Titles Accepted by Accredited Library Schools, 1930–1975* (Ann Arbor, Mich.: University Microfilms, 1976). The "Introduction" to this book reports 195 dissertations completed in the three-year period, 1973–1975. With the decline in federal support for doctoral students, this figure seems likely to decrease. See also Charles H. Davis., ed., "Research Record," *Journal of Education for Librarianship* 17 (Fall 1976): 117–120.
82. ACRL, *Faculty Status for Academic Librarians: A History and Policy Statements* (Chicago: American Library Association, 1975). The ACRL approved the joint statement in 1972 and the AAUP in 1973. The document initially had the backing of the Association of American Colleges, but the AAC declined to endorse the joint statement after having participated in its drafting.
83. Justin Winsor, "The College Library and the Classes," p. 5.

ABOUT THE AUTHOR

Edward G. Holley is Dean of the School of Library Science of the University of North Carolina at Chapel Hill. He has just recently completed a term as President of the American Library Association. He is a graduate of David Lipscomb College, George Peabody College, and the University of Illinois, from which he holds the Ph.D. Active in research and publication, Holley is the author of three books and many journal articles. In 1964 his book *Charles Evans, American Bibliographer* won the ALA Scarecrow Press Award for an "outstanding contribution to library literature." His other publications include *Raking the Historic Coals: The A.L.A. Scrapbook of 1876* and, with Donald D. Hendricks, *Resources of Texas Libraries*.

THE IMPACT OF INSTRUCTIONAL TECHNOLOGY ON THE FUTURE OF ACADEMIC LIBRARIANSHIP

by Damon D. Hickey

The world of American higher education and of academic libraries a century ago was vastly different from today. Education in 1876 was by lecture, book, and laboratory, with libraries playing a minor role. As Guy R. Lyle points out:

> Until the last quarter of the nineteenth century the pattern of college library service was relatively simple. The library was recognized as an important symbol in the establishment of colleges but was honored more frequently in words than in performance. Research on the history of the American college library indicates that the inadequacy of most college libraries was felt so keenly by students that the literary societies, which began to appear after the middle of the century, "undertook to establish student libraries as one of their major purposes." The office of the librarian was one of the first to be differentiated after that of the presidency; but the duties of the librarian, usually a member of the teaching faculty upon whom fell the added responsibility of caring for the library, were largely custodial. He carried the key to the room where the books were kept and saw to it that the room was tightly locked except during the few periods of the week when students were permitted to use the books.[1]

In 1876, two events marked a new beginning for librarianship, for education, and for human communication. The founding in October of the American Library Association (ALA) at the Centennial Exposition in Philadelphia was the first successful attempt to organize librarianship into a national profession. In the following century, the association would establish standards, facilitate communication among libraries and librarians, improve the effectiveness of the library as an educational and cultural institution, and promote free public access to information. The founding of the ALA was one symbol of the height of what has been called the "Print Age," just as the presence of the Great Corliss Engine in nearby Machinery Hall represented the triumph of the "Machine Age." Indeed, for Marshall McLuhan, the two were one, because "Printing from movable type was the first

mechanization of a complex handicraft, and became the archetype of all subsequent mechanization."[2]

Even as the triumph of print and machinery was being celebrated, a revolution had been born in still another exposition building, a technological innovation
that would usher in the "Electric Age" of communication, turn the Great Corliss
Engine into a modern dinosaur, change the context in which education was to take
place, and present librarianship with one of its greatest challenges and opportunities. The event was the first public exhibition by educator and inventor Alexander
Graham Bell of the telephone. Bell's device made possible the first instantaneous
transmission over great distances of audible human communication. It was not the
end of print, but the beginning of an age in which print would no longer dominate
communication, education, or libraries.

THE FOURTH REVOLUTION

Yet more than half a century was required for the revolution in communication
begun by the telephone to have any notable impact on education and librarianship.
As Brown, Norberg, and Srygley have noted, "Technological developments of
the twentieth century, and especially of the last thirty years, have now initiated a
new cycle in communication and instruction. Although this development now proceeds with accelerating speed, it is still a very young revolution and far from
maturity."[3] This young revolution has been called, first by Eric Ashby and later
by the Carnegie Commission on Higher Education, the "fourth revolution." The
first three are identified as the social differentiation of adult roles and the partial
shifting of education of the young from parents in the home to teachers in a
school; the emergence of the written word as a tool of education; and the in-
vention of printing with the widespread distribution of books (corresponding to
McLuhan's "Print/Machine Age"). "The fourth revolution, in Ashby's view, is
portended by developments in electronics, notably those involving the radio, television, tape recorder, and computer."[4] The fourth revolution, then, is the educational equivalent of McLuhan's "Electric Age."

To talk about the impact of the new, electric technology on academic libraries
is merely to focus upon one small part of a very large picture. There is a tendency
to write and speak as though the electric media and their effects were largely
absent from the academic scene and would remain so until formally accepted by
administrators, librarians, and classroom faculty. But if McLuhan is correct, the
true significance of any medium—any technology—is the relationships it creates.
This is the meaning of the statement, "The medium is the message."[5] To speak of
modern academic institutions or modern libraries, therefore, is already to speak of
the effects of the newer media, even if there is not a single electrical outlet or
battery to be found on campus. The changes in academic libraries that will be
described in this chapter are but the most formal, most superficial, and probably

the least significant effects of modern technology on educational institutions and particularly on academic libraries.

This chapter deals with instructional technology, the formal response of American education to the fourth revolution, and with its impact on academic libraries of the future. An attempt will be made to explain what instructional technology is, what its advantages for higher education may be and why higher education has been slow to accept it, which factors now promote the use of instructional technology in colleges and universities, which tools are available to help academic librarians understand it, and what role librarians should play in the educational revolution of which it is a part.

INSTRUCTIONAL TECHNOLOGY

"Instructional technology" is not merely, or even mainly, "audiovisuals." Instructional technology is the systematic application of any and all available means of communication to the process of instruction. "Technology" does not necessarily imply "systematic," but in the literature of instructional technology, it usually does, because instructional technologists seem to be quite eager to establish clearly the fact that they are not merely advocating the use of "audiovisual aids."

The term "systematic" refers to the "systems approach" to instruction. This approach is adapted from the general systems approach to management. According to one authority:

> The systems approach to instructional planning seeks to understand and evaluate the contribution of each of the components of the system to achievement of its stated goals, so that the optimum combination of elements may be chosen for utilization in instruction.[6]

Or, in other words:

> Educational technology, as currently being developed by the professionals in the field, emphasizes a systems approach to instructional development, incorporating specific measurable objectives, diagnostic testing, criteria for student performance and the repeated redesign and re-evaluation of the curriculum materials until the criteria are achieved. It was defined . . . as a way of designing, carrying out, and evaluating the total process of learning and teaching in terms of specific objectives, based on research in human learning and communications, and employing a combination of human and nonhuman resources to bring about more effective instruction. . . . Educational technology, therefore, is currently viewed as a total systems approach to education, incorporating hardware, course materials, and instructional and management techniques.[7]

Its Advantages for Higher Education

What are the advantages of this approach? Several "conservative claims" have been advanced by Charles McIntyre:

(a) the effectiveness of the superior teacher can be extended to more students with little or no diminution; (b) instruction can be systematically structured, revised, and improved in the light of measured student achievement toward agreed-upon goals; (c) the time of teachers can be diverted from lecture, demonstration, and drill and put to better use in instruction requiring the interaction of teacher and student; and (d) teaching can be enriched with a variety and depth of experiences not otherwise available to students.[8]

Instructional technology is a powerful tool. It is synergistic, a fact which is often overlooked or misunderstood by its critics. Having to specify goals and objectives helps a teacher to organize the instructional process. Altogether, applying knowledge of how people learn, testing to determine what students know or which skills they possess at the outset of a course, and continually revising a course in the light of feedback from the student produce an effect much more powerful than would have been anticipated by the simple addition of their separate effects. This extraordinary power of instructional technology as a learning system deserves the respect even of those who dislike it.

Additionally, however, a systems approach to instruction can save time and money in the long term. Faculty time, for example, may be spent in concentrated periods of planning and producing instructional aids rather than in daily lecturing or drilling. Similarly, an investment in necessary and appropriate audiovisual hardware and software may free money that might otherwise be required to pay additional faculty salaries. Cooperative networks for sharing and producing instructional materials could further reduce costs.

Resistance by the Academic Community

The introduction of instructional technology into an educational institution is often too expensive to be added on to existing operating costs. As a consequence, few postsecondary institutions have made use of its great potential. For instructional technology to be economical or even affordable, institutions would have to rethink systematically their entire approach to instruction. Such a change in the tradition of American higher education is only likely to occur if and when: (1) totally new institutions (such as the newer community colleges) are created; (2) there is a breakdown in the existing system (such as that faced by the public schools in trying to prepare students for college mathematics and science in the 1950s); or (3) there is a gradual increase in internal and external pressures to the point where faculty and administrators are forced to consider radical alternatives to the existing system.

The resistance to instructional technology by the academic community and by academic librarians has several possible sources. The approach is often misunderstood, and the words "instructional" and "technology" serve only as red flags. Additionally, the power of instructional technology may be underestimated and trivialized or exaggerated and feared. The approach is revolutionary and, therefore, threatens the status quo. People who have tended to operate in unsystematic or intuitive ways for many years are likely to resist a highly systematic and rational approach.

The formal language of systems management is foreign to most recipients of American higher education, even though some of the ideas it expresses are not. It reflects a behavioristic orientation that grates on the sensibilities of many who have been schooled in the older, humanistic approach to education. It seems somehow to be a language more appropriate for dealing with things than with people. One public school teacher attempted to express his feelings by saying, "A businessman may focus on demonstrable results, but a teacher must focus on people. An unhealthy focus on behavioral objectives has burdened teachers instead of helping them meet the needs of their students."[9] If the point is that a good teacher should be more concerned about the student's needs than about the teacher's own objectives, it is well taken. But the objection may be as much to the connotations of the word "behavioral," which may suggest coldness and lack of personal concern. Rationalization of a process, however, need not entail loss of passion or compassion for persons.

Despite the problems that the use of jargon creates, much of the literature of instructional technology, such as the articles in *AV Communication Review*, the professional journal of the Association for Educational Communications and Technology, generally employs the vocabulary and research techniques of the behavioral sciences. Although any field needs a vocabulary and a methodology, instructional technology suffers because of the way it communicates with educators who are not specialists in the field, do not consider themselves behavioral scientists, and may even dislike the behavioral sciences. It could be argued that the success of academic library faculty members in assisting their classroom faculty colleagues has been due to their ability to remain academic generalists and to borrow freely the vocabularies and methodologies of other fields without making library science captive to any. Instructional technologists would do well to observe their example.

Another objection heard often is that the economics of instructional technology tend to promote uniformity, not diversity, in education:

> The forces promoting uniformity are many. They include: the high cost and scarcity of trained talent to produce high quality, validated materials; the reliance on centrally distributed programs with the concomitant decrease in local production; the consolidation of school districts and the centralization of decision-making; the shift in the financing of local schools from a local to a state and national basis; and the movement toward economic efficiency and productivity.[10]

Although the above argument addresses public schools primarily and although it possibly applies with equal force to the sole use of standardized textbooks in schools, it should be taken seriously in relation to higher education as well, and will be dealt with again later.

Aside from these problems, there are other reasons why instructional technology has not made much progress in higher education. Academic faculties have long used nonprint materials as instructional aids, but they remain for the most part ignorant of the field of instructional technology. This circumstance is due largely to the fact that few have received formal schooling in the field of education. Most teachers tend to perpetuate the teaching methods and to use the learning tools by which they learned. Teachers below the college level are exposed to instructional technology in their undergraduate programs in education, are taught to think of themselves as professional teachers rather than as research scholars, are evaluated and rewarded in relation to their teaching rather than to their research and publication, and may in some school systems be expected to demonstrate their proficiency in the language and according to the model of instructional technology. Such an expectation would seem to many college teachers to be an infringement of their academic freedom. They may tend to identify the preservation of that freedom with the exclusive reliance upon the printed and spoken word in education. James W. Brown suggests that college professors may view the production of educational materials by teams of which they are a part as a threat to their academic privacy and autonomy.[11]

The premium placed by many academic institutions on research and publication may also limit the amount of time that faculty members are willing to devote to producing instructional materials. Charles McIntyre believes that the production of such materials for commercial distribution is analogous to writing a textbook for publication, and may someday be recognized as such, although it is not so recognized now.[12]

It has already been noted that the use of instructional technology is not necessarily a way to save money, especially over the short term. If a school "buys" it with that expectation, it is likely to discover that it must cut back in other critical areas. As Lawrence Grayson points out:

> The high cost of materials development is only one aspect of the total cost of some new technologies. The same level of expenditure is required for the hardware and facilities; for the support of personnel; and for training these personnel as materials producers, media specialists, instructional designers and managers, and utilization specialists.[13]

Grayson could have added the cost and difficulty of servicing equipment; the cost of systems to back up or replace those that are being repaired, have missing parts, or are stolen; the cost of purchasing incompatible systems from rival manufacturers; the cost of cataloging and classifying software; the cost of selection aids comparable to those now available for print materials; and the cost of "mediagraphies" (the analog to bibliographies) for special subject fields. College teachers may have other, more personal reasons for disliking instructional technology, including bad experiences with machines, mechanophobia, or bibliophilia.

On the other hand, there are factors operating to promote the use of instructional technology in higher education. Instructional technology was heralded in the 1960s as the solution to soaring college enrollments and limited numbers of qualified faculty members. Although that situation has changed and will change even more within the next twenty-five years, the experiments begun in the last fifteen years, under the impetus of new federal money, are not likely to be discontinued.

The next decade will probably see a decline in the number of students of "college age" and an increase in the number of "adult" students who are seeking higher education for the first time, resuming an interrupted education, continuing their education, or seeking reeducation for new careers. These students may have educational goals, backgrounds, and abilities that are very different from those of the younger group. It is not likely that higher education will remain unchanged, and one of the changes likely to occur is the introduction of instructional technology for developmental or remedial education. "Learning assistance" programs now provide an opportunity for students whose intelligence has enabled them to complete high school despite basic skill deficits to overcome such deficiencies.[14]

Even where instructional technology has not been formally embraced, elements are usually present that, when combined and augmented, could produce a new system. Many teachers already use audiovisual aids to augment lectures. Some permit students to listen to tape recordings instead of attending lectures. Other teachers are interested in producing their own instructional materials, especially slides and slide-tape presentations. A variety of remedial and developmental programs use a variety of systems. Foreign-language courses regularly employ language laboratories. The faculty development movement in higher education has provided some teachers with the opportunity to examine their teaching systematically and to develop new approaches to instruction. As more students are educated in school systems that utilize instructional technology and come to college having learned as much from television as from either the spoken or the printed word, it is inevitable that educational changes will take place.

These changes could easily be precipitated by a major national development such as provision by the federal government of capital for one or more cooperative regional centers "for the accelerated development and utilization of instructional technology in higher education," as recommended by the Carnegie Commission on Higher Education in June 1972.[15] Such centers would make the production of instructional materials much more economical and would speed the acceptance of instructional technology in higher education. The apparent success of the Ohio College Library Center (OCLC) and other regional bibliographic networks utilizing computer technology to benefit member libraries bodes well for the parallel development of centers for producing instructional materials, possibly also for member libraries.

INSTRUCTIONAL TECHNOLOGY IN THE COMMUNITY COLLEGE AS A MODEL

If one would see a possible image of the future academic institution and its library, the community college of today and its "learning resources center" provides such a model. The community colleges, according to James O. Wallace, evolved from private and public junior colleges and are "usually publicly supported."

> [They] provide a comprehensive curriculum with both academic programs and technical programs, together with developmental programs to remedy previous educational deficiencies and continuing education programs to meet informational, avocational, or vocational training and retraining needs of the local community. Most community colleges offer opportunities at night as well as during day hours to part-time students otherwise in full-time employment.[16]

By the 1970s, community colleges had developed along the following lines:

> The acceptance of the challenge to meet the needs of a diversified and heterogeneous group of students created an interest in the psychology and application of learning principles among many faculty members by the 1970s. Restructuring traditional courses utilizing behavioral techniques, individualized instruction, and application of new technologies received much attention from the faculties. Experimentation in instructional techniques to meet student needs and provision for faculty development programs to make possible adjustments from traditional lecture methods became features of community college educational programs.[17]

It is difficult to say whether the existence and evident success of community colleges in attracting both students and state funds have stimulated four-year and graduate institutions to follow their example or deterred them from doing so. There is a feeling among traditional academic institutions that community colleges are concerned only with "vocational" education and that their methods are not applicable to a "scholarly" or "liberal arts" education. There is at least a grain of truth in this assertion, insofar as community colleges do train people for skills. As the Carnegie Commission on Higher Education points out:

> Some of the informational technology, thus far, seems better at training skills than at general education. The better it is at training skills, the more general education may suffer as a result—particularly if students move off campus and content themselves with skill training. But instructional technology, represented by such media as television and film, can also contribute to general education and to the teaching of concepts.[18]

But even vocational education is not only skill training, and community colleges have not by any means limited themselves to either. The primary reason for employing instructional technology in the community college was that the increasingly widespread variations in background and career goals require an educational approach that is flexible and highly individualized.[19]

Its Learning Resources Center

The library of the community college may be a part of a larger learning resources center (LRC) or, in a few cases, may coexist with one. Management patterns differ, and the library may be under the supervision of an educator/administrator who is not a librarian. The most common pattern seems to be an integrated media collection and service center administered by someone with both library and instructional technology expertise. As a learning, as well as learning resources, center that extends or replaces the traditional classroom, it comes close to the idea of the "library-college" long promoted by Louis Shores.[20]

James O. Wallace provides a description of today's learning resources center which, because of its importance to the topic at hand, is quoted here in full:

> In the first place, there is found a commitment to direct involvement in instruction in programs for library/media technicians and also in the bone and marrow of instructional development.
>
> The learning resources program, in the second place, includes automatic utilization of information for learning in whatever format it can be found—print, microprint, or audiovisual. Again, the learning resources program includes operation of instructional learning laboratories, distribution of equipment, operation of closed-circuit television, as well as providing traditional study facilities.
>
> Staff members in the learning resources program are directly involved in production of instructional learning packages on the community college campus. The administrative head, having had training in both traditional library and audiovisual services, is more often a dean or vice-president than in most four-year institutions. The professional staff usually includes a number of specialists in educational technology as well as those with library school training.
>
> Among the supportive staff will be large numbers of technicians with training not only as library or media technicians but also as television, graphics, electronics, and photographic technicians.
>
> Finally, all traditional library services will be available in the two-year college learning resources program with their effectiveness enhanced by the availability of other informational sources.[21]

AIDS IN DEVELOPING AN INSTRUCTIONAL TECHNOLOGY PROGRAM

The academic librarian who wants to develop a program, however modest, in support of instructional technology will find some assistance in published literature. The Association for Educational Communications and Technology (AECT) publishes a journal-newsletter, *Audiovisual Instruction*, that can be very helpful. The AECT's more scholarly journal, *AV Communication Review*, is much more technical.

The AECT's program standards committee has also cooperated with the American Association of School Libraries (AASL), the Association of College and Research Libraries (ACRL), and the American Association of Junior Colleges (AAJC) in the development of standards for media programs.[22] Until standards are available for such programs in colleges and universities, there are *Guidelines for Audio-Visual Services in Academic Libraries* prepared by the audiovisual committee of the ACRL in 1968.[23]

The ACRL also sponsored the publication in 1975 of *Nonprint Media in Academic Libraries*.[24] This extremely useful book includes essays on "bibliographic" organization; selection and acquisition; standards; sound recordings; slides; film; filmstrips; maps and map collections; pictures, photographs, and prints; and a comprehensive bibliography arranged to correspond with the chapter topics.

The standard textbook in the field of audiovisual education is Brown, Lewis, and Harcleroad, *AV Instruction: Technology, Media, and Methods*.[25] Although geared mainly to elementary and secondary education, this textbook is still useful in describing the applications of different media. James W. Brown, the principal author, has also collaborated in three other works of importance: *Administering Educational Media: Instructional Technology and Library Services*[26] contains several chapters of interest to the academic librarian, including one on "Media Services in Colleges and Universities"; *College Teaching: A Systematic Approach*[27] is a good introduction to use of the systems approach to college teaching; and *New Media and College Teaching*[28] gives case studies and inventories programs involving a variety of media. Also of use is Brown's annual *Educational Media Yearbook*.[29]

In addition to these print resources, the librarian who is interested in learning more about instructional technology can take advantage of workshops, formal courses offered by schools or departments of library science and education or by community colleges, and consultation with people who are involved in media services and instructional technology. The proliferation of such specialists through community college systems should leave few librarians without a nearby consultant.

As has already been suggested, the academic librarian who seeks to promote instructional technology in his or her institution will find both allies and opponents. The use of nonprint educational resources is already a fact in virtually every institution, and a desire on the part of the library staff to assist faculty members in locating and obtaining software, servicing hardware, and in some cases centralizing media services will probably be welcomed.

Brown, Norberg, and Srygley suggest that the two things needed to make instructional technology succeed in higher education are: (1) "an institutionwide commitment to efforts to improve instruction, including those aimed at its general systematization"; and (2) "provision of an adequately staffed, adequately supported educational media center to provide leadership and services essential to this effort."[30] Obtaining the first is a difficult task for the librarian working alone. As an educator without a classroom, the librarian may be thought presumptuous to suggest to colleagues that they commit themselves to improving instruction with her or his assistance. It may be possible, however, for librarians to bring together support for instructional improvement and to promote the efforts of their colleagues. The second factor mentioned above is of utmost importance to librarians who intend to include a "media center" in their facilities. Nothing turns a skeptical faculty member away from audiovisual media faster than a mechanical breakdown in front of a class. If librarians want to promote the effective use of all learning resources, they must do well whatever they do.

THE FUTURE ROLE OF INSTRUCTIONAL TECHNOLOGY IN ACADEMIC LIBRARIES

The future of instructional technology in academic libraries is difficult to chart. It is possible that the question is really, "What is the future of academic libraries in instructional technology?" That was the question faced by libraries in community colleges. It may even be that the question concerns the future of academic institutions themselves. Certainly, advanced level research will continue, and major universities (at least some major universities) will continue to produce research and researchers for as long as anyone can foresee. It is at the level called "college" or "undergraduate," where research is not the major enterprise, that the question of the future is most critical. The community college provides one clear model. Whether the four-year school adopts the community college's goals or its approach to education remains to be seen.

Academic libraries cannot, of course, pursue educational goals that contradict those of the schools they serve, although they can be, and have sometimes been, leaders in educational innovation among faculties reluctant to change. Long advocates and practitioners of individualized instruction, they should certainly welcome technological advances that promote this cause. Yet, one often finds a distressing lack of involvement of librarians, whether from intention or exclusion, in educational planning. Librarians sometimes seem to accept the judgment of classroom colleagues who view them as clerks who do not teach and who, because they are not "subject specialists," are not qualified to make educational judgments. The only argument advanced in some places for putting librarians on faculty committees has been that if curricular changes are planned, the librarians should not be the last to know. It is assumed that librarians have little to contribute to the educational planning process itself.

Related to this distance from educational decision making is what sometimes appears to be a lack of interest by librarians in the use of nonprint educational media. There are several possible reasons for this attitude. Librarians may, as some instructional technologists have claimed, be interested mainly in print and suspicious or afraid of "machinery." Electric media are certainly more complicated and troublesome than books, and more expensive. Academic librarians may have a justifiable fear that those media could intrude upon already limited book budgets and introduce into the staff "media specialists" who will compete with them for scarce salary dollars, just as community colleges are competing with traditional colleges and universities for scarce educational dollars.

But it is possible that the real problem is the "four-wall syndrome," the distance of many academic librarians from the instructional process. The very fact that the introduction of nonprint media into the library is as likely to bring groans as cheers from the staff testifies to this distance. The academic library has not entirely ceased to be a passive repository of books, despite reserve collections, reference rooms, open stacks, undergraduate libraries, and library instruction. The idea of "selling" the library and its services to the classroom faculty, of working with these colleagues, not just in teaching students how to use the library, but also in assisting them to prepare and improve their own materials, has not caught on with most academic librarians. It is not surprising that some administrators of community colleges have said that they want educators, not librarians, to run their learning resources centers.

Academic Librarians as Educators

One problem, of course, is that many librarians do not see themselves as educators. Educational design and planning is not an important part of the professional, graduate education of many academic librarians, although it features prominently in the preparation of school librarian/media specialists. Since few college teachers are ever trained in the skills of teaching, it is sad that academic librarians are not trained to assist their underequipped colleagues.

It has been remarked more than once that the image of librarians is fragmented and changing. Is the librarian an educator, social scientist, media specialist, educational consultant, systems analyst, information specialist, classifier of the world's knowledge, manager, builder of collections, all of the above, or more? Certainly, the academic librarian can be pardoned some confusion about roles, and library schools must be forgiven for not being able to include everything in one short, master's degree program. The future is likely to bring more diversity to the librarian's role and task, not less.

There are, however, some very good reasons why all academic librarians should know something about instructional technology and should be involved to some extent in media services. Instructional technology and media services are bound to affect colleges and universities sooner or later. They can become competitors with the library, or its allies. Enmity threatens the position of both in an era of scarce resources, whereas alliance can strengthen both.

Library services and instructional technology also have an affinity. Both involve a system for delivering information to points of need. Reference/information services are similar to mediated, individualized instruction. Circulation systems are necessary for both. Acquisitions, collection development, and cataloging problems are related.

Academic librarians also need, in this librarian's opinion, to be more actively involved in instruction if their claim to professionalism and to faculty status is to be taken seriously. If the instructional technologists are teaching and helping others to teach while librarians catalog and check out books, both groups will be judged by their works, not by their claims.

The main reason why librarians ought to be involved in instructional technology, promoting its application to college teaching, is that instructional technology is too important to be left to instructional technologists alone. Not everyone agrees. As Doris Timpano rages:

> The librarians and their respective educational association—in their quest for SURVIVAL, STATUS, and POWER—have been driven beyond ethical consideration and practices to achieve their ultimate ends; the domination and control of modern educational technology and its funds.[31]

Seldom have librarians been viewed with such fear or regarded as so assertive!

As has already been noted, serious questions have been raised about instructional technology, questions with which librarians may be particularly well equipped to deal. There is the question of whether educational objectives may become more important than the students' needs. Lawrence P. Grayson, chief of the technical applications division of the National Institute of Education in Washington, D.C., expands on this concern:

> As a technology is adopted and widely used, however, it creates new options or makes previously unattainable options feasible. Changes take place in what is done and why it is done, and technology thus begins to modify the goals on which the original objectives were based. As this happens, technology has an effect *on* education. This is a social issue, not an educational one, for it directly affects the ends that education is to achieve. In this case, the people who will be most directly affected must have the primary role in deciding on the new uses of technology.[32]

In other words, technology creates new moral choices, whether in warfare, in medicine, or in education. Grayson continues:

> Numerous scenarios can and have been created describing what education could be like in the future. The difficult question, however, is what *should* education be like. Because of the uncertainty that exists about the potential effects of education innovations and the radical changes that are possible, it is important that as technology is introduced into education, actions be taken to ensure that the rights of the individual student and his family are protected and that the principles of human freedom are maintained.[33]

Grayson's appeal is basically that instructional technology remain the servant, not the master, of those who employ it; that its potential for expanding the range of choices available to students be exploited; and that the temptation to economize by limiting choices of instructional materials, and thereby effectively producing uniformity, be consciously avoided.

It is interesting that these remarks are addressed to an audience of instructional technologists, in their professional journal, by a leader in their field. They are concerns and sentiments that one would expect to find in library literature, not simply because some librarians are fearful of new technology (many are not), but primarily because of the history and values of the profession. Librarianship is an old profession, and, in America, it has long been a champion of the freedom of the mind. Authorities as diverse as Marshall McLuhan and Daniel Boorstin, the Librarian of Congress, have pointed to the printed word as the handmaiden of individualism. It is not surprising that librarianship should hold individual freedom in such high regard.

Librarianship is also grounded in humanistic studies and values. One of the reasons why many older librarians have resisted being called "information specialists" may be that they see themselves as transmitters of culture, beauty, and civilization, not merely of information. That is, they have sought to bring their patrons into contact with men and women whose writings reflect their struggle to find the Good, the True, and the Beautiful. Librarians have tried to help their patrons to learn from those struggles.

Librarianship is also syncretic and eclectic. Academic librarianship may be the last refuge of the academic generalist and the first rallying point for the new interdisciplinary spirit. It has already been said to be one of few fields that have borrowed methods and materials from many disciplines without having become the captive of any. It is, therefore, particularly able to interpret unfamiliar subjects to those schooled in other disciplines. If anyone can "sell" the use of instructional technology to a skeptical faculty, it should be the librarian.

Librarians are also experienced in the selection of materials. If they apply equally to all media the same critical judgments that they usually apply to books, no administrator or educator need fear that materials will be purchased simply because they are "audiovisual" or ignored because they are not books.[34]

Libraries and librarians have a much larger social role to play in the uses of instructional media than members of the profession have sometimes acknowledged. In the controversies that have raged about the "vast wasteland" of television, the effects of network control of television news, the proper role of government as arbiter of conflicting rights in broadcasting (and, therefore, as possible censor), the control of public, noncommercial broadcasting, and the development of cable television, librarians have not always seen the issues at stake as inseparable from the "right to read" and the promotion of "good literature." It is sad when librarians fear the displacement of books by television more than they fear the displacement of "good" television by "bad"—the displacement of television that offers a wide range of alternative programming for audiences of all types and sizes by television that offers little but propaganda, sensationalism, boredom, or inanity. One still hears in academic circles the disdainful comment, "I never watch television," as if that were somehow superior to watching television critically. It is precisely this capacity to review and select critically from among books, records, tapes, filmstrips, journals, maps, and prints, with an eye toward the needs of students and the goals of a humanistic, liberal, democratic education, that is the great potential contribution of the academic librarian.

Such decisions will not be made by librarians alone. Instructional technologists will play an increasingly important role, as they should, in recommending resources and producing new ones. But the academic librarian should be a very important part of a team of instructional resource persons that may include instructional technologists, technicians, classroom teachers, special-education people, guidance counselors, diagnosticians, library paraprofessionals, and students themselves.

In considering the impact of instructional technology on the future of academic librarianship, the only certainty is that it will have an impact. But the most important issue may be, after all, the impact of academic librarianship on instructional technology: whether academic librarians will have the moral courage to bring to bear on this new technology the professional judgment and professional values that they have striven to apply to the technologies of print, even though, in so doing, they may have to leave familiar roles behind.

It may be that the accidental juxtaposition of the founding of the American library profession, the birth of the "Electric Age," and the centennial celebration in Philadelphia in 1876 of the birth of American freedom will be extended by design in the deliberate commitment of academic librarians to the application of new technologies of education to the process of liberating the human mind.

NOTES

1. Guy R. Lyle, *The Administration of the College Library*, 4th ed. (New York: H. W. Wilson, 1974), p. 1.
2. Marshall McLuhan, *Understanding Media: The Extensions of Man* (New York: McGraw-Hill, 1964), p. 170.
3. James W. Brown, Kenneth D. Norberg, and Sara K. Srygley, *Administering Educational Media: Instructional Technology and Library Services*, 2nd ed. (New York: McGraw-Hill, 1972), p. 101.
4. From Eric Ashby, summarized in Carnegie Commission on Higher Education, *The Fourth Revolution: Instructional Technology in Higher Education* (New York: McGraw-Hill, 1972), p. 9.
5. McLuhan, *Understanding Media*, p. 7.
6. James W. Brown and James W. Thornton, Jr., *College Teaching: A Systematic Approach*, 2nd ed. (New York: McGraw-Hill, 1971), p. 62.
7. Lawrence P. Grayson, "Instructional Technology: Diversity in Education," *AV Communication Review* 24 (Summer 1976): 121.
8. Charles J. McIntyre, "The Impact of New Media on College Instruction," *Journal of Higher Education* 34 (February 1963): 85.
9. David E. Garner, "Are Teachers Professionals?" *Greensboro Daily News*, November 28, 1976, p. B5.
10. Grayson, "Instructional Technology," pp. 121–122.
11. Brown, Norberg, and Srygley, *Administering Educational Media*, p. 100.
12. McIntyre, "The Impact of New Media on College Instruction," p. 89.
13. Grayson, "Instructional Technology," p. 123.
14. "Help for the Brightest," *Time* 107 (February 2, 1976): 44.
15. Carnegie Commission on Higher Education, *The Fourth Revolution*, pp. 54–58.

16. James O. Wallace, "Newcomer to the Academic Scene: The Two-Year College Library/Learning Center," *College & Research Libraries* 37 (November 1976): 503–504.
17. Ibid., p. 509.
18. Carnegie Commission on Higher Education, *The Fourth Revolution*, p. 5.
19. Richard Benton and Mertys Bell, "Today's Learning Resource Center: Theory or Practice?" *North Carolina Libraries* 34 (Fall 1976): 40.
20. Louis Shores, ed., *The Library-College*, Drexel Library School Series, no. 16 (Philadelphia: Drexel Press, 1966).
21. Wallace, "Newcomer to the Academic Scene," pp. 511–512.
22. Pearce S. Grove, ed., *Nonprint Media in Academic Libraries*, ACRL Publications in Librarianship, no. 34 (Chicago: American Library Association, 1975), p. 68.
23. Audiovisual Committee, Association of College and Research Libraries, American Library Association, *Guidelines for Audio-Visual Services in Academic Libraries* (Chicago: American Library Association, 1968).
24. Grove, *Nonprint Media in Academic Libraries*, p. 68.
25. James W. Brown, Richard B. Lewis, and Fred F. Harcleroad, *AV Instruction: Technology, Media, and Methods*, 5th ed. (New York: McGraw-Hill, 1977). Also available are James W. Brown and Richard B. Lewis, eds., *AV Instructional Manual for Independent Study*, 5th ed. (New York: McGraw-Hill, 1977), an instructor's manual, and transparency masters.
26. Brown, Norberg, and Srygley, *Administering Educational Media*, pp. 97–123.
27. Brown and Thornton, *College Teaching: A Systematic Approach*, p. 62.
28. James W. Thornton, Jr., and James W. Brown, eds., *New Media and College Teaching* (Washington, D.C.: Department of Audiovisual Instruction, National Education Association, 1968).
29. James W. Brown, ed., *Educational Media Yearbook* (New York: Bowker, 1973–). Published annually.
30. Brown, Norberg, and Srygley, *Administering Educational Media*, p. 100.
31. Doris M. Timpano, *Crisis in Educational Technology* (New York: Gilbert Press, 1970), p. 13.
32. Grayson, "Instructional Technology," p. 119.
33. Ibid., p. 124.
34. Lester Asheim, "Introduction" to "Differentiating the Media: A Focus on Library Selection and Use of Communication Content," *The Library Quarterly* 45 (January 1975): 1–12.

ABOUT THE AUTHOR

Damon D. Hickey is Assistant Library Director for Public Services at Guilford College in Greensboro, North Carolina. He holds degrees from Rice University, Princeton Theological Seminary, and the University of North Carolina at Chapel Hill. He assisted Jerrold Orne with editorial work on the third edition of *The Language of the Foreign Book Trade* and has published articles in *English Language Notes* and *North Carolina Libraries*. He serves as an Associate Editor of the latter journal.

THIS TEACHING/LEARNING THING:
LIBRARIANS AS EDUCATORS

by A. P. Marshall

> But the place where we are to get knowledge, is the Books Themselves! It depends on what we read, after all manner of Professors have done their best for us. The true University . . . is a collection of Books.*

A NEW TYPE OF STUDENT BODY ENTERS COLLEGES AND UNIVERSITIES

The Higher Education Act of 1965, which reflected a growing natural concern for the nontraditional student, hastened the need for reexamination and reevaluation of institutional missions that were previously designed for traditional students. The concurrent influx of young people who lacked traditionally required academic preparation caused charges and countercharges about overlooked educational standards. Though college enrollments had been on the increase, particularly since the return of the World War II veterans, no period in history had witnessed such a large number of the so-called nontraditional students as that from 1955 to 1970. Though there had always been a smattering of college students with deficient preparation and backgrounds, this lack of training could be largely overcome by the sheer determination of some students to achieve academic respectability, promising upward social and economic mobility. Students who were unable to cope with the somewhat rigorous demands of college were simply forced out by the system, which showed little concern for those who could not compete successfully.

During this period, librarians in general and college librarians in particular began an examination of their roles in the educative process as they sought to exert greater influence in the academic development of students. In order to be more impressive in their demands for equal recognition with faculty, they sought membership on college and university committees, became more active with other programs in which faculty were involved, and sought to increase their general knowledge about higher education and its problems. They saw the expanding acceptance of higher education as an immediate contender for their attention. Every

*Thomas Carlyle, "The Hero as Man of Letters," in *On Heroes, Hero-Worship, and the Heroic in History*, ed. by Carl Niemeyer (Lincoln: University of Nebraska Press, 1966), p. 162.

problem facing education became a challenge to their ingenuity, with the rapid growth of student enrollments as a major concern.

In 1950, 26.9 percent of the population between the ages of eighteen and twenty-one were pursuing degree credit courses. By 1960 the percentage had increased to 33.8, and by 1970, to 47.6.[1] The number of public community colleges more than doubled during the ten years between 1960 and 1970.[2] The increase of students enrolled for college credit from 3.6 million in 1955 to 7.9 million in 1970 represented an annual growth rate of 8 percent.[3] This meant not only a need for new buildings, but also the assembling of libraries if instructional programs were to reflect normal dependency upon books and materials. Just as the teaching profession was beginning a frantic search for prepared teaching personnel, library schools were being pressed to increase enrollments in order to meet the demands for more professionally prepared librarians.

Concurrently, another phenomenon was taking place on the American scene, one that was to have a lasting effect upon American life, and eventually upon the traditional programs of higher educational institutions. The 1954 Supreme Court decision was a harbinger of many unprecedented challenges to practices that had previously been accepted as a part of the country's pattern. As blacks and other minorities were determining to gain long sought-for rights and privileges, the general mood favored correction of such societal shortcomings. There was disagreement as to how this would be accomplished and how long it would take, but little disagreement on the fact that the more obvious discriminatory practices must be eliminated. A seeming avalanche of minority or nontraditional students enrolled at institutions where previously there had been only a trickle. These students began immediately to make demands for increased opportunities in education as well as in other facets of campus life and culture. Most institutions were ill prepared to meet such problems. The old system had provided opportunities for the admission of small numbers of minority students, particularly in northern states, whereas the pattern in southern states was generally total separation. For a number of years there had existed a quota system at several midwestern and eastern schools to which by previous agreement only a stated number or percentage of minority students, including blacks, native Americans, and Spanish Americans, were allowed to enroll during any given year. Neither system was prepared to welcome with any degree of readiness or enthusiasm the sizable number of minority students demanding admission, many of whose educational preparations failed to match their ambitions.

There was a third development that had an important influence on the direction of institutional missions. The country was moving rapidly toward a need for more trained workers than the educational system was prepared to supply. The computer industry, for example, was experimenting with applications of its equipment to many types of business, industrial, and educational operations. A growing social concern had helped to create a greater awareness of health problems, and more manpower was needed to meet increased demands for services. There was recognition that many of the less sophisticated responsibilities of professionals in numerous fields could be performed by persons trained in narrow aspects of the general field, giving rise to a need for technicians and paraprofessionals. Though this kind of work required some training beyond the secondary school, it did not require the depth necessary for the traditional professional, nor were the long periods of study and large outlays of funds a prerequisite for certification. Many of these newly developing programs were particularly attractive to the less affluent students, including minorities.

Finally, as the social attitudes of the country gave way to change, business and industry began to open doors of opportunity by extending employment opportunities previously limited to whites. This brought about a gradual change and broadening of educational objectives among minorities.

NEW INTEREST IN THE LIBRARIAN AS EDUCATOR

Librarians became increasingly aware of the greater opportunity to give meaning to their interests and training. They, too, were keeping up with the general mood of the emerging social revolution and were anxious to become a part of it. They saw the influx of minorities as an opportunity to contribute to the educational preparation of all students in general, and minority students in particular. The process of seeing themselves as educators resulted partially from the long desire for professionalization. They now began to seize upon opportunities to make libraries meaningful in the lives of all students. Recognizing the general failure of long existent orientation practices, they began to experiment with and to discover new approaches that placed emphasis on the librarian as a partner in the educational process.

Fortunately for librarians concerned with ineffective student use of resources, there were several trailblazers. A cursory examination of the literature of librarianship, particularly since 1930, reveals that several other librarians had become interested in the inability of students to make proper use of library resources. B. Lamar Johnson had introduced elements of the idea of a library-oriented instruction program at Stephens College in Columbia, Missouri, in the 1930s.[4] Louis Shores approached the idea in a different manner by introducing the concept of The Library College in a speech at the American Library Association (ALA) Chicago World's Fair Convention in 1933. This plan proposed to center all learning around the library and its resources.[5] Though practical application of this idea was slow, many librarians began turning to various segments of the concept as they innovated programs that emphasized the book as the foundation for formal learning. Harvie Branscomb called attention to the ineffective use of libraries by teachers who simply do not know how to get the best out of their students.[6] He further stated: "There has been lacking a sense of common purpose and, consequently, attention to the problem of the most effective coordination of effort."[7]

Verna Melum had been involved with library instruction for fourteen years at Northern Illinois University. In that position she had developed techniques and methods for introducing library materials to unoriented students, providing for them an understanding of library usage that would serve not only for college years, but throughout life. Southern Illinois University at Edwardsville had seen the need for such a program almost from its day of opening and had employed Millicent C. Palmer as Library Instruction Librarian. In this role she served full time developing methods and techniques for working with a student body, the majority of which was from the St. Louis metropolitan area, and many of whom were without the general knowledge of using libraries to the best advantage. Patricia B. Knapp had been instrumental in integrating library usage in Monteith College,[8] an experimental instructional unit of Wayne State University in Detroit, Michigan. Jesse H. Shera at Case Western Reserve University had for some years been interested in directing library school students toward the teaching of library usage as a way of achieving educational goals.

FUNDED PROGRAMS FOSTERING COURSE-RELATED LIBRARY INSTRUCTION

In 1969 the Council on Library Resources (CLR) began a program of funding library programs designed to encourage orientation efforts to increase college students' use of library materials. Known as the College Library Development Program, it encouraged librarians to consider and develop techniques for helping students to improve their own learning through the wide use of the resources of libraries, including dependency upon the expertise of librarians. The grants were for a five-year period, were as varied in application as were the objectives of the institutions, and were coordinated with the National Endowment for the Humanities, which matched CLR grants.

On May 7–8, 1971, a national Orientation Conference was held at Eastern Michigan University. This was an effort to promote a new concept in library instruction and to impress librarians with the idea that they had an important role to play in the teaching/learning process. The stated purpose of the conference was "to explore a number of practical solutions to such problems as: how to motivate students to use the library, how to teach proper methods of research, and how to assist teaching faculty in the maximum usage of library resources for curriculum planning."[9] The keynote address was presented by Millicent C. Palmer of Southern Illinois at Edwardsville, who talked about the necessity of "demythologizing" the card catalog. "Students," she said, "needed to know what the card catalog is as well as what it is not."[10]

Verna V. Melum of Northern Illinois University emphasized some of the myths of library instruction, particularly for freshmen, and went on to outline some of the special techniques she had developed for improving library instruction.[11] James Kennedy gave an overview of "course-related library instruction" at Earlham College as opposed to separate bibliography courses provided in a vacuum.[12] Finally, the two Orientation Librarians at Eastern Michigan University told how that program sought to teach faculty involvement in introducing the rich library resources to students as a way of improving the teaching/learning process.[13]

Over the last several years there has developed a wide interest in library instruction as an instrument to widen the horizons of students. Special sections to concentrate upon the subject have been introduced into regional and state organizations, followed by similar groups within the ALA. The six annual conferences that have been held each spring since 1971 at Eastern Michigan University have served to encourage the development of new techniques for dealing with library instruction. One outgrowth of those conferences has been the establishment of LOEX (Library Orientation Exchange), which, with a grant from the CLR, provides information and guidance for librarians interested in what others have done and are doing. Once the grant period ends, libraries are expected to continue the exchange through membership fees and service charges.

The College Library Development Program was begun as a catalyst. Each recipient institution was expected to have complete support of the administration as well as of the library staff. The variety and richness of the programs are illustrated by the following examples:

1. Brown University's program used a group of graduate students from various disciplines who trained rather intensively as advisors to undergraduates and prepared themselves by undertaking reading and research projects. During a two-month summer period the students were given rigorous training in reference techniques, filing, searching, and serving at the reference desk. They rotated between departments while pursuing research in library science. This training completed, they worked fifteen hours each week in the program, nine hours on the desk where they were available for student consultations, and six hours as liaisons with the department of their specialty.[14]

2. Jackson State College in Mississippi inaugurated an intensified learning program called "Project Lamp" that utilized selected courses in literature, music, philosophy, and the social sciences. It was designed to involve students, teachers, and library staff. Books and material resources of the library were foundations of the program. Team-teaching between classroom teachers and librarians was emphasized, along with monthly book reviews, a lecture series, art exhibits with gallery talks, and a listening program. Teachers were encouraged to invite librarians to visit classrooms where instruction was given in the use and interpretation of the card catalog. Special and subject indexes were explained, and relevant bibliographical materials were discussed. Teachers were also encouraged to make library assignments that corresponded with library holdings.[15]

3. Dillard University in Louisiana sought to strengthen academic work in the humanities and social sciences by relating the library more directly to the programs and courses and by becoming concerned particularly with the needs of students engaged in independent study. Introductory courses were designed to be

class related, but in addition, cooperative programs were developed with faculty. Involved in the development of the program were faculty, administration, library staff, and students.[16]

4. Swarthmore College in Pennsylvania created the position of Divisional Librarian in an effort to increase the quality and quantity of service provided students and faculty. The program was designed to counsel faculty on bibliographical aspects of teaching as well as to provide assistance to students involved with independent study projects. The Divisional Librarian also served as a liaison between the library and faculty on such responsibilities as interdepartmental purchases, reserve books, and collection building.[17]

5. North Carolina Central University undertook the development of an effective method of communicating to faculty the richness of resources already available as well as of newly acquired materials. The orientation librarian arranged for other librarians to work closely with teachers in order to bring to their attention the rich resources bearing upon the subject at hand.[18]

6. Washington and Lee University in Virginia provided "for faculty and student participation in making the University community more knowledgeable about the total resources of the library system, its reference services, the relative strengths and weaknesses within disciplinary collections, and the ways to make most effective use of the resources at hand and those available through interlibrary cooperation. The program provided for an interplay of administration and faculty guidance, student initiative, and the support of the library and its staff with resources and services." The major objective of the plan was to have it develop into a "permanent, University-wide system designed to integrate maximum familiarity with the library into every student's undergraduate education."[19]

7. The University of Richmond in Virginia called its program the "Library-Faculty Partnership" and used three to four faculty members in the humanities and social sciences each year. These faculty devoted one-half of their time to specific library-teaching duties under the supervision of the University Librarian. Their duties included: (a) the development of library-centered teaching; (b) the provision of assistance in reference services; (c) the development of a program of instruction in the use of the library; and (d) the planning and inauguration of a ten-year collection development program.[20]

8. Miles College in Alabama developed a procedure to strengthen its program for orienting students to the library by coordinating instruction in library usage with the college curriculum. Using representatives from each instructional division as an advisory committee, a full-time professional member of the staff was assigned to coordinate the program, including team-teaching.[21]

9. Davidson College in North Carolina was given support for its newly developed Extended Studies Program, which required each student to complete a special project during each year of enrollment. A Coordinator of Library Resources for Extended Studies was employed to assist students with reference work. In addition, the Coordinator advised faculty and students on reference questions and on the practicality of student projects. From three to five subject specialists were chosen from the emeritus professors of the college to assist the Coordinator.[22]

10. Hampden-Sydney College in Virginia employed an additional reference librarian who was charged to "work with students, faculty, and library staff in creating an awareness of library resources," to integrate "library work with the teaching program," and to upgrade "the professional qualifications of the library staff." During each summer, "an eminent librarian" offered a "week's refresher course to members of the faculty and the library staff."²³

11. Hampshire College in Massachusetts started a program to "orient the library to the user instead of orienting the user to the library." Interrelated activities included "investigations of what users do and do not do in libraries; a multimedia orientation program intended to instruct users in self-help; and the training of student reference assistants for service in the library and outside of it."²⁴

12. At Eastern Michigan University a new position of "Orientation Librarian" was created. Working with small groups, speaking to classes, and holding follow-up sessions with students, the program attempted to "identify for the teaching faculty the contributions librarians are prepared to make to the students' learning, to encourage their working together to achieve this goal, and to demonstrate the role librarians can play in the motivation of students."²⁵

In 1975, the CLR instituted a revised form of the College Library Development Program grants, calling the new approach the Library Service Enhancement Program. Continuing the concept of catalyst programs, the twelve recipients were to place emphasis on strengthening library involvement in the teaching/learning process. In each case the library was required to designate a project librarian "to explore with faculty, students, and administrators ways of integrating the library more fully into the teaching/learning process of its institution, and to design and implement creative programs that, in a faculty-library partnership, will expand the library's role in the academic life of the college or university." The salary of the designated librarian was paid for one year so that full time could be devoted to researching and planning the program. Released funds were to be used "to appoint for the year a beginning professional librarian and to pay for necessary travel and related project expenses."²⁶

Some of the recipients of the Enhancement grants were building on programs already in operation, but others were initiating steps that represented a departure from their traditional library services. Each of the libraries was visited by representatives of the CLR in order to determine if the applicant institution had the support of administration and faculty for the project.

REEXAMINING OBJECTIVES AND PURPOSES OF HIGHER EDUCATION

"Universal access to higher education to all persons and to enlarge the creative capacity of our society" is the keynote thought behind the Carnegie Foundation for the Advancement of Teaching's *More Than Survival*.²⁷ This study reflects the concern of higher education for the present downward trend in enrollments and also sounds a warning that "the great public purposes" of education must continue to be served.[28] "For higher education to remain fully vital requires effective public policies as well as individual institutional efforts. The nation has a great stake in the vitality of its system of education."[29]

As librarians look at some of the problems confronting higher education, there must continue to be strong desires to provide innovative ideas on how their services can contribute to the vitality in education that society seems to be demanding. This means more than complaining about the lack of library usage by faculty and students. It means that librarians must become involved with the long-range planning process in order to help determine the direction of policies and planning for their institutions.

Most colleges and universities are now reexamining their missions in order to determine their individualities, purposes, and goals. This fact is reflected in evaluations. The institutions are not being measured on the basis of what other institutions are doing, but on how well they are following their own objectives. The North Central Association of Colleges and Secondary Schools publishes the following statement about the individual purposes of institutions of higher education:

> They provide a frame of reference for decisions about student admission and retention policies, the curriculum and other educational experiences made available to students, the faculty, the organization of the institution, the physical facilities, and the financing of the enterprise. In addition to the institution's instructional function, the stated purposes should include reference to research and service where such activities are carried on by the institution.[30]

The missions of libraries are necessarily based upon the total programs of the institutions they serve. Because librarians have reached the point of being considered educators with valuable ideas to contribute, it is important that they participate in any institutional evaluations that might emerge. The North Central Association goes further by directing its evaluators to consider the following:

> The faculty's attitude toward the library is important. The library can be a significant component of the programs of instruction and research only to the extent that it is recognized as such by the faculty.[31]

There are some general "missions" or "purposes" that are considered as vital to higher education, though there is constant change. For the most part, most may be identified with higher education in general, particularly in publicly supported institutions. They are:

1. To maintain, support, critically examine, and to enforce the existing social and political system.
2. To train students and faculty for leadership and superior service in public service, science, agriculture, commerce, and industry.
3. To develop students to well-rounded maturity, physically, socially, emotionally, spiritually, intellectually, and vocationally.
4. To develop, refine, and teach ethical and cultural values.

5. To provide fullest possible realization of democracy in every phase of living.
6. To teach principles of patriotism, civil obligation and respect for the law.
7. To teach the practice of excellence in thought, behavior, and performance.
8. To develop, cultivate, and stimulate the use of imagination.
9. To stimulate reasoning and critical faculties of students and to encourage their use in improvement of the existing political and social order.
10. To develop and teach lawful methods of change and improvement in the existing political and social order.
11. To provide by study and research for increase of knowledge.
12. To provide by study and research for development and improvement of technology, production, and distribution of increased national goods and services desirable for national civilian consumption, for export, for exploration, and for national military purposes.
13. To teach methods of experiment in meeting the problems of a changing environment.
14. To promote directly and explicitly international understanding and cooperation.
15. To provide the knowledge, personnel, policy for planning and managing the destiny of our society with a maximum of individual freedom.
16. To transfer the wealth of knowledge and tradition from one generation to another.[32]

Commitment to Equal Opportunity

Based upon the above goals (or similar ones), librarians of the future will have to develop supportive goals and then determine the objectives necessary to meet them. There must be an assessment of the local environment in order to make such determinations. Most current goals now include some commitment to "equal opportunity," usually referring to varying degrees of attention to nontraditional students. It sometimes means that the institution will use every means at its disposal to provide educational opportunities to those whose educational backgrounds may be short of the ordinary standards of admission.

There are some trends already on the horizon that, to the discerning librarian, will indicate the direction higher education will take over the next few years. In a recent article in *The Chronicle of Higher Education*, colleges and universities are reminded that they "must not lose sight of their commitment to quality education."[33] There has been a continuous argument in the educational press over whether the admission of large contingents of nontraditional students must necessarily be detrimental to academic standards. This is a particularly timely question because of the increased public concern over educational expenditures. Since 1970, the number of states and territories that provide money for student-aid programs has increased from nineteen to fifty-three, according to a recent study by the National Association of State Scholarship Programs. The actual dollars awarded rose from $199.9 million in 1969–1970 to an estimated $645.4 million in

1976–1977. The number of recipients over the same period rose from 470,800 to 1,095,300.[34] The fact that so many of these states are making scholarship aid available to students in private schools and to part-time students is particularly important when considering what the total educational needs of these students are. There will certainly be a large number who need instruction in the use of library resources if they are to complete their work successfully. This fact places an additional load upon librarians who are concerned about their role in the teaching/learning process.

Of course state grants-in-aid are supplementary to the Basic Educational Opportunity and other grants being offered through colleges and universities by the federal government. The effects of inflation make higher educational costs range far ahead of the earning power of American citizens, calling attention to the plight of the so-called middle-income families, who, despite their affluence, must find ways of matching their educational budgets with available federal funds.

Another factor to be considered with the increased and inflationary cost of education is the plight of the working student. There are perhaps more students seeking employment in order to support their college studies now than at any other time in our history. Though these are often part-time students, they are nevertheless as much a challenge to those concerned with library usage as they are to regular classroom instructors.

One of the more significant contributions that librarians can make over the next twenty-five years is involved with the liberal arts. If the arguments of some of the leading exponents of liberal education prevail among librarians, then their major role in the formulation of institutional missions will be to emphasize the symbiotic relationship between democracy and liberal education.[35] Because even today, by experience if not by training, librarians tend toward liberal education, and because they take seriously the transmission of ideas and culture from one generation to the other, it should not be surprising that they will be advocates of the idea that in a democracy people "live by ideals they themselves have conceived and given legal embodiment."[36]

Many of the new concepts of equality, conceptually advocated by various Supreme Court decisions, will definitely influence the direction of our way of life in the future. Sexual equality, racial equality, and religious freedom are only now being hammered into the American system as ideals no longer impossible. Though the ideas have been around for many years, it is only the liberally read who are likely to ferret them out. The ideas of Carlyle, for example, who talked about the limitations on the amount possible to learn at the feet of a professor, as compared to the unlimited horizons to be reached through books, are readily available. Further reading of such ideas from Plato—"The educator as the excavator of the soul, exploring its depths, discovering its many dimensions, and raising to the light of consciousness the rich ore it conceals"[37]—and Socrates—"Our human character is an ideal attained through critical inquiry"[38]—will lead librarians and faculty influenced by the library ideal to select from the major ideas of all time the core around which a real education should be built.

The campuses of tomorrow are developing today. The presence of formerly nontraditional students will be accepted fact. Just how long it will take for our educational systems to reverse the current trends toward job-oriented educational programs is not certain, but on isolated campuses the changes are already taking place. A recent study by the U.S. Office of Civil Rights indicated that "minority-group students attending colleges and universities in the United States rose 11.7 percent between 1972 and 1974."[39] This came at a time when traditional student enrollment was estimated to be down by at least 1 percent.[40] Enrollment of minorities in engineering colleges was predicted to reach 18 percent in 1982, and then to hold steady.[41]

As our society does away with the old concept that members of minority groups are inherently inferior, a concept foisted upon the American people by an unfortunate bit of historical circumstance, the values of higher education for anyone who can contribute to our social, economic, and political development will be evident. No other profession is so well equipped to promote such ideas as are librarians. It is they who are called upon to guide the prospective "educated person" into the higher realms of thought. By unlocking the doors to their storehouses of knowledge, they can provide the student with the tools for intellectual development that can bring to our societies the kind of cultural and social change that we seek.

Much of the change that has taken place within recent years is peripheral, in that we were concerned with the basics. Before we could be concerned with how well students at the lower level of our society could take advantage of higher education, there had to be opportunities to participate fully. The complex problems facing today's world should have been a concern of all of the minds capable of doing so. Too much of our human energy was being wasted by turning our collective backs upon those whose outer characteristics were different. Many people of the present generation can remember too vividly the necessity for well-educated minorities to seek employment at menial tasks in order to have food for their families.

Specific Role for the Librarian in the Education Process

Librarians who promote such programs as Library Enhancement, Library Orientation, or any other such programs by varying names, are merely expressing a concern for the future of our society. They are horrified by the waste of talent this society has seemingly condoned. Though their thoughts are certainly not limited to racial minorities, they are not disturbed that those groups are included. They see literally hundreds of students being forced from educational institutions because they may not have developed proper methods of study, or, they may not have been introduced to the parameters of knowledge always waiting in libraries. They see our educational systems as having a responsibility to at least open the doors and to provide the stimulus that quite often leads to higher levels of contribution to society and to themselves.

Any such objectives on the part of librarians must also take into account the teaching faculty. Quite often they are unable to fathom the real issues involved. Perhaps they have been so involved in reaching their own narrow parameters that they have had little time to think about how they can awaken the same kind of intellectual curiosity in others. As a result, many library programs must be geared to enlisting the help of sympathetic faculty who want to find a way to improve their own effectiveness. Librarians have long been concerned with this problem, but until recent years too many have given up the effort too soon.

A concern was expressed recently at a meeting of the College Entrance Examination Board, when it was said that the time has come "to reassert academic values and be sure that gifted and able young persons are intellectually challenged in their schools."[42] One of the speakers at the 1972 Orientation Conference at Eastern Michigan University said:

> Librarians who have never tried to convince faculty that students need bibliographic instruction might wonder how we can suggest that working with faculty is one of our trials. Surely instructors believe that students should learn how to investigate a subject independently and surely that means learning to use library resources, at least in most subjects. What we are doing is offering to help faculty educate students; the faculty ought to welcome us into the classroom. But they do not.[43]

In another instance, a library-oriented organization reported:

> The libraries of our colleges and universities are central to the educational process that can and must produce the reservoir of national leadership to take us safely through the decades ahead. . . . The academic library's function goes well beyond mere support for the teaching program. It has the potential to sharpen a student's intellectual curiosities to the point where they will demand satisfaction all his life. It must use that potential and apply its resources to make itself the full partner in the education of the student.[44]

In each of the above quotations, the major concern is the development of individuals who can think critically about issues, and from whom can come the varied leadership demanded by a changing society. By challenging intellectually those students who have the potential of providing leadership, at whatever level, colleges and universities will have made a major contribution. The point is that librarians have definite contributions to make to the process that can provide depth to the whole teacher/learning program.

"Education has been, and probably will continue to be, an expression of a civilization and of a political and economic system," writes John W. Porter. Further, he notes that "Each person faces problems of self-fulfillment and self-development."[45] Though he was discussing vocational education in particular, Porter was not unmindful of the varied aspects of self-fulfillment. If this is to be the goal of all education in its various applications, then librarians will have earned their place as educators by the end of this century.

NOTES

1. The Carnegie Foundation for the Advancement of Teaching, *More Than Survival: Prospects for Higher Education in a Period of Uncertainty* (San Francisco: Jossey-Bass, 1975), p. 27.
2. Ibid., p. 58.
3. Ibid., p. 25.
4. Byron Lamar Johnson, ed., *The Librarian and the Teacher in General Education: A Report of Library Instructional Activities at Stephens College* (Chicago: American Library Association, 1948).
5. Louis Shores, *Library College USA: Essays on a Prototype for an American Higher Education* (Tallahassee, Fla.: South Pass Press, 1970), pp. 191–198.
6. Harvie Branscomb, *Teaching with Books* (Chicago: Association of Colleges of the American Library Association, 1940), p. 8.
7. Ibid., p. 196.
8. Patricia B. Knapp, *College Teaching and the College Library* (Chicago: American Library Association, 1959). ACRL Monograph no. 23.
9. *Library Orientation*, papers delivered at the First Annual Conference on Library Orientation held at Eastern Michigan University, May 7, 1971, ed. by Sul H. Lee (Ann Arbor, Mich.: The Pierian Press, 1972), p. viii.
10. Millicent C. Palmer, "Why Academic Library Instruction?" in *Library Orientation*, pp. 1–17.
11. Verna V. Melum, "Motivating Students and Faculty," in *Library Orientation*, pp. 29–35.
12. James Kennedy, "Question: A Separate Course in Bibliography or Course-Related Library Instruction?" in *Library Orientation*, pp. 18–28.
13. Ann Andrew and Hannelore Rader, "Library Orientation Is Reaching Out to People," in *Library Orientation*, pp. 36–45.
14. Council on Library Resources, *News Release*, no. 290, April 27, 1970.
15. Ibid.
16. Ibid.
17. Ibid., no. 315, October 22, 1971.
18. Ibid., no. 328, June 16, 1972.
19. Ibid., no. 305, May 17, 1971.
20. Council on Library Resources, *Recent Developments* 1 (July 1973): 1.
21. Council on Library Resources, *News Release*, no. 347, July 27, 1973.
22. Ibid.
23. Ibid.
24. Ibid., no. 296, October 4, 1970.
25. Ibid.
26. Ibid., May 20, 1976.
27. The Carnegie Foundation for the Advancement of Teaching, *More Than Survival*, p. 4.
28. Ibid.
29. Ibid., p. 7.
30. North Central Association of Colleges and Secondary Schools, *Guide for the Evaluation of Institutions of Higher Education* (Chicago: 1965), p. 1.
31. Ibid., p. 7.

32. Kern Alexander, *College and University Law* (Charlottesville, Va.: The Michie Company, 1972), pp. 471–472.
33. "Universities Are Urged to Reassert Values," *Chronicle of Higher Education* 13 (November 1, 1976): 10.
34. Jack Magarrell, "State Appropriations Up 24 Pct. in Two Years," *Chronicle of Higher Education* 13 (October 25, 1976): 9.
35. Bernard, Murchland, "The Eclipse of the Liberal Arts," *Change* 8 (November 1976): 22–26.
36. Ibid.
37. Ibid., p. 23.
38. Ibid., pp. 22–23.
39. Ellen K. Coughlin, "Minority Enrollments Up 11.7 Pct. in Two Years," *Chronicle of Higher Education* 13 (November 8, 1976): 7.
40. "If Enrollments Are Down, It's First Drop Since 1951," *Chronicle of Higher Education* 13 (October 25, 1976): 3.
41. "Engineering Schools Claim Gain in Numbers of Minority Students," *Chronicle of Higher Education* 13 (October 4, 1976): 7.
42. "Universities Are Urged to Reassert Values," *Chronicle of Higher Education* 13 (November 1, 1976): 10.
43. Mary Jo Lynch, "Trials, Tactics, and Timing: Some Thoughts on Library Instruction Programs," in *A Challenge for Academic Libraries*, Second Conference on Library Orientation held at Eastern Michigan University, ed. by Sul H. Lee (Ann Arbor, Mich.: The Pierian Press, 1973), p. 9.
44. Council on Library Resources, *14th Annual Report* (Washington, D.C.: 1970), p. 14.
45. John W. Porter, "Articulation of Vocational and Career-Oriented Programs at the Postsecondary Level," in *Formulating Policy in Postsecondary Education: The Search for Alternatives*, ed. by John F. Hughes and Olive Mills (Washington, D.C.: American Council on Education, 1975), pp. 212–213.

ABOUT THE AUTHOR

Albert P. Marshall served as Dean of Academic Services at Eastern Michigan University from 1972 until 1976. A graduate of the University of Illinois, he has served as Editor of the *Missouri Library Association Quarterly* and President of the Missouri Library Association. An active writer, he has also served on the Executive Board of the American Library Association.

THE EFFECT OF THE REVOLUTION OF 1969–1970 ON UNIVERSITY LIBRARY ADMINISTRATION

by David Kaser

Just as the first American Revolution is dated from the "shot heard round the world" at Concord Bridge, so, for academic librarians, does the nation's second "revolution" date from the American Library Association's Annual Conference in Atlantic City in June 1969. Skirmishing and sabre rattling predated the conference, but it was there that the battle was irrevocably joined. When hostilities many months later began to subside and the smoke began to clear, it was apparent that much in university libraries was different from what it had been before. It is the purpose of this paper to note some of the changes that occurred in the administration of academic libraries as a result of that revolution and to speculate upon the likelihood of their permanence.

Perhaps it is redundant to call the period 1969–1970 one of "romantic revolution"; every revolution is a romantic revolution. The twentieth century's revolution possessed in abundance all of the romantic trappings of the revolution of the eighteenth century. Disaffection with structure, as in religion, art, and government; a quest for the transcendental, as through drugs, mysticism, and other mind-expanding exercises; a search for serenity, as in the uncorrupted "noble savage" or through life in a forest yurt or a bucolic commune, all pervaded society then and now. A key striving in both times was to reestablish the importance of the individual, a motivation which in 1969–1970 bestirred large libraries mightily.

The revolution of 1969–1970, at least as it affected libraries, was aggravated by perhaps only one atypical characteristic—only one factor that was different from those of previous revolutions. This was the frustration of unrealized expectations—expectations that had for the most part been unrealistic in the first place. It is difficult today to reconstruct the total sense of unbridled optimism that permeated the "Great Society" days of the early and mid-1960s. Somehow we had come to believe that we held all the aces, that we knew what society needed, that we knew how to deliver it, and that we had the resources to get the job done. As regards libraries, the press and public expected them to purvey extended services through instant computerization. University presidents expected them to cut costs. Faculty expected them to deliver everything they needed. Students expected them to stay open all night. Staff expected that work should never be dull and that salaries should rise 10 percent per year.

American university libraries in the aggregate may have come closest to meeting those diverse and irreconcilable expectations around 1965, but soon thereafter library directors began to realize that they were attempting to navigate troubled waters—that their budget increases were no longer adequate to meet the need. In 1966, 1967, and 1968 they were increasingly able to stave off disaster only by mortgaging their futures. They found themselves in each successive fiscal year exhausting budgeted funds a month or two earlier—May, April, February. In retrospect, it seems incredible that the profession did not get nature's message as the Association of Research Libraries (ARL) watched its member directors fall one after another, during those three years, to coronaries and other stress-induced diseases. Individually, and in most cases also subconsciously, those directors recognized long before the rest of the library community that a day of reckoning was sure to come, that they were expected to do things for which the resources no longer existed, that there was no more straw for the making of bricks. It is doubtful that anyone else in the university community, save perhaps a few perceptive presidents, had access to such clear omens. In the spring of 1969 everyone foreclosed at once, the revolution began, and by the time it ended some clear alterations had occurred in university library management.

THE FLOW OF AUTHORITY CLARIFIED

A key modification in the basic administration of academic libraries in immediately subsequent years was the clarification of the sources and flow of authority in library decision making. The period began with an ambient social obsession with "power," although there was great unspecificity and ambiguity in the use of the term.

In the academic world, no one had any power, but everyone felt that because he or she did not have any, someone else must have it all, and ought to share it. Much of the unrest on campuses during the revolution of 1969–1970 took the form of a quest for power. In order to take power, however, the revolutionists had first to find it, and in their search they were largely frustrated as they came naïvely upon countless checks and balances of which they had not previously been aware. Inability to find the power source turned sit-ins to riots and turned riots to building-burnings. Presidents and library directors especially found themselves unseated because of their alleged failure to share their power. They, on the other hand, believed they had little real power to share—or were uncertain as to which, if any, of their limited powers they were legally able to share.

Had the revolution been confined to libraries, the number of toppled directorships during the period would have been far fewer. In ordinary times, a director in trouble can count upon some public support (perhaps with chastisement in private) from the president's or provost's office, or from the director's next subordinate colleagues. The revolution was so total in the university community, however, as to place the entire administration in a state of rout. No one had any spare strength to lend to anyone else. Everyone had to look out for his or her own skin, and "devil take the hindmost." They were parlous times.

The drive to gain a share of power appears to have ended quickly. As a matter of fact, it ended as soon as the revolutionaries, rummaging around in the debris of a sacked director's office, found how powerless the office had been—a paper tiger, not worth the sharing. But the experience precipitated, often for the first time, a salutary examination of just where academic authority comes from and what can (and cannot) be done with it. By 1975 most had come to identify two kinds of authority: (1) statutory authority, flowing from the charter or other legislation, with executive responsibility lodged in the president and delegated by him, with an appropriate segment allocated to the director, to implement the will of the proprietors (the state or trustees) as expressed through budgetary constraints; and (2) natural authority, reposed by the group in its leader to administer its affairs as the group proceeds in concert toward contracted goals.

Although it was frequently challenged, the outworking of statutory authority in academe was not changed much by the revolution of 1969–1970. Concern for natural authority however, which had been largely dormant in libraries, was stimulated by the revolution. Natural authority, always limited to the will of the group, is usually granted by degrees and recalled *en bloc*—granted by evolution and recalled by revolution—and such was the case in many large libraries. Some staffs apparently felt constrained during that time to withdraw past concessions to the library administration, thereby bringing about the collapse of the directorate, an event often accompanied by organizational trauma and crises of confidence.

Confidence in the administrative structure of the organization was often demolished. "Scrap the structure," became the watchword; seek all decisions in the "committee of the whole," just as Rousseau in a previous revolution had envisioned group decision making as calling for the community to gather under an oak tree. Robert's *Rules for Order* became "those goddam Robert's *Rules for Order*," thought now to be not for facilitating group dynamics, but for impeding or obfuscating them. Trust in established processes was gone.

Slowly a new generation rediscovered itself. There were too many decisions to be made in the "committee of the whole," and so "work groups" were set up (not "committees," which had become in the minds of many a term that smacked of past establishment obstructionism), and small bits of trust were delegated charily to them. All documentation was reviewed, and in many areas where past action had been based solely on practice or precedent, new documentation was developed. Processes were reexamined and revised. New forms of governance, with considerably greater group involvement—indeed too much for some—and more rigorous checks and balances were conceived, shaped, and adopted.

No aspect of library administration was scrutinized with greater care than was the source and flow of authority. Charters, trustee minutes, old correspondence, appointment letters, and job descriptions were pored over in the effort to sharpen the detail of understanding of this phenomenon. This understanding was in many institutions further enhanced by such exercises as negotiating collective-bargaining contracts or drafting constitutions. The greater clarity of thinking regarding this issue is certain to facilitate library administration during the decades ahead.

THE ADMINISTRATIVE STRUCTURE CHALLENGED

Also brought under scrutiny, debated, and challenged during the early 1970s was the basic administrative structure by which large libraries had implemented their affairs. That structure had traditionally been the conventional pyramid, with each echelon divided by function, or in some cases by subject. This structure had many virtues, of which the major was doubtless that everyone in a library so structured could know precisely to whom he or she was responsible and for what. It had the added advantage of being infinitely expansible, as witness the Department of Defense and General Motors. It was exactly, however, its similarity to these two organizations that brought down greatest calumny upon it. Somehow society concluded in the late 1960s that "the military industrial complex" was responsible for many of its ills and that it, and everything that looked like it, including libraries, needed to be changed.

Actually, of course, the pyramidal organizational structure is much older than either the Department of Defense or General Motors. Its first appearance in recorded history was in the Sinai Peninsula some 1500 years before Christ when Moses found the Israelites coming to him at all hours of the day and night with the myriad problems of their forty-year sojourn in a hostile desert environment. According to Exodus 18:18–21, it was Moses' father-in-law, Jethro the Midianite, who pointed out to him that "thou wilt surely wear away, . . . for this thing is too heavy for thee." Appoint, he suggested, "rulers of thousands, and rulers of hundreds, rulers of fifties, and rulers of ten," a plan that Moses subsequently followed and that virtually all large organizations have followed for three and one-half millennia thereafter.

At any rate, by 1970 some felt that the pyramidal administrative structure had outlived its social utility and needed to be laid aside in favor of some new format. There ensued a flurry of experimentation with alternative structures. A matrix structure, which had experienced some successful application in project-oriented industries, was tried in some libraries and, although found to be ill-adapted to their production responsibilities, was of some use on particular tasks with natural termini. An orbital structure was suggested, although in use it appeared to be rather like a curvilinear representation of the conventional pyramid. Some toyed with concepts of three-dimensional organization charts, but no one seems to have succeeded in the application of one to a real-life library. Doubtless most radical were proposals for free-form and fluid structures, called anarchic by some and "ad hocratic" by Toffler, wherein ad hoc leaders would rise from the group for the occasion and then merge back into the group when the task was complete. An inherent weakness of such a scheme is that most people require a little more certainty in their lives than it affords.

Early in the hubbub over administrative structure, it became clear that a major problem with the pyramid was not an inherent one but rather a weakness borne of its misapplication, recognition that the pyramidal structure is an implementing structure rather than a decision-making structure. Mosaic law was not determined in Jethro's proposed structure, but was rather implemented there; the law itself was writ by the hand of God on Sinai's heights. In the absence of divine intervention, however, decisions have required the will of the group. Two hundred years after Moses, Agamemnon convened the Greeks in council to determine if the war against Troy should be pursued. Following affirmative council decision, he again became their commander-in-chief to implement their decision. The executive branch of our government today, with its pyramid of departments, bureaus, and agencies, can only implement laws made by Congress, which is a delegate assembly.

This critical distinction between implementing and decision-making mechanisms in libraries was an outcome of the unease over structure. Most large libraries have subsequently established or invigorated some kind of general or representative assembly for deliberation and determination of large issues, strategic long-range plans, goals and objectives, and self-governance. The pyramid appears to remain largely intact but with much clearer ambient understanding than existed in the 1960s of its true function and virtue as a device for implementing decisions made not within it but elsewhere. This recognition has in many institutions brought about the affirmation of librarians as a faculty and elicited a change in the title of the library's principal officer from director to dean, thought by most to be a more precise definition of his or her true responsibility.

As debate on this issue continues to subside, the degree of serenity in many large libraries continues to rise. The newly recognized dual nature of library organizational structure of course discomfits some. Some individuals obviously opted to come into librarianship in the first place because they were *not* expected to involve themselves in broad, global bibliothecal theory, and they resent the incursion into their productive time. Others are troubled that too many, or too few, decisions are being allocated to the implementing structure rather than being made in the peer assembly. Still others rue the return to any kind of structure at all, preferring the adventure of swashbuckling from decision to decision. It does appear to some observers, however, that little else is likely to occur in the years immediately ahead that will precipitate quantum modifications in library administrative structure. Of course, fine tuning will always be necessary, but it now seems likely that any malcontents remaining in libraries will find themselves compromising to accommodate the requirements of the structure rather than the reverse. As ever in the past, romanticism declines and classicism rises.

THE PREPARATION OF LIBRARY DIRECTORS SOMEWHAT CHANGED

A couple of efforts have been made in recent months to determine how the incumbents in research library directorates since the 1969–1970 revolution differ—in terms of their preparation for the role—from those of a decade or two ago. In view of the great turmoil that consumed that office following 1969, there is surprisingly little change to report. Today's directors seem to have served one-third longer in subordinate roles (averaging sixteen years as compared to twelve earlier) before becoming directors, a change that bespeaks the more intricate complexity of today's research libraries and the greater knowledge that must be mastered before one is considered qualified to direct them. More of today's directors are trained in librarianship than was true formerly, a difference largely reflective of the same thing. Fewer of today's directors hold the doctoral degree. Little else seems to have changed.

Perhaps some useful observations can be made, however, about these changing external characteristics of research library directors. It is perhaps a reasonable and noteworthy generalization, for example, that the leadership of the nation's large academic libraries in 1960 had come almost entirely out of the Graduate Library School (GLS) at the University of Chicago. Parker of Missouri, Lundy of Nebraska, McCarthy of Cornell, Branscomb of Ohio State, Powell of Duke, Stanford of Minnesota, Purdy of Wayne State, Eaton of Washington at St. Louis, Miller of Indiana, Logsdon of Columbia, Ellsworth of Iowa, Fussler of Chicago, Hintz of Oregon, Moriarty of Purdue, Swank of Stanford, all came through the GLS and all save one or two at the doctoral level. A small but impressive group— Wagman of Michigan, Dix of Princeton, Wyllie of Virginia, Cameron of Rutgers, for example—lacked library training per se but held doctor's degrees in other disciplines.

All of these directors had been, in their doctoral experience, imbued with the rigor of scholarly method, yet it is interesting and perhaps meaningful to note that with the exception of one or two, none of them pursued scholarly research in their later lives. Virtually all of them remained prolific authors. They were active commentators in the professional forum, powerful shapers of librarianship through their writings, articulate advocates of progress in the field, but almost none of them sustained in their postdoctoral careers what could be called, even with generosity, even a modest regimen of the research to which they were trained.

If it was not their research skill that benefited their tenures as library directors, then what did these men learn at the GLS that enabled them so effectively to guide the world's greatest university libraries in the period of their most optimistic growth? It may be that in a time when America's library schools were still stressing technique at the M.L.S. level, these men had an opportunity to learn principles at the Ph.D. level. When others were learning the "how" of librarianship, they were learning its "why"—an understanding critically important in the front office, which must carry the banner into the hurly-burly of budget struggles, among alumni and into board rooms, and against the hard buffeting of often hostile questions of broader society. Not everyone, after all, is as convinced as librarians are that society really needs libraries in the first place. These directors were probably also able, with their doctorates, to relate more easily to the professoriate only recently come itself from library control and still uncomfortable in the company of people who insisted upon calling themselves redundantly "professional librarians."

At any rate, today only about 10 percent of the large library directorships are occupied by people holding Ph.D. degrees. Clearly, whoever is selecting directors today no longer feels that the doctorate is essential to success in that office. If such a degree was needed a decade or two ago, and so dramatically is not today, then something about the position has obviously changed quite drastically in a short time.

Any, or a combination, of several reasons may account for this change. It may be due, for example, to the people making the selection. Traditionally, the teaching faculty was primarily responsible for selecting library directors, with some substantial input from the university administration, but that appears no longer to be true. Now staff committees are heavily involved, and staff may just be a bit afraid of Ph.D.'s. University administrators, moreover, now that campuses are replete with latter-day quasiacademics, seem no longer to think of library directorships as scholarly posts. The assignment is thought to be largely administrative with little relationship to the "hard-core" professoriate.

Or the change may be due to the different character of library training today from what prevailed a quarter-century or more ago. At the M.L.S. level, technique has been increasingly subordinated in most library schools to theory and philosophy, thereby diminishing the earlier advantage held by those with GLS doctorates. This kind of "democratization" of the profession may account for other recent changes in the profession as well, such as the decline in the need for surveyors and consultants, also once come largely out of the GLS trained cadre.

Still a third possible explanation for the decline in the perceived utility of the doctor's degree for library directors suggests that perhaps training in scholarly method may indeed even be inimical to the administrative exercise. "Administration," it has been said, "is decision making in the absence of data." Where there are data, they presumably make their own decision almost automatically, on a "go/no go" basis. Few administrative problems, however, are blessed with this kind of "researchability." Research training, with its emphasis on rigor, exactness, caution, and suspended judgment, often tends to make scholars uncomfortable in administration, where emphasis is more often on haste, compromise, political expedience, and, at best, partial data. The mismatch, according to this view, was less apparent two decades ago when research libraries were smaller and less complex than they are today.

At any rate, and for whatever reason, the very rapid decline in the importance of the doctorate for top posts in research libraries is a remarkable phenomenon. It seems likely, in the eternal squabble between university administrations and teaching faculties, that the change will hasten the library director's alienation from the latter and his or her alliance with the former. The director's traditional neutrality in this standoff seems destined to become increasingly difficult to maintain, whether he or she wants it to be or not, and the resulting identification with the administration will be viewed by the professoriate as simply another manifestation of the continuing erosion of its traditional domain. The director may, as a result, have to find new relationships and mechanisms for sustaining the scholarly quality of the library, as his or her dialogue with the teaching faculty diminishes.

THE QUALITIES OF LEADERSHIP LITTLE CHANGED

It deserves to be noted that the two comparative studies of present and former directors mentioned earlier concerned only their externals—the scholarly and experiential paraphernalia of the individuals involved—rather than their subtler but vastly more significant qualities of leadership. As usual, the latter have thus far proved elusive, defying quantification and laboratory analysis in the library environment as they have everywhere else. Such a comparison moreover can probably never now be made, because no "baseline data" exist for the earlier period. A study of this kind would be exceedingly valuable if a method for its accomplishment could be devised.

Can nothing useful be said, short of such a study, about library leadership? Is leadership completely an inscrutable mystery? A handful of observations will be made here, although they will probably prove to be little more enlightening than any of the other writings on this tantalizing topic. It is indeed difficult to think of a more exciting subject with a less exciting body of literature concerning it.

There appears to be a vast chasm between what society says it wants in its leaders and what its actions demonstrate it wants. The plaint "We want human leaders" is frequently recited, only to be belied by subsequent actions. When he first took office, much of President Ford's popularity was attributed to his "humanity"; his popularity, however, lasted only a very few days until his humanity got the best of him and he pardoned President Nixon. Thereafter, he was unable to walk and chew gum at the same time. Society's actions indicate that it wants human leaders only when leadership is not needed; when leadership is needed, it wants messiahs. A shuffling, bumbling nice guy in charge is easy to take most of the time, but when the troops are charging the hill in the face of withering enemy fire—and there are such days in libraries as in any other enterprise—no one wants to be following some accident-prone clod whose shoelaces keep coming untied or whose magazine keeps dropping inexplicably out of his carbine. At such times, and only at such times, we want superhuman "six-million-dollar men," "cool-hand Lukes," leaders who are error-free, dauntless, courage personified. But then what do we do with messiahs? We crucify them. Our egos cannot really handle them. They are always there to remind us of our own mortality.

Perhaps for this very reason we take great glee in finding the tragic flaws in our leaders. We feel a perverse sense of relief when we discover that Achilles has his heel or that Napoleon has his peptic ulcer. Nonetheless, evidence of humanity is also our excuse to disfranchise them. This phenomenon even functions *ex prius facto*. If they have not yet erred, we disbelieve them anyway because we *know* by faith that it is only because we have not yet given them enough time. Sooner or later they will show their true colors. We stand poised to chop them off at the knees as soon as their feet of clay appear. For whatever reasons, this process of running through leaders seems vastly to have sped up in recent years. The cry for leadership seems never any longer to abate, as household names one week are targets for opprobrium the next.

The phenomenon of life cycle among leaders is worthy of review here. John Jones, young person with incipient leadership qualities, rises from the group and if he can express the group's concerns with greater clarity or confidence than anyone else, is sent by the group to the next echelon to, as the expression goes, "tell it like it is!" This he does, sometimes with cracking voice, but perhaps also effectively. The next echelon recognizes effective leadership when it sees it too, and so it tends to reason with him, not only listening but also explaining its perceptions of the situation. Being a reasonable person, the fledgling leader returns to his group and explains that things were not quite as they had all previously thought. Immediately a process of disaffection with the group begins. "Look at that," the group murmurs, "we sent him over there to tell it like it is, and he went native. Already he's talking like an administrator."

And he is. His perceptions can never again be the same as those who sent him forth. Moreover, the next time a leader is needed at the next echelon, where he demonstrated his effectiveness, he becomes a prime candidate. The next echelon thinks of it as a promotion; the group views it as co-option. At each such successive level, the individual's perceptions change somewhat, until finally he can no longer communicate with the group whence he came. When this happens, his fall is imminent. There is no reason for the group any longer to sustain him the next time his tragic flaw becomes evident.

Nature is replete with analogies: the young bull elephant rising to become leader of the herd, only himself someday to be toppled; the inexorable fall of the hero in a Greek tragedy; the inevitable death of Othello when he no longer perceives reality as it is perceived by others. Perception, as Robert Browning so dramatically portrays in *The Ring and the Book*, can be a monumental force in the fortunes of men. A person who would lead must have always two perceptions: those of the group he is leading and those of the Promised Land that is his goal. And he can lead from only a little distance ahead of the group. If he gets too far ahead he is viewed as a Jeremiah rather than a Tamerlane, and no one follows a Jeremiah. The difference is a razor's edge.

It seems unlikely that even with our latter-day wisdom, the basic qualities of successful leadership will be much different during the next quarter-century from what they have been since the beginning of time. It also seems unlikely that the requisite leadership qualities in librarianship will differ much from those necessary in any other human endeavor. If these assumptions be true, what characteristics do we find the great leaders of the past holding in common that we can predict will remain essential to success in the future? A list can be developed, but it has an embarrassingly unscientific ring about it; "muscular Christians" they seem to describe, right out of *Tom Brown's School Days*.

Saul and Achilles ruminating in their tents to the contrary notwithstanding, *incisiveness of mind* seems to have been a virtue common to leaders. So also have most demonstrated great *spiritual strength*, as in a George Washington or a Gautama Buddha. Marcus Aurelius and George Patton epitomize a *self-discipline* found in most if not all leaders. Leaders have possessed Albert Schweitzer's *industry* and Thomas Jefferson's realistic *faith in man* and Gandhi's *tenacity* and John Wesley's *humility*. With such exceptions as Moses and Demosthenes, they have manifest the *ability to communicate* their perceptions and concerns. All have had profound *knowledge* of the fields in which they have worked. In addition, a *sine qua non*, a philosopher's stone, a *je ne sais quoi*, has been common to them all; it is *charisma*, whatever that is. In short, the qualities sought by Moses in the people he appointed to leadership positions in the organizational structure proposed by Jethro remain fairly good predictors of success in library leadership today. "Able men," they were, "such as fear God, men of truth, hating covetousness." That is not a bad recipe for library leaders today—people of ability, principle, and honesty, who can place the commonweal above personal gain.

Is nothing then different? Has nothing changed? Although the answer to such questions must be heavily in the negative, some limited differences can probably be detected. Patience, for example, although ever a homely virtue, has not always been a requisite for successful leadership in the past. It appears certain, however, to be one in the future, as decisions and actions will be required by law or contract to suffer much more time-consuming scrutiny, review, and challenge than they have for the most part endured in the past.

Compassion, on the other hand, which has been an important although secondary quality of leadership in the past, appears to have little place in its future. Apparently out of apprehension that it might degenerate into pernicious paternalism, compassion is rapidly being eliminated, also by law or by contract, from the administrative scene. "Equity" has become the watchword, regardless of the possibility of differing circumstances. The administrator who slips and implements a decision with his heart is destined for difficulty. This change ironically has been concurrent with a rising clamor for people to be treated as individuals rather than as statistics. Too bad, however. The laws and contracts dictate otherwise.

Still another modest change in the lives of leaders results from rising social insistence that whatever they do must be a matter of public information. President Johnson must show the scar of his recent surgery, and President Carter must tell how many times a day he prays. The same phenomenon to a lesser degree is affecting library leaders. They must be prepared to live in glass boxes, to come on like professional Rotarians. Essentially private persons are likely to be increasingly uncomfortable under the probing public's "right to know."

But that seems to be about all. Little else on the horizon seems destined to modify the kinds of qualities to be required of library leaders between now and the end of the century. Eagle Scouts then; Eagle Scouts now, with for the most part the same old merit badges. Less privacy, less compassion, more patience, with the last factor introducing still another irony. Although more patience will be required of leaders, less patience is likely to be accorded them by others.

COMPOSITE VIEW OF FUTURE LIBRARY ADMINISTRATION

When these four areas of change are brought together, a composite perception of future university library administration begins to emerge, imperfect perhaps and not wholly clear, "as through a glass darkly," but of some value nonetheless.

As was noted earlier, the struggle for power seems largely to have subsided. The economic recession of 1974–1975, if nothing else, jolted most of us back to more realistic expectations. The nature of authority is probably as well understood now as it is going to be for awhile, although some jockeying will continue over the appropriate loci within the library for small bits of it. The administrative structure, as has been stated, appears to have resolved itself for the most part into a bipartite mechanism composed of a decision-making section and an implementing section, the latter being the same old pyramid. Three refinements continue to influence the exact shape of this mechanism, some libraries opting for the faculty model, some for the corporate model, and some for the collective-bargaining model. The first of the three models appears to have the greatest momentum at the present time, although concurrently the first is coming increasingly to look like the third. Both the first and third have an inherent flaw that may yet rise up to haunt the community, in that they both are built upon an "elite," the librarians.

As regards the individuals destined by fate to direct university libraries, they seem likely hereafter to be older than their counterparts in the past because they are now expected to have worked longer in subordinate roles before qualifying for directorates. This may, on the other hand, be offset by a tendency for them to remain for shorter tenures in the director's office, if staff impatience continues high. It seems certain that their educational accoutrements have changed, the doctorate no longer being "required," although it is not yet apparent just what the new preparational requirements of the office will be. No clear educational pattern for them has as yet emerged.

It might be speculated that, because "scientific managers" and administrators imbued with the social sciences have recently failed to live up to our exaggerated expectations of them, we may try looking for humanist leaders. After all, Douglas McGregor did not invent Theory X and Theory Y. He just gave it a new name. St. Paul called it "the old man" and "the new man," and the medieval scholiasts wrote long commentaries on man's "natural depravity" and his "natural goodness." It is understanding the phenomenon that is important, rather than what it is called, or whether its existence is learned in a school of business or in a school of religion. There is some evidence elsewhere in society as well that the concept of a "servant leader" is currently somewhat attractive. At any rate, the qualities of leadership appear to remain largely the same.

At best, it seems likely that promising young leaders will have greater difficulty rising to the top in libraries in the next few years than they have in the past because: (1) the past approach through doctoral preparation seems no longer to be deemed important by society, but no new model can yet be discerned for them to pattern themselves upon; (2) the past practice of grooming promising young administrative talent for leadership assignments may have become so encumbered of "equity" requirements as to render the process impracticable; and (3) leadership positions may now appear to some to be so shorn of psychic rewards as to be rendered unattractive to persons of unusual potential. They may simply come to believe with Candide that it is easier and infinitely safer to hoe cabbages in their gardens. If this third eventuality actually occurred, it would be a pity, for it would leave a vacuum in library executive suites that could attract demagogues, spoilers, and persons covetous solely of its financial benefits.

Finally, it must be recognized that indeed the days of great librarians, as are the days of heroes, may indeed be over. Such, after all, has been the fate of other complex industries. Who, for example, invented the atom bomb or the ability to land on the moon? Individuals, to be sure, can be identified who were associated with both of those massive developments, but the Manhattan Project is credited with the bomb and the Apollo Project with the moon landing, both vastly too complex for the influence of a single individual to stand out above others.

Perhaps the same will become true of libraries, that one or another institution will come to be recognized as a "leadership library," with the myriad egos and personalities of its human beings—the individuals who laugh, and cry, and pray, and strive, and think—submerged totally in its impersonal corporate thrust. Perhaps some of us will live to hear our professional progeny ask, "What was it like Grandfather, when there were library giants in the earth?"

ABOUT THE AUTHOR

David Kaser, former Director of Libraries at Cornell University, is now professor in the Graduate Library School of Indiana University. He holds degrees from Houghton College, the University of Notre Dame, and the University of Michigan where he received the Ph.D. An active researcher, Kaser has been a Guggenheim Fellow and has published eleven books and numerous articles. He is a former president of the Association of College and Research Libraries, Beta Phi Mu International, and the Tennessee Library Association. Between 1962 and 1969, he was Editor of *College and Research Libraries*.

OPERATIONS RESEARCH
AND THE ACADEMIC LIBRARY

by Herbert Poole and Thomas H. Mott, Jr.

To those who have read the Carnegie Foundation report entitled *More Than Survival* cited by Edward G. Holley in the lead essay and contemplated the less-than-secure future of colleges and universities in this country, it should by now be apparent that no aspect of higher education will be more important to its future than the certainty and facility with which those of us working in it learn to make decisions. To some this statement will appear to be tautological, but more than superficial consideration of it may lead many to the hypothesis that prompts this paper honoring Jerrold Orne. We maintain that many crucial decisions made by management, whether in the academic library, in the office of the academic dean, or elsewhere on the campus are made on the basis of insufficient information and with little objective effort to consider alternative courses of action and their economic consequences. In fact, one writer maintains that "the vast majority of business decisions, like the bulk of purely personal decisions, are made on the basis of very little data, figure work, and thought."[1]

Other than the beating of one's heart, the process of respiration, or the continuous activity of the brain, there is probably for none of us a function more constant than decision making. Our every act is the result of some decision made in either a voluntary or an involuntary fashion. There seems, in fact, no way to avoid decisions, because as someone so aptly stated: "Not to decide is to decide."

Why then have so many of us failed to learn how to make decisions more objectively? One of the most apparent reasons in the library profession seems to be that in the literature of library service there is little writing of an instructive nature about decision processes and what we do possess is most often insufficiently or only descriptive. This chapter is an attempt to correct this circumstance.

We recognize clearly that some categories of decisions fall within the mundane. The results of many are admittedly inconsequential.

A relatively few business decisions are of sufficient importance to merit more extensive and perhaps more formal consideration. In such cases the executive is apt to obtain and write down some figures pertaining to the matter, perform some calculations or analysis, and put together a report, recommendation, or other document intended to justify the selection of one course of action in preference to others. The amount of time needed to prepare and present his analysis and conclusions will depend mainly on how much is at stake in the decision (as the executive sees it) and on how difficult it is to see and prove which course of action is the "right" one.[2]

Our desire in the span of pages allotted here is to focus attention on a general class of decisions that we define as "consequential" in their economic impact upon the academic library's budget. We wish to demonstrate the increasingly critical nature of the decision process which we think justifies our belief in the need for greater objectivity, to provide a brief history of the development of decision science, to introduce the reader to several quantitative decision-making techniques, to explore one of them in a depth that those newly introduced can understand, and finally to furnish those interested with a brief annotated bibliography that should equip them for further study.

Some of the most prolific and respected writers in the field of decision science today contend, and in this we concur, that "managerial decision problems have increased in both number and complexity over the past thirty years."[3] They attribute this largely to two trends: the changing nature of management itself and the more rapidly changing and increasingly complex nature of the environment within which management operates. At the same time, in higher education and elsewhere throughout most of our economy, we have enjoyed nearly unlimited resources, however defined, without which the growth aspect of the changes experienced by us would not have been possible.

Now, as we turn into the last quarter of this century, we are confronted by organizations that have grown large, complex, and relatively expensive to operate. We are also confronted by the prospect of slowing growth or no growth for several years to come and of an increasing trend toward stricter managerial accountability. In the future, few boondoggles will be tolerated or afforded.

TYPICAL STAGES OF ORGANIZATIONAL GROWTH

Students of bureaucracy are quick to recognize the classic position in which higher education and its component agencies find themselves today. One of the best sources that we have discovered as a remarkably clear exposition of this position is a text by Alan Filley and Robert House entitled *Managerial Process and Organizational Behavior*.[4] In a chapter devoted to organizational growth, they describe a theoretical organizational model that has been tested on several occasions by longitudinal studies of industrial firms and nations as well. They have found that, given certain sets of characteristics, organizations tend to follow a typical pattern of growth that may exhibit up to three separate and distinct stages. These they label as a traditional craft stage, a second stage of dynamic growth, and a third stage of "rational" administration. It is the last of these in which many academic libraries find themselves today and on which our attention will focus here. To see why we arrive at this conclusion, it might be well to take a closer look at an organization in each of the three stages. Stage I organizations are

> characterized by the absence of rational formalization of objectives, policy, and structure. The personal objectives of managers are the continued success of the operation, plus the well-being of major participants, and the managers tend to look to the past rather than the future for measures of success. If the firm remains in business and continues to provide a comfortable living for the owner-manager, he probably feels that it is successful.[5]

At some point while the organization is in Stage I, the traditional stage, opportunities for expansion or innovation may occur. If certain prerequisites for growth are present, the firm will move into a dynamic phase described as Stage II. The characteristics of Stage II are primarily growth oriented and entrepreneurial. The firm in this stage is sustained by increasing shares of the market, which are its primary resource and cause for being. Having grown in ever-increasing increments initially, it eventually begins to grow at a decreasing, asymptotic rate resulting from the natural process of entropy, a stabilizing market, or both. If these forces can be counteracted, successive growth is possible. If they cannot be overcome, then a transition into the rational phase of the firm's existence, Stage III, will begin.[6] As noted, the organization in this latter stage is the one that interests us most, although the techniques that we intend to introduce are equally applicable to organizational decisions at any stage of an agency's growth.

Stage III organizations display classical, bureaucratic characteristics. They are large and complex; their period of dynamic growth has been replaced by institutionalization; entrepreneurship has been succeeded by the executive bureaucrat who performs the classical rational tasks of planning, organizing, directing, and controlling; attitudes are conservative; and action is undertaken only after careful consideration of alternatives and their possible consequences. Gains in this stage are

> derived more from internal efficiency and less from external [sources]. The firm cannot compensate for internal weaknesses by the natural benefits of rapid growth, as it did earlier. Rather it must reap the benefits of its larger size by reducing costs and increasing economies of operation.[7]

Many, if not most, of our institutions of higher education and the libraries that serve them, it is submitted, fit neatly and unmistakably into Stage III of Filley and House's organizational model. We believe that a moment's reflection on the past fifty years of American academic library history will support this contention. Academic libraries today are larger and more complex than they were as recently as twenty years ago; their period of rapid, dynamic growth is coming to, or is already at, an end; their executives fit the bureaucratic image; and organizationally they are more "bureaucratic" in every sense. If this is true and if growth ceases to be the modus vivendi for our colleges and universities, then the library will ultimately feel the impact of stabilizing or declining budgets for personnel, services, and collections. Just as with other Stage III organizations, "keeping up," let alone "getting ahead," will require many greater degrees of internal efficiency; and the need for more certainty in the decision process thus seems obvious. Although mistakes and the economic consequences of poor decisions have never been desirable, they have been, in fact, more affordable in the past. This is not likely to be the case in the future. How then do we avoid poor decisions and the possible disastrous economic results that they could ultimately produce for our academic libraries?

OPERATIONS RESEARCH IS THE SCIENTIFIC APPROACH
TO DECISION MAKING

The term used most commonly to denote the scientific approach to decision making or decision analysis is operations research (OR). Operations research is primarily concerned with the use of quantitative forms of analysis to assist the manager in making decisions. It is

> a discipline for systematic evaluation of alternative actions as a basis for choice among them . . . its application involves setting up models of the problems to be analyzed, selecting inputs to the models that quantify the judgments of those responsible for the decisions, and deriving the models' outputs from the inputs.[8]

Synonyms for it are to be encountered frequently, depending upon the text one is using. It is often referred to as management science, systems analysis, systems science, operations analysis, quantitative analysis, managerial analysis, and decision science.[9]

For most library school students as well as practicing librarians, OR is a topic about which they know little. There are several reasons for this. First of all, OR is not frequently part of the curriculum of the country's graduate library schools. Until now the teaching of it has been carried on mainly in schools of management and engineering. Secondly, there is not as yet a substantial core of OR literature within the literature of library science. Except for the January 1972 issue of the *Library Quarterly*, which was devoted entirely to articles on it, the results of OR studies appear infrequently in our professional journals. Finally and perhaps most unfortunately, those publications about OR that do exist have been far too sophisticated and esoteric to attract and hold reader interest. Ours is not the only field where this is true, however; and although it does not improve the situation to know that others share our plight, it is comforting to realize that we are not alone.

When examining other texts in this area, we often were irritated; we always were disappointed. Prefaces boasted, "Only college algebra is needed." On one occasion, however, we had read fewer than ten pages before being confronted by complex notations. Certainly we hold no grudge against notation; we recognize that it is the accepted language of mathematicians. But in our opinion, the villain discouraging so many students in their attempt to grasp the fundamentals of operations research is the complexity of notation—not the complexity of the subject matter.[10]

Until the appearance of this paper, we have found no attempt in the literature of librarianship to instruct the uninitiated in an elementary fashion in OR techniques. Quite inadvertently then, we seem to have failed to "sell" this scientific approach to decision making simply because it has been too difficult to explore and too needlessly complex to understand.

The introduction of a course in OR into the doctoral curriculum in library service at Rutgers University several years ago was greeted with curiosity on the part of some and with dismay on the part of others. For most its application to practical librarianship was obscure. That it has real and practical value is one of the theses of this paper, and we hope to demonstrate later by example how this is true.

Operations research as a recognized field of study and an accepted technique for decision making is just over a quarter-century old. Beyond the field of library service, especially in those of engineering and management, it has established itself firmly as an activity that has fostered new attitudes, new concepts, and new techniques of research into everyday management problems. Its ability to assist with solutions to complex problems, and hence with major decisions, is far-reaching.

Characteristics of OR

Before describing the origins of OR, it might be best to list its major characteristics. Until now the majority of practitioners in the field have been trained in the basic sciences and in schools of engineering and management. As a result, OR reflects not inappropriately a strong orientation toward the classical scientific method. In process, it is experimental.

The scientific method, as most will recall, begins with the observation of a phenomenon that suggests or identifies a problem. Once identified, the problem is defined explicitly in exact proportions. The causal relationship between the phenomenon and the problem is also identified, because failure to do so could result in erroneous and costly attacks on the wrong problem. Following clear articulation of the problem, one usually reviews how others have dealt with identical or similar problems, if indeed they have. Eventually, in OR, one uses trial-and-error techniques to formulate a solution that it is hoped will be the "one best solution." In OR, this is known as the optimal solution. Typically a symbolic mathematical model is constructed to test the solution. Symbolic models, as opposed to iconic models, are abstract representations of reality that employ figures, symbols, or numbers. Such models are precise, and they lend themselves to experimental manipulation. The advantageous feature of such an experimental model is that should the hypothetical solution prove less than ideal, the variable values and parameters of the model can be altered until the configuration producing the one best, or optimal, solution can be identified. Once an optimal solution to a problem is determined, it can be verified in a more general situation.[11] This may not always be possible, however.

A second major characteristic of OR is its departure from the "scientific" school of management of Frederick W. Taylor, Frank Gilbreth, and Henry L. Gantt and its primary concern with every aspect of an action system rather than with one or two narrow segments. Around the turn of the century, Taylor performed a series of industrial engineering studies which subsequently resulted in his recognition as the father of scientific management. Some of these studies are described in his book *The Principles of Scientific Management*. He was followed by Frank Gilbreth who expanded Taylor's motion studies to include time studies as well. Gilbreth's work was popularized by his book *Cheaper by the Dozen* and others written by his wife, Lillian. Henry Gantt, coming later still, became best known for his contributions to production scheduling. All of these men were interested in the "best way" of approaching single managerial problems within action systems. The work of each expanded successively upon the work of the others. Eventually, the interests of industrial researchers who followed them shifted beyond the scope of all of these men toward consideration of entire complex operations. This gradual shift represented a change in emphasis that gave rise to OR. As Ellis A. Johnson noted in *Operations Research for Management*:

> In general the older professions that exist to serve management have made a second, healthy application of scientific principles to separate elements of action systems. Operations research is more concerned with improving operations within one division thereof.[12]

A third major characteristic of OR that is usually cited by writers on the subject is that it makes use of a team approach to problem resolution. This has been true of the field since its earliest beginnings. By team approach it is meant that a formal OR effort may need the talents of a variety of individuals with separate scientific skills such as mathematics, engineering, and the like. The composition of such a team will vary with the magnitude and complexity of a given problem or set of problems. The degree to which this characteristic is or must be present in library-related research is directly dependent upon this last set of conditions. Many library-related problems can be attacked by only one person using OR techniques.

Historical Development of OR

Although, as noted earlier, OR as a formal field of study goes back barely twenty-five years, there is evidence to indicate that as early as World War I Thomas Edison was performing work that would currently be categorized as OR. Working for the United States Navy, Edison attempted to determine "which of the possible maneuvers of merchant ships would be most effective in minimizing shipping losses to enemy submarines."[13] In 1914 and 1915, F. W. Lancaster, an Englishman, published papers on the relationship between victory, numerical superiority, and the superiority of firepower.[14] In 1917, A. K. Erlang, a Danish mathematician, developed numerous formulae using OR techniques that are used still in planning circuits and traffic flow in telephone exchanges.[15]

In the 1930s, a natural scientist named Horace C. Levinson carried out a rather fascinating OR project for L. Bamberger and Company in an attempt to determine the significant variables affecting customer refusals of C.O.D. mail-order packages:

> as would be expected, the more expensive orders were more frequently re-fused. Analysis of a very large sample of orders revealed that the time be-tween receipt of the order and shipment of the merchandise was quite important. It was so important, in fact, that shipment 5 days after the place-ment of the order was not worthwhile; on the average, orders older than 5 days did not break even. From this point, of course, it was relatively easy to compare the cost of rejections with the cost of faster shipping and thus deter-mine the optimum shipping effort.[16]

Although interest in OR grew between 1914 and the 1930s, it was not until the outbreak of World War II that several of the then active workers in this area formed themselves into a research section within the headquarters of the Royal Air Force Fighter Command at Stanmore, England, to study radar detection and related military operations. Studies by this group and others that were formed shortly thereafter became the prototypes for future investigations. Likewise, a research group formed by the RAF Antiaircraft Command and dubbed "Black-ett's Circus" established the model for OR teams of the future. P. M. S. Blackett, a member of the faculty at the University of Manchester, was chosen to study a problem related to the coordination of antiaircraft artillery with radar. To examine the problem in its many aspects, Blackett organized a team composed of three physiologists, two mathematical physicists, an astrophysicist, an army officer, a surveyor, a general physicist, and two mathematicians. The value of this mixed team approach was soon proved, and within two years of the outbreak of hostilities each arm of the British military had an established OR group.[17]

Florence Trefethen, a widely known writer in the field of OR, co-editor of *Operations Research for Management*, and perhaps the best single chronicler of the early historical development of OR, was never able to describe with full accuracy the growth of OR in the United States. According to an article that appeared in *Combat Forces Journal* in 1951,[18] James B. Conant (then chairman of the National Defense Research Committee) became acquainted with OR in 1940 on a trip to Great Britain. By the time the United States entered the war a few months later, both the Army Air Force and the United States Navy had already initiated OR activities. As in England, early military interest in OR was stimulated by problems with radar coordination. By the autumn of 1942, several OR teams had already been established, and by war's end hundreds of military personnel were actively involved.

As an illustration of the value and effectiveness of this type of investigatory endeavor, two examples, one from British and another from American records, serve well. They demonstrate clearly how OR benefits managerial decisions. The first is taken from a volume entitled *Science at War*, by James G. Crowther and Richard Whiddington, as recounted by Florence Trefethen.

As German U-boat attacks on English shipping in the early 1940s increased their pace and toll, the British Admiralty was confronted with the problem of deciding which merchant convoy size would be most effective in simultaneously minimizing losses from U-boat action and escort requirements. At that time, convoy sizes averaged forty vessels with six escorts. Losses were high. More escort protection, it was believed, would reduce losses, but England had no more planes or ships. The single variable in this rather austere equation with which the research team assigned to the problem could experiment was that of convoy size. A three-year record of convoy losses indicated that groups sailing with fewer than forty-five ships suffered from a mean attrition rate of 2.6 percent, while those with more than forty-five ships sustained losses of only 1.7 percent even though the number of escort vessels had not varied and the size of the attacking submarine packs had been approximately the same. Research indicated quite clearly that the variable of convoy size was significant, and when it was subsequently increased, shipping losses were reduced markedly.[19]

How OR benefited the U.S. forces can be seen from the following example taken from a lecture delivered in 1947 at a Meeting of the Institute of Mathematics Statistics and the American Historical Association.[20] The Coastal Command Operations Research Section of the Royal Air Force had shown in French coastal waters that with carefully selected patrolling times and routes, a remarkably small number of aircraft could detect all alien ships within a given search area. The United States Navy's Operations Research Group conducted similar studies and decided to replace the random method of search activity that had been the modus operandi with carefully planned and scheduled search patrols. This new system was instituted in the South Atlantic early in 1944. The entire area was covered by only four long-range daily sorties of B-24 Liberators and PBM's. The capture of five German blockade runners confirmed the effectiveness of this OR-derived method of conducting wartime operations.

Following the close of the war in 1945, military OR groups continued to function, but as might be expected some units were phased out while others were combined or absorbed by various agencies of the armed services. Provision for postwar operations varied from branch to branch. Postwar plans for continuing OR activities in Britain were formulated as early as 1942. In the United States, both the navy and the Army Air Force moved ahead shortly after the war to continue their activities in this area. One example, the RAND Corporation, is a direct outgrowth of General Arnold's efforts in 1946 to establish a scientific organization to assist the air force in its need for assistance in making decisions. Initially, ten million dollars were provided by the air force for the RAND (an acronym for research and development) project. In 1948, the RAND project became the RAND Corporation and moved from Douglas Aircraft to its own quarters in Santa Monica, California. As could be anticipated, the Korean conflict stimulated a resurgence of interest in OR among the various arms of the U.S. military.

Nonmilitary OR grew more quickly in Britain than it did in the United States. The reason for this has been attributed by Richard Levin and C. A. Kirkpatrick to the low state of the British economy at the war's end. Inventories had been destroyed along with factories in many instances, machinery that had survived was most often badly worn, and the nation's balance of payments placed the economy in a precarious position. As a result new methods for increasing productivity were highly attractive.

American industry on the other hand was not so quick to accept OR after the war, even though it had traditionally sought techniques for making operations more efficient and more profitable. Again, according to Levin and Kirkpatrick, this seems to have been due largely to communication problems between scientists and managers. Neither traditionally spoke the other's language, and a certain distrust was natural due to the language barrier and OR's normal staff position within the organization. Managers in the United States were inclined to trust consulting firms, however, because management consulting was an established way of life. After a few companies began using OR, it became more respectable. Following the war, firms like Booz, Allen, and Hamilton were able to absorb some of the mathematical and engineering talent returning from the services and thus to expand the scope of their services to include OR. About the same time, information on the value of OR to wartime activities and successes began to be published. These converging factors soon took effect and civilian postwar OR in the United States began to grow.

Because of the burgeoning interest in OR in military, government, and industrial circles at the end of World War II, formal study of the subject made its way into the country's universities by the late 1940s. In 1948 the Massachusetts Institute of Technology established a course in nonmilitary applications of OR, and other universities both in this country and abroad were soon to follow.[21] As far as we can ascertain, formal study of OR is offered in only a few graduate library schools in the United States.

COMMONLY USED TECHNIQUES FOR DECISION MAKING

The field that we have chosen to label OR is at present a broad one. As one might have gathered earlier from the litany of titles by which it is sometimes known, it encompasses numerous strategic, quantitative techniques for decision making, or rather for indicating which among several decisions is the optimal one.

Although the illustration we provide in the pages to follow focuses narrowly on one particular technique, we would at least like to introduce the reader by name to several of the most commonly used methods and provide a brief description of others. We realize that brief descriptions are sometimes tantalizing, but space is limited in a volume of this sort. Further information about any of them can be found in titles that we cite in our review of what in our opinion is the best textual literature for introducing oneself to OR.

Each of the techniques that we describe falls into a class of techniques more appropriate for some conditions than others. Problems have two basic characteristics: their own peculiar nature and the environment in which they exist. Of the latter there are four basic states: risk, certainty, uncertainty, and conflict.[22]

Examples of techniques used with problems under conditions of risk are: probabilistic linear programming, chance-constrained programming, the stochastic model of goal programming, queuing theory, Markov analysis, simulation modeling, and probabilistic inventory modeling. Risk exists when only the probabilities of certain outcomes are known.[23]

Examples of techniques used with problems under conditions of certainty are: break-even analysis, deterministic linear and goal programming, transportation and assignment models, and inventory models under certainty. Certainty exists when "the information required to make a decision is known and available."[24]

Techniques used with problems under conditions of uncertainty have yet to be developed. As one writer has put it: "Decision under uncertainty remains the academic virgin land of decision science."[25] Uncertainty exists when the probabilities of certain outcomes are not known.

The chief technique for decision making under conditions of conflict is known as game theory. It "provides a framework for analyzing competitive situations, in which competitors (or players) make use of logical thought processes and techniques of mathematics in order to determine an optimal strategy for 'winning.' "[26]

Techniques of Practical Value to the Library Administrator

We would now like to describe several techniques for solving problems under conditions of certainty, because they seem to us to be of more practical (as opposed to theoretical) value to the library administrator. For such a class of problems the following OR techniques would be appropriate.[27]

1. *Break-Even Analysis.* This technique is sometimes referred to as cost-volume profit analysis, because it analyzes the relationship of cost to volume to profit to determine the point of break-even volume. The break-even point is, of course, where cost and revenue are equal. Within the library setting, the operation of copying machinery is a prime example of an area where this technique would have ready application. Assuming that a librarian had to justify the proposed installation of a copying device that would provide copies to the public for a nominal fee, this analysis would provide an answer to the question of how many copies at

which price would need to be made before the fixed and variable costs of the machine's operation would be equalized.

2. *Linear Programming*. This is a method of determining from among a large number of system components the best (optimum) combination to produce a specified objective, for example, the maximization of profits or the minimization of costs. A typical decision problem facing library management is the optimum allocation of limited resources.

3. *Goal Programming*. Whereas linear programming has as its objective a single goal of determining the optimum configuration among a set of variables and program constraints so as to maximize profits by minimizing costs, goal programming (as an extension of linear programming) has as its objective the satisfaction of several goals in as optimum a configuration as possible.

According to classical economic theory, profit maximization is the sole objective of management. This view has been tempered in recent years by the realization that organizations may be forced to accept multiple objectives of which profit maximization is only one.

4. *Transportation and Assignment Methods*. The latter of these techniques is actually a particular case of the former. Both represent special types of linear-programming problems. The transportation method is used to determine the lowest expense for transporting or assigning goods or services from several sources to a number of locations when either sources, destinations, or supply and demand are unequal. The assignment method is used when sources and destinations are equal and supply and demand are the same. Both techniques have high applicability to the kinds of problems currently encountered by some libraries, and their use in a future when income may stabilize or even decline could become critical.

A single example, though simple, of how the assignment method can be used is as follows. Let us suppose that Library X has six qualified employees who are able to operate an equal number of machines, all of which are different. Because of the varied training and experience of the employees, the cost of operating any of the machines will vary for each employee. The assignment method would permit the library administrator to determine which configuration of employees and machines would produce the minimum cost to the library. The value of such a technique seems obvious.

5. *Inventory Modeling*. This is an aid to controlling inventory costs. For many firms the cost of inventory production and maintenance may be the most significant variable in the survival equation. Management of large inventories demands a high degree of skill and accuracy. A firm's profit (or operating cost in the case of a library) is directly affected by the way in which it manages its supply inventory. Two inventory decisions are basic: (a) how much to order and (b) when to order it. Too little too late can be as bad or worse than too much too early. Inventory modeling seeks to determine the optimum course of action.

6. *Queuing Theory*. Although queuing theory belongs to that class of problems resulting from conditions of risk, its appropriateness to library situations is sufficiently obvious to merit attention. This technique is used in the analysis of waiting-line problems. Most importantly for the librarian, it can assist in determin-

ing the optimum number of staff required to serve a given point by assessing the cost of providing a service versus the cost of not providing a service. Cost is defined as actual cost or the loss of goodwill—both important to libraries.

APPLYING OR TO A TYPICAL LIBRARY PROBLEM

For purposes of illustration, we would now like to set up an imaginary problem of a type common to some libraries. The difficulty with such a problem is that if a practicing librarian has never experienced an identical or a similar situation, it may appear to be too theoretical. We ask these persons to allow the imagination to expand upon actual experience.

Library X is confronted by a storage problem for its collection, which has outgrown stack space. Neither the university librarian nor the university administration sees much prospect for a stack addition paid for by legislative appropriation, regular university budget, or private donor. Collection growth continues to outpace an active annual weeding program.

Careful review of the collection has helped to determine that (A) 3,000 full shelves of books in philosophy and religion, (B) 4,000 full shelves of books in the social sciences, and (C) 4,000 full shelves of books in history could be stored outside the collection because they have not been used within the past ten years. The faculty library committee insists that they not be discarded.

With the assistance of the university administration, the librarian has found three cellar areas of different dimensions on the campus which, if properly equipped, could each accommodate a portion of the 11,000 shelves of volumes that are candidates for storage. Demands (if any) for the materials thus stored could be serviced with moderate speed by the circulation department of the library. Because the available areas cannot accommodate all of the volumes available for storage, the university's administration has asked the librarian to develop and present a study of which books should be stored and of what the minimum cost for moving them to storage from their different areas of the library would be.

Upon examination the librarian finds that Location 1 has a storage capacity of 2,500 shelves. Taking into account the moving and handling charges for relocating books from their present stack locations to specified storage areas, the librarian determines that the per-shelf cost for moving (A) philosophy and religion volumes to Location 1 would be $1.20. For moving (B) social science volumes to Location 1, the cost would be $0.80 per shelf, and for moving (C) volumes in history, the cost is estimated to be $1.40 per shelf.

The librarian finds that Location 2 can accommodate the storage of 2,000 shelves at expected moving costs of $0.75 (category A), $0.50 (category B), and $0.90 (category C).

Similarly, Location 3 is determined to have a capacity for storing 4,500 full shelves of volumes, where the associated unit shelf cost for moving is calculated to be (A) $0.90, (B) $0.60, and (C) $1.05.

In comparing volumes available for storage to space available, the librarian notes that the total space available will be short by 2,000 shelves, and therefore, will be inadequate to fully house the entire 11,000 shelves of volumes earmarked for storage. Moreover, only one storage location at most (Location 3) has the capacity to house completely either of three collection areas to be stored. The others must be stored in multiple locations, or only partly stored.

The problem before the librarian then is to determine an optimal choice of the volumes to be moved so as to produce the lowest expense for relocating them. So stated, the problem provides an excellent illustration of the applicability of the classical *transportation or distribution method* to problems facing library operations and management. To see how the method can be applied to provide a working solution to the librarian's problem of relocating books will be the task of the next several pages.

THE TRANSPORTATION OR DISTRIBUTION METHOD

The transportation method involves the following five steps:

1. Define the problem and set up the transportation table;
2. Develop an initial solution;
3. Test the solution for optimality;
4. Develop an improved solution; and
5. Repeat steps 3 and 4 until the optimum solution is reached.

A method of solving a problem that is purely mechanical and of such a nature that it can easily be followed or programmed for a digital computer is called an *algorithm*. As seen from step 5 above, the transportation algorithm consists of a series of repetitions of the same basic procedure, where each repetition is called an *iteration*. Hence, the transportation algorithm is iterative in nature. We shall now follow the five basic steps of the method to solve the book storage distribution problem presented above.

Define the Problem and Set Up the Transportation Table

The transportation table provides a convenient framework for representing all the relevant data in a concise manner and serves to facilitate the search for increasingly improved solutions.

The transportation table for the book storage distribution problem is shown in Table 1.

The categories of volumes available for storage are listed by rows in Table 1. Thus the volumes in philosophy and religion available for storage are represented by row A. Row B represents social sciences volumes, and row C volumes in history. The storage locations are listed in the table by the columns 1, 2, and 3. The last column of the table, available shelves for storage, shows that 3,000 full shelves of A volumes (philosophy and religion), 4,000 shelves of B volumes (social

TABLE 1

TRANSPORTATION TABLE FOR BOOK STORAGE DISTRIBUTION
PROBLEM (UNBALANCED)

Category of Volumes	Storage Locations			Available Shelves for Storage
	1	2	3	
A	1.2	.75	.9	3,000
B	.8	.5	.6	4,000
C	1.4	.9	1.05	4,000
Storage Capacity	2,500	2,000	4,500 (=9000)	11,000

sciences), and 4,000 shelves of C volumes (history) are available for storage. The bottom row of the table, storage capacity, shows that at Location 1, 2,500 shelves of book material can be stored, 2,000 shelves at Location 2, and 4,500 shelves at Location 3.

Because there are three categories of the volumes to be stored and three storage sites, the middle section of the table has nine spaces (3 × 3 = 9) to record the unit moving costs based on the categories of the volumes slated for storage. Thus A1 = 1.2 refers to the fact that the cost of moving a shelf of philosophy and religion books to Location 1 is estimated to be $1.20. Similarly, C3 = 1.05 indicates that a cost of $1.05 is estimated for moving a shelf of history volumes to Location 3, and so on.

The space in the lower right-hand corner of the table refers to the total number of shelves of A, B, and C volumes available for storage as well as the total shelf capacity of the three storage facilities. The two numbers appearing in this space refer to the fact that a total of 11,000 shelves of A, B, and C book material are available for storage, whereas the total shelf capacity of the three storage sites is only 9,000 shelves. An *unbalanced condition* is thus said to exist in the problem, whereby the total quantity of book material available for storage exceeds the combined capacity of the three storage locations.

The Unbalanced Transportation Problem

In the real world it is a rare exception to encounter the balanced form of the transportation problem where supply and demand are equal. Usually, in most actual situations supply and demand are unequal—supply may exceed demand or demand may exceed supply. Translated into the terminology of the book storage problem, this means that there are more shelves of book material to be moved than storage shelves for holding them. In other words, in the problem as given, supply exceeds demand. In other situations the reverse could have been the case: the storage capacity could exceed the quantity of book material available for storage.

The transportation method requires that a balance between supply and demand always exist. This is accomplished by the addition to the transportation table of either a dummy row or a dummy column (or occasionally both). In the book storage problem a dummy column means that some of the shelves of book material available for storage will not be stored (except at the dummy storage site—in this case they would remain in the university library); contrariwise, a dummy row would mean that not all storage shelves will be used to store the volumes available for storage (except to store shelves of dummy volumes that do not exist).

In the library problem at hand, in order to balance the supply and demand requirements, we must allow the university library to serve as the dummy storage site to absorb/retain the excess supply of 2,000 shelves of book material available for storage that cannot be stored at Locations 1, 2, or 3. Referring to this dummy storage site as Location 4, we add a new column to Table 1 to get Table 2. The costs of variables in a dummy row or column must be the same and are usually made equal to zero. In our problem, the unit costs for moving the extra shelves of available books to dummy Location 4 shall be zero.

With the book storage problem now in balanced form, we are ready to develop an initial solution for it.

Develop an Initial Solution

In the transportation method, as in linear optimization techniques generally, an initial solution must be developed as the starting point of the algorithm. There are several methods available to develop an initial solution to the transportation problem. It is obvious, however, that the closer the initial solution is to being optimal, the fewer the number of iterations required to reach the optimum solution. A simple yet extremely useful and quick way to develop an initial solution is through use of the *northwest-corner rule*.

TABLE 2

BALANCED FORM OF TRANSPORTATION TABLE FOR BOOK
STORAGE DISTRIBUTION PROBLEM

Category of Volumes	Storage Locations				Available Shelves for Storage
	1	2	3	4 (Dummy)	
A	1.2	.75	.9	0	3,000
B	.8	.5	.6	0	4,000
C	1.4	.9	1.05	0	4,000
Storage Capacity	2,500	2,000	4,500	2,000	11,000

Northwest-Corner Rule

The northwest-corner rule may be stated as follows:

1. Starting at the northwest corner (upper left-hand corner) of the solution table, assign as many shelves as possible consistent with meeting the row and column requirements for shelves as we move horizontally and/or vertically toward the southeast corner of the table.
2. Check that all row and column requirements for the storage of available shelves are completely satisfied.

For the book storage distribution problem the initial solution by the northwest-corner rule is shown in Table 3. How each assignment is made in the initial solution is explained below.

A1 = *2,500*. We assign to the northwest corner (row A, column 1) of the solution table as many shelves of A material as possible consistent with meeting the shelf capacity of Location 1. Three thousand shelves of A books are available to be stored, but the storage capacity of Location 1 is only 2,500 shelves. Hence, the maximum number of shelves of A material that can be stored at Location 1 will be 2,500. While this assignment exhausts the storage capacity of Location 1, it leaves 500 shelves of A material still to be stored elsewhere. Therefore, staying in row A we move to the right to the second column to A2.

A2 = *500*. Location 2 has a capacity to store 2,000 shelves of material. Because 500 shelves of A volumes still remain to be stored, they can be stored at Location 2. When this is done, all A materials will have been stored, leaving a partial capacity of 1,500 open shelves at Location 2 for storing B or C material. Hence, we stay in column 2 and move down the column to row B to B2.

B2 = *1,500*. None of the 4,000 shelves of B material have yet been stored. Since 1,500 shelves of storage remain at Location 2, we store 1,500 shelves of B material at this location. This assignment will exhaust the storage capacity of Location 2, leaving 2,500 shelves of B material still to be stored. Therefore, we stay in row B and move directly across the row to the next column to B3.

TABLE 3

NORTHWEST-CORNER SOLUTION FOR BOOK STORAGE
DISTRIBUTION PROBLEM

	1	2	3	4	
A	2,500 $\longrightarrow$	500 $\downarrow$	0	0	3,000
B	0	1,500 $\longrightarrow$	2,500 $\downarrow$	0	4,000
C	0	0	2,000 $\longrightarrow$	2,000	4,000
	2,500	2,000	4,500	2,000	

B3 = 2,500. Two thousand five hundred shelves of B material still remain to be stored, and the storage capacity of Location 3 is 4,500 shelves. Assigning 2,500 shelves of B material to Location 3, we have now stored all B material while leaving a partial capacity of 2,000 unused shelves remaining at Location 3. This being so, we move vertically down column 3 to the next row to C3.

C3 = 2,000. None of the 4,000 shelves of C material have so far been stored, and 2,000 unused shelves remain at Location 3. Assignment of 2,000 shelves of C material to Location 3 will exhaust the storage capacity of Location 3 while leaving 2,000 shelves of C material still to be stored. Thus we stay in row C and move directly across the row to the next column to C4.

C4 = 2,000. Column 4 is the dummy storage site we have added to the transportation table in order to balance the storage capacity with the volume of material available for storage. To balance these unequal conditions (11,000 shelves of material to be stored and only 9,000 storage shelves at hand), the transportation algorithm requires that we create a dummy Location 4 with a fictitious storage capacity of 2,000 to "accommodate" the 2,000 shelves of excess material to be stored. Assignment to dummy Location 4 of the 2,000 shelves of unstored C material will ensure that all C material has now been "stored," albeit some of it at a dummy location. At the same time this assignment also ensures that no unused "storage capacity" remains at dummy Location 4. In reality, of course, the assignment C4 = 2,000 means that 2,000 shelves of C material are never placed in actual storage. But this is a reality imposed by the problem because the three categories of materials to be stored exceed the combined capacity of the three storage sites by 2,000 shelves.

The northwest-corner rule has allowed us to traverse the solution table by making assignments of materials to storage locations in a stepwise fashion from the northwest corner (A1) to the southeast corner (C4) in such a manner that all row and column requirements for the storage of the materials are satisfied. This completes our account of the northwest-corner rule. As seen above, it provides us with a quick and easy starting solution for relocating little-used books at minimal moving expense.

Cost of Initial Solution

In order to determine whether a given solution table represents an optimum cost assignment or not, it is necessary to compute the cost (C) of each solution we generate. To compute the cost of this first solution, we multiply the assignment values arrived at in the solution in Table 3 by the respective unit moving costs cited in Table 2, and add the results, as follows:

$$C_1 = (1.2 \times 2,500) + (.75 \times 500) + (.5 \times 1,500) + (.6 \times 2,500) + (1.05 \times 2,000) + (0 \times 2,000)$$
$$= 3,000 + 375 + 750 + 1,500 + 2,100$$
$$= \$7,725$$

Some Useful Terminology

Before proceeding to the next step of the transportation algorithm—namely, testing the solution for improvement—we should introduce some useful terminology. From the theory underlying the algorithm, it is known that an *optimum solution* to the transportation problem always consists of a so-called *basic feasible solution*. The northwest-corner rule always produces such a solution, and indeed, the initial solution shown in Table 3 above is basic feasible. The transportation algorithm itself is so designed that only basic feasible solutions are generated in the process of producing new and improved solutions from preceding ones.

A solution is said to be *feasible* if the assignments of all variables in the solution table are either zero or positive in value. The initial solution developed in Table 3 by the northwest-corner rule, while not necessarily optimum, is feasible: none of the solution variables have negative values.

A solution is called *basic* if the number of positive-valued variables (excluding all zero-valued ones) in the solution is equal to the number of row conditions plus the number of column conditions less one, that is: column variables + row variables − 1. For the book storage problem there are three row conditions corresponding to the numbers of shelves of A, B, and C materials available for storage, and four column conditions corresponding to the shelf capacities of the three actual storage locations and the one dummy location. Hence, the formula becomes:

$$(3 + 4) - 1 = 6$$

Because there are *six* variables in the initial solution shown in Table 3 that have positive values, namely:

$$A1 = 2,500, A2 = 500, B2 = 1,500, B3 = 2,500, C3 = 2,000, C4 = 2,000$$

and all remaining variables are zero, the initial solution generated by the northwest-corner rule is indeed a basic solution.

It is customary to refer to the positive-valued variables in a solution as *basic variables* and zero-valued variables as *nonbasic variables*. Thus A1, A2, B2, B3, C3, and C4 above are the basic variables of the solution shown in Table 3, and the zero-valued variables (A3, A4, B1, B4, C1, and C2) are the nonbasic variables for that solution. Basic variables are said to be *in* the solution, whereas nonbasic (zero-valued) variables are considered as being *out of* the solution. A new solution is generated from the old solution by removing one basic variable from the old solution as the outgoing variable (driving it to a value of zero) and introducing a nonbasic variable from the old solution as an incoming basic variable in the new solution (driving it to a positive value). In this way we are assured that if the old solution is basic feasible, the new solution will be also, and we shall thus eventually reach an optimum solution. The strategy underlying the next two steps of the transportation algorithm—testing the current solution for optimality, and developing a new improved solution—is to identify the particular basic variable and nonbasic variable in the current solution whose roles will be *exchanged* in the new improved solution.

Occasionally, we shall encounter a basic feasible solution that will be said to be *degenerate*. This will occur when there are fewer than the required number of basic variables appearing in the solution as called for by the formula above. Thus a solution to the present problem would be degenerate if it contained fewer than six basic variables. And, indeed, optimum solutions can be degenerate in this sense, as we shall see later.

It is time now to move to the next step of the transportation algorithm.

Test the Solution for Optimality

Once an initial solution is obtained for the transportation problem, the next step is to evaluate whether or not the solution can be further improved in terms of reduced total cost. As explained above, the test for determining whether the solution can be improved involves examining each zero-valued (nonbasic) variable in the current solution to determine whether its introduction into the new solution as an incoming basic variable would result in overall lower cost for the new solution. Two alternative methods have been developed to so evaluate the nonbasic variables: the stepping-stone method and the MODI (modified distribution) method. The MODI method is more algebraic in nature than the stepping-stone method and provides a more efficient means of evaluating zero-valued variables for cost improvement. However, because the stepping-stone method forms the basis for the MODI method and provides a good introduction for an easier understanding of it, it would be advantageous to devote discussion here to an explanation of the stepping-stone method. Lack of space precludes any further discussion of the MODI method.

It should be pointed out that the transportation problem is a special case of the general linear-programming problem and could be solved by the more complicated *simplex algorithm* developed for linear-programming problems. Because both algorithms follow basically similar steps, familiarity with the transportation algorithm will serve to enhance one's understanding of the simplex algorithm for solving more general linear-programming problems. In this sense, we invite the reader to view the transportation algorithm as having value not only as an independent tool for solving problems such as the book storage problem and others, but also as an introduction to the simplex algorithm for solving a more general and even broader class of library-related problems. For both algorithms, the goal is to start with an initial basic feasible solution and, through an iteration of steps, to generate successively improved solutions until the optimum solution is obtained. In both algorithms the iteration consists of two basic steps that we have alluded to earlier:

1. Evaluating all zero-valued variables of the current solution for possible cost improvement, and selecting the one showing greatest cost improvement to introduce as the new incoming basic variable in the next solution.

2. Identifying the basic variable in the current solution that, by virtue of the selection process in step 1, must now go out of the next solution by having its value reduced to zero. At the same time, we increase the new incoming basic variable to the maximum value possible.

Step 1, selecting the incoming variable, assures us that progress is always made toward the optimum solution. In the simplex algorithm this step is accomplished by the so-called *rule of steepest descent* and corresponds to the stepping-stone and MODI methods of the transportation algorithm. Step 2, identifying and removing the outgoing variable, assures that feasibility is always retained. Called by many authors the *θ rule* in the simplex algorithm, step 2 corresponds in the transportation to tracing a closed "+,−" path for the incoming variable that will serve to identify which basic variable in the current solution will be reduced to zero as the outgoing variable of the next solution.

Let us now turn to step 1, selecting the incoming variable for the next solution, and see how this is accomplished in the transportation algorithm by the stepping-stone method.

Stepping-Stone Method

We have already seen that among the zero-valued variables of the current solution, the one selected as the incoming variable for the next solution must always show the greatest cost improvement. To choose a variable with a smaller cost improvement factor would violate the rule of steepest descent. The stepping-stone method employs the so-called closed "+,−" path technique for computing the cost improvement factors of zero-valued variables. We shall now explain the technique.

Closed "+,−" Paths. Given a solution table that is basic feasible, there is associated with each zero-valued variable in the table a *unique* closed path that starts at, and returns to, the variable in question, extends horizontally and vertically only, and contains only basic variables as the other components of the path. Starting with the zero-valued variable first and labeling it with a plus (+) sign, let us label every node in the closed path alternately with plus (+) and minus (−) signs. If we now assign to each node of the path the corresponding unit moving cost from the transportation table, and add and subtract these cost elements around the "+, −" path in accordance with their signs, the result will be the *cost improvement factor* for the zero-valued variable in question. The significance of the cost improvement factor is that it affords a ready means for measuring the change in the cost of the solution if the zero-valued variable in question were brought into the next solution as the new basic variable. It should be emphasized that for each zero-valued variable in the current solution, there exists one and only one closed "+,−" path.

If, after their computation from the "+,−" paths, all the cost improvement factors for a given solution table are shown to be *zero or positive*, then no reduction in cost is possible and the given solution represents the *optimum solution*. However, if any of the cost improvement factors is negative, an improved solution with reduced cost is possible. The stepping-stone method calls for selecting as the new incoming variable the zero-valued variable showing the *largest negative cost improvement factor*.

Before turning to the next step of the transportation problem—developing an improved solution by increasing the value of the new incoming variable as much as possible while driving a basic variable out of the solution—we will illustrate the stepping-stone method in the context of the book storage distribution problem. Given that the initial solution as shown in Table 3 has been derived by use of the northwest-corner rule, we now wish to employ the stepping-stone method to test whether the initial solution is optimal, and if not, to select the appropriate zero-valued variable of the initial solution as the incoming variable for an improved solution.

For each zero-valued variable of the initial solution, we shall need to do two things:

1. Trace the unique closed "+,−" path associated with the variable.
2. Compute the cost improvement factor for the variable by adding and subtracting the unit storage cost elements around the "+,−" path.

With this information in hand, we shall then be in a position to select the incoming variable for use in the next step of the transportation algorithm.

Referring to Table 3, we see that the zero-valued variables for the initial solution are A3, A4, B1, B4, C1, and C2. It is these variables whose "+,−" paths must now be traced in order to compute their cost improvement factors for determining whether a new improved solution is possible.

Let us begin with A3 = 0. Examination of the solution in Table 3 shows that the "+,−" path for A3 = 0 is:

$$+ \ A3 \ - \ A2 \ + \ B2 \ - \ B3$$

This path tells us that if we wish to introduce A3 as an incoming basic variable in a new solution by assigning at least one shelf to it so that new A3 = 1 (more shelves would be assigned later), then in order to satisfy the total storage requirement for row A, variable A2 = 500 must be decreased by one shelf; hence new A2 = 499. However, to meet column 2's total storage requirement, the reassignment of A2 forces B2 = 1,500 to be increased by one shelf, hence new B2 = 1,501. This reassignment, in turn, requires that B3 = 2,500 should be decreased by one shelf in order to maintain the storage requirement for row B, hence new B3 = 2,499. Because new A3 = 1 and new B3 = 2,499, the storage requirement for column 3 continues to be met.

This "+,−" path thus provides the beginnings of a new solution table in which A3 would enter as an incoming basic variable. To determine whether the emerging new solution would have an overall reduced cost, we need to refer back to the "+,−" path for A3 in order to compute A3's cost improvement factor. A look at the transportation table (Table 2) shows that the unit storage costs associated with the nodes of the path for A3 are:

$$+ .9 - .75 + .5 - .6 = + .05$$

Adding and subtracting these costs around the "$+,-$" path, we find that the cost improvement factor for A3 is $+.05$. This amount indicates that if we were to reassign one shelf from A2 to A3, while carrying out the other reassignments dictated by the path in order to continue to satisfy row and column storage requirements, the total storage cost would *increase* by $0.05. Thus, a reassignment of, say, 500 shelves to A3 would increase the total storage cost by $.05 \times 500$, or $25.00. Clearly, the selection of A3 as the incoming variable will not lead to a solution in which total storage costs are reduced.

We now continue to compute the cost improvement factors for the other variables. Examination of the solution in Table 3 shows that the "$+,-$" path for A4 = 0 is:

$$+ A4 - A2 + B2 - B3 + C3 - C4$$

The unit storage costs associated with this path are:

$$+ 0 - .75 + .5 - .6 + 1.05 - 0 = + .2$$

The cost improvement factor for A4 is thus $+.2$. If we were to reassign some shelves from A2 to A4, we would find that the total storage costs would rise by $0.20 per reassigned shelf.

The closed paths and cost improvement factors for the remaining variables are:

$$B1 = 0: + B1 - A1 + A2 - B2$$
$$+ .8 - 1.2 + .75 - .5 = -.15$$
$$B4 = 0: + B4 - B3 + C3 - C4$$
$$+ 0 - .6 + 1.05 - 0 = +.45$$
$$C1 = 0: + C1 - A1 + A2 - B2 + B3 - C3$$
$$+ 1.4 - 1.2 + .75 - .5 + .6 - 1.05 = 0$$
$$C2 = 0: + C2 - B2 + B3 - C3$$
$$+ .9 - .5 + .6 - 1.05 = -.05$$

The largest negative cost improvement factor is seen to be $-.15$, and is associated with the variable B1 = 0. If we reassign shelves from B2 to B1, the total storage costs of the initial solution could be *reduced* by $0.15 per shelf. Thus if we were to assign, say, 1,500 shelves to B1, the total storage costs would decrease by $(1.5 \times 1,500)$ or $225.

Of all the variables that are zero in the initial solution, only B1 and C2 offer any opportunity for developing a new solution table with reduced costs. Because B1 offers the greater opportunity of the two, it will therefore serve as the incoming variable to enter a new solution. The next step, then, is to develop the new solution around B1.

Develop an Improved Solution

In order to develop a new basic feasible solution around B1 that represents, for the moment, the best possible cost improvement over the initial solution, B1 must enter the new solution at the maximum value possible at the same time that one of the current basic variables is driven out of the solution. An exchange of roles between B1 and the yet unidentified basic variable to be removed is required in order to guarantee that the new solution will be a basic solution. By driving this outgoing variable to zero, but never negative value, we further guarantee that the new solution will also be feasible as well as basic. The "+,−" path is useful in identifying both the basic variable to be removed and the maximum value to be assigned to the incoming variable B1. Recall that the "+, −" path for B1 is:

$$+ \ B1 \ - \ A1 \ + \ A2 \ - \ B2$$

Replacing the variables in the path by the values assigned to them in the current solution table (Table 3), we obtain:

$$+ \ 0 \ - \ 2,500 \ + \ 500 \ - \ \widehat{(1,500)}$$

We saw earlier that the "+,−" path exhibits a "ripple" effect due to the necessity of meeting row and column storage requirements. Thus if we wish to increase B1 by some amount, it is necessary for us to decrease both A1 and B2 by comparable amounts. Similarly, any decrease in A1 or B2 results in comparable increases for A2 and B1. The alternate assignment of "+" and "−" signs along the path serves to identify in easy fashion the concomitant increases and decreases that are required if the row and column storage requirements are always to be satisfied. What is equally important, the distribution of signs along the path also serves to facilitate easy identification of the basic variable to be removed from the new solution by limiting the choice to those variables in the path that are prefixed by a minus sign. Thus, in the path for B1 above, only two variables are eligible to qualify as the basic variable to be removed from the new solution: A1 = 2,500 or B2 = 1,500. Because the new solution must remain feasible, we choose the variable with the smaller value in the current solution table. In this instance it is B2 = 1,500, and we add and subtract that amount around the path in accordance with the "+" and "−" signs, as follows:

$$+ \ (0 + 1,500) \ - \ (2,500 - 1,500) \ + \ (500 + 1,500) \ - \ (1,500 - 1,500)$$
$$+ \ 1,500 \ - \ 1,000 \ + \ 2,000 \ - \ 0$$

Hence B1 = 1,500, A1 = 1,000, A2 = 2,000 and B2 = 0 represent the values to be assigned to these variables in the new solution. The values for all the other variables will remain unchanged from the current solution table (Table 3), namely, A3 = 0, A4 = 0, B3 = 2,500, B4 = 0, C1 = 0, C2 = 0, C3 = 2,000, C4 = 2,000. The solution table for the new solution appears in Table 4.

TABLE 4

THE SECOND SOLUTION

	1	2	3	4	
A	1,000	2,000	0	0	3,000
B	1,500	0	2,500	0	4,000
C	0	0	2,000	2,000	4,000
	2,500	2,000	4,500	2,000	

Cost of Second Solution

The total moving cost of the improved solution is \$7,500, as shown below, a reduction of \$225 from \$7,725 of the initial solution. Because the cost improvement factor of B1 was $-.15$, and the number of shelves reassigned to B1 from B2 was 1,500, the total cost improvement has to be $.15 \times 1,500$, or \$225. The calculations are as follows:

$$C_2 = (1.2 \times 1,000) + (.75 \times 2,000) + (.8 \times 1,500)$$
$$+ (.6 \times 2,500) + (1.05 \times 2,000) + (0 \times 2,000)$$
$$= 1,200 + 1,500 + 1,200 + 1,500 + 2,100$$
$$= \$7,500$$

Reach the Optimum Solution

Repeat Steps 3 and 4 until the Optimum Solution Is Reached

Having completed one iteration of the transportation algorithm, we now go back to step 3 to determine whether further improvement is possible. Using the stepping-stone method, we trace the closed paths and compute the cost improvement factors for A3, A4, B2, B4, C1, and C2 in the second solution (Table 4) as follows:

$$A3 = 0: + A3 - A1 + B1 - B3$$
$$+.9 - 1.2 + .8 - .6 = -.1$$
$$A4 = 0: + A4 - A1 + B1 - B3 + C3 - C4$$
$$+ 0 - 1.2 + .8 - .6 + 1.05 - 0 = +.05$$
$$B2 = 0: + B2 - A2 + A1 - B1$$
$$+ .5 - .75 + 1.2 - .8 = +.15$$
$$B4 = 0: + B4 - B3 + C3 - C4$$
$$+ 0 - .6 + 1.05 - 0 = +.45$$
$$C1 = 0: + C1 - B1 + B3 - C3$$
$$+ 1.4 - .8 + .6 - 1.05 = +.15$$
$$C2 = 0: + C2 - A2 + A1 - B1 + B3 - C3$$
$$+ .9 - .75 + 1.2 - .8 + .6 - 1.05 = +.1$$

Looking at the cost improvement factors computed above, we find only one variable with a negative factor, namely A3 = 0, indicating that further improvement is possible. For each shelf reassigned from A1 to A3, total costs will be reduced by $0.10. To determine the maximum number of shelves that can be assigned to A3 from A1, we follow the procedure discussed earlier in step 4 by choosing the smallest variable in the "+,−" path for A3 that is prefixed by a minus sign, and then adding and subtracting that amount around the path as follows:

+ A3 − A1 + B1 − B3
+ 0 − (1,000) + 1,500 − 2,500
+ (0 + 1,000) − (1,000 − 1,000) + (1,500 + 1,000) − (2,500 − 1,000)
+ 1,000 − 0 + 2,500 − 1,500

For the third solution we see that the maximum number of shelves that can be assigned to A3 is A3 = 1,000 with A1 = 0, B1 = 2,500, B3 = 1,500, and all other variables remaining unchanged from the second solution. The solution table for the third improved solution is given in Table 5.

TABLE 5

THE THIRD SOLUTION (OPTIMUM)

	1	2	3	4	
A	0	2,000	1,000	0	3,000
B	2,500	0	1,500	0	4,000
C	0	0	2,000	2,000	4,000
	2,500	2,000	4,500	2,000	

Cost of Third Solution

The total moving cost of the third solution is $7,400, as shown below, a reduction of $100 from the cost of the second solution. This fits with the fact that the cost improvement factor of incoming variable A3 was −.1, and the number of shelves assigned was 1,000. Thus, the cost reduction for the third solution is .1 × 1,000, or $100.

C_3 = (.75 × 2,000) + (.9 × 1,000) + (.8 × 2,500) + (.6 × 1,500)
      + (1.05 × 2,000) + (0 × 2,000)
   = 1,500 + 900 + 2,000 + 900 + 2,100
   = $7,400 (minimum)

Again it is necessary to return to step 3 to determine whether further improvement of the solution is possible. We will thus need to trace "+,−" paths and compute cost improvement factors for A1, A4, B2, B4, C1, and C2 appearing in the third solution table (Table 5). These computations are carried out as follows:

$A1 = 0:$ + A1 − A3 + B3 − B1
         + 1.2 − .9 + .6 − .8 = +.1
$A4 = 0:$ + A4 − A3 + C3 − C4
         + 0 + .9 + 1.05 − 0 = +.15
$B2 = 0:$ + B2 − A2 + A3 − B3
         + .5 − .75 + .9 − .6 = +.05
$B4 = 0:$ + B4 − B3 + C3 − C4
         + 0 − .6 + 1.05 − 0 = +.45
$C1 = 0:$ + C1 − B1 + B3 − C3
         + 1.4 − .8 + .6 − 1.05 = +.15
$C2 = 0:$ + C2 − A2 + A3 − C3
         + .9 − .75 + .9 − 1.05 = 0

It is readily evident that none of the above zero-valued variables appearing in the third solution (Table 5) have negative cost improvement factors. In other words, there is no way we can improve the solution shown in Table 5 by devising new assignments that will further reduce the total moving cost. Therefore, we have reached the optimum solution with its minimum cost.

Alternate Optimal Solutions

An examination of the cost improvement factors used to establish the optimality of the third solution to the book storage problem will reveal that the cost improvement factor for variable $C2 = 0$ is zero. This means that if C2 were selected as the incoming variable for a new solution, new and different storage assignments would result, and yet the total cost would be the same. Thus it would not matter if we reassigned one shelf or 2,000 shelves of C material from Location 3 to Location 2; the total moving cost would be the same as that for the optimal assignment in Table 5. We may conclude, then, that in addition to the optimal solution just computed, another equally cost effective storage assignment exists.

To determine what this alternate optimal solution looks like, we follow the procedure of step 4 used for bringing any incoming variable into the solution. To bring C2 into a new solution, we need to trace its "+,−" path and select the smallest variable in the path that is prefixed with a minus sign, so that it may be added to, and subtracted from, all elements of the path, as follows:

+ C2 − A2 + A3 − C3
+ 0 − (2,000) + 1,000 − (2,000)
+ (0 + 2,000) − (2,000 − 2,000) + (1,000 + 2,000) − (2,000 − 2,000)
+ 2,000 − 0 + 3,000 − 0

Thus the maximum number of shelves that can be assigned to C2 is $C2 = 2,000$ with $A2 = 0$, $A3 = 3,000$, $C3 = 0$, and all other variables remaining unchanged. The solution table for this alternate optimal solution is shown in Table 6.

TABLE 6

ALTERNATE OPTIMAL SOLUTION

	1	2	3	4	
A	0	0	3,000	0	3,000
B	2,500	0	1,500	0	4,000
C	0	2,000	0	2,000	4,000
	2,500	2,000	4,500	2,000	

Cost of Alternate Optimal Solution

The cost of the solution in Table 6 is computed as follows:

$$C_4 = (.9 \times 3,000) + (.8 \times 2,500) + (.6 \times 1,500)$$
$$+ (.9 \times 2,000) + (0 \times 2,000)$$
$$= 2,700 + 2,000 + 900 + 1,800$$
$$= \$7,400 \text{ (minimum)}$$

The total moving cost of this alternate optimal solution is exactly the same as the total moving cost of the original optimal solution presented in Table 5. Were the cost improvement factors to be computed for the new solution, they would all show positive values except for variable C3, whose cost improvement factor is zero. As might be expected, introducing C3 into a new solution results in the original optimal solution shown in Table 5. Hence, we know that no other alternate optimal solutions exist. From a practical standpoint, alternate optimal solutions can provide valuable flexibility to the library director in deciding which assignment plan to follow in removing little-used material from active circulation and storing it.

Degeneracy

We end our discussion of the book storage problem by observing that the alternate optimal solution developed in Table 6 contains fewer than six (3 rows + 4 columns − 1) basic variables. As mentioned earlier, when such a condition arises in a solution, the solution is said to be *degenerate*.

Although the term "degeneracy" generally has unfortunate connotations, implying as it does an undesirable or unsavory condition, degenerate basic feasible solutions to the transportation problem are perfectly good solutions, and, as we have seen, may even be optimal. However, when degeneracy develops in a transportation problem, it causes a breakdown in the stepping-stone and MODI methods, resulting in the need to apply standard recovery techniques for resolving the degeneracy. In this regard, degeneracy is of little or no concern to us here.

In the book storage problem, it should be noted that some slight preference may exist for the alternate optimal solution that is degenerate in that it allows both A and C materials to be stored in their entirety in single storage locations, whereas the nondegenerate optimal solution allows only C materials to be so stored. In any case, if the library director has a preference for a given solution, an analysis of alternate optimal solutions may be valuable from several standpoints.

The transportation and simplex methods have proved themselves to be reliable and versatile management tools outside the library field. However, like other quantitative techniques with which the library director may be more familiar, these two OR algorithms will be only as good as the quality of judgment that must be exercised in applying them with skill to library problems. The book storage and distribution problem illustrates a single application of one of the OR tools available to library directors and staffs.

In closing this presentation of a library OR problem and in passing on to the final segment of this chapter, we wish to make one final observation about OR problems. The researcher will find that once variables and constraints exceed a certain number, the assistance of an electronic digital computer will be needed. Unless this step is taken, the time required for problem resolution becomes far too great. In some instances it is, in fact, practically impossible to operate otherwise. At the same time, however, a host of library-related problems of limited size lend themselves to resolution by hand. Common sense should be the best indicator of the appropriate course of action.

ANNOTATED BIBLIOGRAPHY OF BASIC SOURCES

In conclusion, we believe it would be helpful to refer the reader to what we consider to be "the" several basic sources in this area. Indeed, there are many good sources; and we would like to recognize them all, space permitting. Those that follow appear to us to be most appropriate for beginners who wish to learn on their own without the need to enroll in a formal course. We shall describe them in the order in which we recommend they be consulted.

Levin, Richard I., and Kirkpatrick, C.A. *Quantitative Approaches to Management*. New York: McGraw-Hill, 1965.
This is a splendid introductory text for the OR beginner. It demands little background in mathematics and makes no use of the complicated notation that has heretofore discouraged most from reading OR articles, let alone from studying the subject. In our opinion, the chapters on vectors and determinants, matrix algebra, and proceeding through the simplex method of linear programming are among the best to be found for clarity of explanation and a relatively painless, simple approach to understanding somewhat tricky concepts. Their chapter on queuing theory is also a "best" introductory approach. This is an excellent introductory text in the OR field at the present time.

Lee, Sang M., and Moore, Laurence J. *Introduction to Decision Science*. New York: Petrocelli/Charter, 1975.

After *Quantitative Approaches to Management*, by Levin and Kirkpatrick, this comprehensive volume is the next step. Although it treats many of the same topics, it does so in a slightly more sophisticated manner for which the student-manager should now be ready. It also introduces in a relatively painless fashion the symbolic notation that is eventually inevitable. Although some of its coverage (for example, break-even analysis and game theory) is identical to Levin and Kirkpatrick, the Lee and Moore approach is easier to comprehend. It also contains chapters on goal programming and network modeling.

Wagner, Harvey M. *Principles of Operations Research, with Applications to Managerial Decisions*. Englewood Cliffs, N.J.: Prentice-Hall, 1969.

If any single volume contains everything, this may well be the one. In something more than 1,000 pages, Wagner has produced an OR text for "college students who have no previous background in operations research." The most cogent reason for consulting Wagner, in addition to his comprehensive approach, is the attention that he has given to detail and example, both of which are valuable supplements to the basics explained by Levin and Kirkpatrick and Lee and Moore. He has not, however, been able to do this without the use of symbolic notation.

McCloskey, Joseph F., and Trefethen, Florence N., eds. *Operations Research for Management*. Baltimore: Johns Hopkins Press, 1954.

One of the early works on OR to appear in this country, this work contains many individual chapters by persons prominent in the OR field some twenty or more years ago. The chapter by Florence Trefethen entitled "A History of Operations Research" may be the one most helpful to students new to OR. Although it is not imperative that this work be consulted, study of it will provide the interested person with a historical perspective that should heighten one's appreciation for the value of OR.

Library Quarterly 42, no. 1 (January 1972).

This is the best single exposition to date of OR as it relates to libraries. Although it contains some symbolic notation, it presents more importantly ten excellent papers on OR in a variety of library settings. Contributors to the number include notables such as C. West Churchman, Ferdinand Leimkuhler, Michael Buckland, Ben-Ami Lipetz, Philip Morse, and others. Vladimir Slamecka's contribution is a selective, but fundamental bibliography on OR in libraries covering a fifteen-year period. Although they are not as basic as the texts described earlier, reading of each of these papers will improve one's grasp of OR in the library.

Churchman, C. West, Ackoff, Russell L., and Arnoff, E. Leonard. *Introduction to Operations Research*. New York: Wiley, 1957.

For many years this served as the best introductory text in the field. Information contained in it was developed over a period of several years for a course in OR at the Case Institute of Technology. It touches in somewhat greater depth on most of the topics presented in the foregoing pages, and it is especially recommended for study of allocation models. Its chief shortcoming is the use of symbolic notation, which, as we have noted, has a tendency to discourage many who lack mathematical training.

Our purpose here, as stated earlier, has been a multiple one. In this short paper, we have attempted to introduce the reader and library manager to the use of a decision tool that, if adopted, could greatly enhance the decision processes of both the present and the future. We have attempted also to establish a rationale for employing quantitative decision methods, to provide a brief historical account of the development of the same, to demonstrate their efficacy by example, and finally to point the way to a highly useful body of literature that is not so vast as to be discouraging.

Clearly this paper has been directed toward, and written for, the novice and the uninitiated. It claims no sophistication of technique, intending as it does to illustrate the application of one basic though useful tool of OR in the simplest terms possible. We hope to make it clear that we are practitioners sharing with our colleagues something that we think is useful. Despite any indication to the contrary, we would close this paper by reemphasizing that although OR can be a highly useful tool, it is only that. It cannot make decisions; they must first and last be made by people. We are simply advocating a more objective way of making them.

NOTES

1. Rex V. Brown, Andrew S. Kahr, and Cameron Peterson, *Decision Analysis for the Manager* (New York: Holt, Rinehart & Winston, 1974), p. 3.
2. Ibid.
3. Sang M. Lee and Laurence J. Moore, *Introduction to Decision Science* (New York: Petrocelli/Charter, 1975), p. 1.
4. Alan C. Filley and Robert J. House, *Managerial Process and Organizational Behavior* (New York: Scott, Foresman, 1969).
5. Ibid., p. 443.
6. Ibid., pp. 444–448.
7. Ibid., pp. 449–450.
8. Brown, Kahr, and Peterson, *Decision Analysis for the Manager*, p. vii.
9. Lee and Moore, *Introduction to Decision Science*, p. 7.
10. Richard I. Levin and C. A. Kirkpatrick, *Quantitative Approaches to Management* (New York: McGraw-Hill, 1965), pp. v–vi.
11. Ibid., pp. 2–5.
12. Ellis A. Johnson, "The Executive, the Organization, and Operations Research" in *Operations Research for Management*, ed. by Joseph F. McCloskey and Florence N. Trefethen (Baltimore: Johns Hopkins Press, 1954), p. xiii.
13. Levin and Kirkpatrick, *Quantitative Approaches to Management*, p. 7.

14. F. W. Lancaster, *Aircraft in War: The Dawn of the Fourth Arm* (London: Constable and Company, Ltd., 1916) as cited in *Operations Research for Management*, ed. by McCloskey and Trefethen, p. 4.
15. Levin and Kirkpatrick, *Quantitative Approaches to Management*, p. 8.
16. Ibid.
17. Florence N. Trefethen, "A History of Operations Research" in *Operations Research for Management*, ed. by McCloskey and Trefethen, p. 6.
18. Ibid., p. 12.
19. Ibid., p. 9.
20. Jacinto Steinhardt, "Operations Research" a lecture delivered at the New York Meeting of the Institute of Mathematical Statistics and the American Historical Association (December 29, 1947) as cited in *Operations Research for Management*, ed. by McCloskey and Trefethen, p. 17.
21. Florence N. Trefethen, "A History of Operations Research" in *Operations Research for Management*, ed. by McCloskey and Trefethen, pp. 33–34.
22. Lee and Moore, *Introduction to Decision Science*, p. 41.
23. Ibid.
24. Ibid.
25. Ibid., p. 42.
26. Ibid., p. 419.
27. Background for this review of techniques is drawn from Lee and Moore, *Introduction to Decision Science* and Levin and Kirkpatrick, *Quantitative Approaches to Management*.

ABOUT THE AUTHORS

Herbert Poole is Director of the Library at Guilford College in Greensboro, North Carolina, where he also serves as Special Assistant to the President for Admissions and Financial Aid. He holds degrees from the University of North Carolina at Chapel Hill and is a candidate for the Ph.D. at Rutgers University in New Brunswick, New Jersey. He is currently vice-president of the North Carolina Friends Historical Society and has authored or edited several articles and monographs. Since 1972 he has served as editor of the quarterly journal, *North Carolina Libraries*.

Thomas H. Mott, Jr., is Dean of the Graduate School of Library Service at Rutgers University in New Brunswick, New Jersey, where he is also professor of library service and computer science. He holds degrees from Rice University and from Yale, where he received the Ph.D. He is co-author of *Introduction to FORTRAN IV Programming* and *Introduction to PL/I Programming for Library and Information Science*. He is founder of the Applied Logic Corporation, Princeton, New Jersey.

PERSONNEL NEEDS FOR LIBRARIANSHIP'S UNCERTAIN FUTURE

by Richard M. Dougherty

The 1970s have become a time of disquiet for the library professional. After two decades of unprecedented growth for library collections and staff, conditions have changed dramatically. Library school graduates, once so eagerly recruited, find it difficult to secure their first professional positions. Now graduates of accredited library schools are often willing and sometimes eager to accept library assistant positions. Even the experienced, accomplished librarian has become less mobile. Signs of the general disquiet are all about us. At professional conferences, one listens to the complaints of frustrated job seekers who resent the "bazaarlike" atmosphere pervading the job placement centers. Organizations similar to CLOUT (Concerned Librarians Against Unprofessional Trends) have been formed to counteract tendencies that threaten to undermine recent gains in professional status. Other professionals who feel their status threatened seek means to ensure and reinforce compliance with proper standards of professional competence—for example, certification. All of the above developments are a reflection of the tightened job market and the related perception that opportunities for professional employment and advancement have lessened.

All occupational groups experience periodic oversupplies of personnel. The current imbalance in the library profession will gradually be corrected by adjustments in the marketplace. Nonetheless, all indicators suggest that we are in the midst of a severe personnel surplus. Entering professionals are likely to experience restricted employment opportunities for several more years. In order to fully understand the current situation it may be instructive to review some of the events that occurred in the mid-1960s.

OPENING THE FLOODGATES

In 1965, there was a shortage of librarians, not a surplus. In the judgment of the leadership of the profession this shortage was one of extreme concern, so much so that under the auspices of the American Library Association (ALA), President

Edwin Castagna commissioned a national inventory to study personnel needs.[1] The results of the inventory were presented at a general session meeting of the 1965 Detroit annual ALA conference. Specifically, it was estimated that a shortage of 100,000 professionally trained staff existed. To eliminate the shortage, $320 million would have to be added to the aggregate budget of the nation's libraries. This influx of additional funding was mandated in order to bring staffing and collection sizes up to the then existing ALA standards for libraries.[2] President Castagna's lament seemed to reflect the attitudes of many leaders: "The decades ahead will be gloomy unless we prepare for a radical stepping-up of library support."[3] It has become increasingly apparent in the intervening years that the profession estimated its personnel deficit on the number of vacancies that *would* be created if financial support to libraries increased to the degree recommended rather than on the number of vacancies that *actually* existed. In effect, the profession was gearing itself to fill positions that had not been, and in fact never were funded.

Two years later, at the ALA conference in San Francisco, Mary V. Gaver noted that divisional programs, in one way or another, had focused on the theme of "crisis in library manpower; myth and reality."[4] The San Francisco conference also explored the nature of the shortage, and a report was presented that pointed out the need to conduct community studies so as to heighten professional awareness of what services the library should actually be providing its users. If community analyses were conducted, the report recommended, it would then be possible for the library to identify the new types of positions that should be created in order to better serve its community.[5] It was reasoned that if specific needs could be identified, library schools would then be better able to gear their programs to meet the personnel needs of libraries as identified in the field.

Gradually others took up the cry, and soon group after group began to address the question of how to overcome the personnel shortage. The profession's leaders created a general perception of the problem. The *National Inventory of Library Needs*, along with other assessments, added a quantitative parameter. Quite understandably, the profession began to marshal its resources to solve the "perceived" crisis.

Librarians were not the only group to misjudge the magnitude of the shortage. In 1966, Congress enacted the Higher Education Act, which, among other provisions, provided for scholarship and fellowship funds to library schools. This governmental pump-priming served to stimulate a growth in and proliferation of library school programs. The momentum generated by this pump priming was still evident in the 1970s, long after the shortage itself had disappeared. In 1964, 36 accredited library schools graduated 3,115 students. In 1968, the number of accredited library schools had increased to 45 graduating 4,625 students. By 1974, 62 accredited schools graduated 6,370 students.[6]

Library educators, with the encouragement of both the profession and the stimulus of federal aid, successfully created the capacity to double the prior rate of library school graduates. But as librarianship and higher education entered the 1970s, a number of warning signs, unheeded by most, began to appear on the educational horizon. Allan Cartter cautioned educators that they were creating an oversupply of Ph.D.'s. In general, educators agreed with Cartter's theses; unfortunately, his warnings did not lead educators to institute preparations for a period of no growth, or what has come to be termed a period of "steady-state."[7] As a group, librarians, like most other educators, failed to grasp the warning signs; growth in library education programs continued into the 1970s.

The actions of library educators contributed to the current personnel surplus. These actions, however, were quite reasonable given the circumstances that existed during the 1960s. It must be remembered that the profession placed a high priority on increasing the number of graduates, and the government, through federal aid programs, had stimulated larger enrollments and additional programs. In short, the profession successfully mobilized itself to wipe out the personnel deficit through its influence on public policy and by convincing large numbers of students to attend library school. Unfortunately, the profession did not give evidence of a capability to control the juggernaut it had helped to create.

BOOM TO BUST

In 1971, Carlyle J. Frarey reported that positions for new graduates were still available. He went on to caution that the deficit between demand and supply had visibly narrowed. He noted that the placement picture that emerged during the spring of 1970 indicated that there was no longer an acute shortage of librarians.[8] In spite of a growing recognition that demand had substantially diminished, the number of accredited library schools continued to grow. Library educators showed little tendency to modify their programs in response to available supply-and-demand indicators. In 1974, Frarey and Learmont reported that although 1974 graduates experienced slightly more job opportunities than had their counterparts in 1972 and 1973, the employment picture remained tight and did not offer the wealth of opportunities that so many had become accustomed to in the 1960s.[9]

With the benefit of hindsight it is safe to conclude that the shortage of the 1960s was not nearly as severe as had been believed. The shortage was, in part, a product of inadequate data and incorrect interpretations of that data. A shortage existed but not of sufficient magnitude to justify a twofold increase in the number of library school graduates.

Although we have focused on only one cause of the current personnel surplus, namely, the factors that have led to an overabundance of library school graduates, there were other important contributing factors. First, the desire to improve professional status led many libraries to develop more effective methods for staff utilization. Many tasks traditionally performed by professionally trained librarians were assigned to equally capable library assistants. Second, computer-based production systems and the development of networks such as the Ohio College Library Center (OCLC) and BALLOTS enabled libraries to reduce gradually the number of professional positions in the technical services areas. These reductions have been achieved either by reassignment of professional staff or through a process of attrition. In either case, the result has been a reduction in the number of advertised vacancies. Third, the gradual withdrawal of federal support for library education and innovative library programs has further reduced professional opportunities.

THE UNCERTAIN PRESENT

Today, the academic library professional is faced with an uncertainty that is inexplicably bound to countless external factors; however, enough information is available for us to suggest certain possibilities.

The austere budgets of the 1970s may not be a permanent fixture, but it does seem clear that our nation has entered into an era in which we must learn to cope with more limited financial and natural resources. This warning was voiced recently by the governors of Michigan, William G. Milligan, and California, Edmund G. Brown, Jr. Governor Brown points out that "it is now a question of reordering our priorities and choosing one program over another, based on a rigorous standard of equality and common sense."[10]

Educators and academic librarians must recognize the folly of continuing the practice of basing the quality of programs and services on factors primarily associated with growth. Some readers might view the foregoing statement as haranguing the obvious, for so many, for so long have echoed similar sentiments. Nonetheless, academic library budgets are still in large measure based on factors related to size or growth, for example, circulation of library materials, size of collection, the number of students a library serves. In a very real sense, college and university libraries are paying the price in 1977 for failing to develop in the 1960s the means to measure their qualitative accomplishments.

The fortunes of most academic libraries are closely bound to those of their parent institutions. Today, the future of higher education seems uncertain. Based on a recent assessment of higher education prepared for the Carnegie Commission on Higher Education one can confidently predict far-reaching changes.[11] For example, the enrollment projections of a few years ago were unduly optimistic. The U.S. Office of Education projected a 3.9 percent growth rate. It now appears that a 1.3 percent growth rate is more realistic.[12] The picture presented, however, should not be cause for undue pessimism. Some selective growth has been projected. For example, educators believe that some growth in enrollment may occur at community colleges because more students are interested in learning practical vocational skills and in taking nondegree credits that will help them advance in their chosen careers.[13]

The development of institutional strategies for reallocating existing resources is one of the major challenges facing academic administrators. The authors of *More Than Survival* enumerate some of the options available to the academic administrator. For example, administrators can capture faculty positions once they become vacant through retirement and resignation and reallocate these positions to programs with higher institutional or educational priority. Another possibility is to make more extensive use of temporary and part-time faculty. The use of part-time positions will become more important as permanent faculty positions become scarcer. As the proportion of tenured faculty grows, the opportunities for newly graduated Ph.D.'s will correspondingly diminish. To the extent that administrators are able to (1) increase the use of joint appointments between departments; (2) recruit scholars with subject flexibility; and (3) encourage faculty to shift fields through retraining and through granting extended leaves for study, they may now be able to ameliorate this emerging problem.[14]

The problems confronting the library administrator are analogous to those just described. It is already less common for library administrators to secure successfully additional dollars to underwrite new programs. The library administrator who wishes to initiate a new service must frequently carve support for that program from existing activities. Moreover, in order to be responsive to constituent demands and confronted with the prospect of a long period of reduced growth, library administrators must create more effective ways to reallocate funds. Regardless of the strategies employed, all academic administrators must make every effort to maximize flexibility in the use of uncommitted staff and dollar resources.

Society, consciously or unconsciously, has begun to reassess the role that higher education is to play during the next decade. A few educators are beginning to fear that we have created an "overeducated" society. Spiraling costs have prompted both funding agencies and critics alike to question the economic benefits of a college degree. Regardless of one's position, today's web of controversial issues is likely to produce an altered societal role for higher education. The library profession too must continue to address the question of what role librarianship should play in society. What can librarianship offer to society? Has librarianship developed a professional body of knowledge and expertise that will enable it to contribute to the solution of society's needs?

Library leaders have long recognized the need for the profession to develop a working definition. In the 1960s, educational leaders struggled to develop library school programs that could best respond to the operational needs of libraries. At one conference, co-sponsored by the ALA Office for Library Education and Library Administration Division, the conferees recommended that a "clear definition of librarianship and the role of the library in society" be established. "Without this [definition] . . . every approach to the manpower problem is hampered. Recruiters do not know what they are recruiting for; administrators do not know what the organization of jobs and positions should be; educators do not know what constitutes the needed content for their curricula."[15] In other words, the absence of a clearly understood definition of the profession's role has hampered efforts to formulate professional education programs.

In his classic exposition on librarianship, Pierce Butler expressed the same problem but in slightly different terms. Butler underscored the importance of evolving a true science. One of the benefits envisioned if that goal was achieved would be the ability to distinguish among various professional activities. A person, Butler noted, could perhaps gain a clearer insight into the confusion that has prevailed in librarianship by picturing to himself or herself how the medical field would appear if no distinction could be made between the physician, the nurse, and the hospital orderly.[16] The ambiguity in professional roles that Butler discussed is all too prevalent in librarianship forty years later.

The failure of the library profession to define the nature of roles and careers could suggest that the profession is unsure about its path and the direction in which it should be moving. Regardless of the cause(s), the failure to define roles has also contributed to other personnel problems. One specific example is a growing rift in the relations between professionals and other library staff.

Role Confusion between Professionals and Other Staff

Library assistants have become increasingly dissatisfied with their status. Their complaints can be attributed to several factors. Librarians, preoccupied with the desire to improve their own lot, have shown little concern over either the economic welfare or the workplace role of the library assistant. Librarians, in an effort to improve the utilization of staff, assign tasks identified as unprofessional to their subordinates.[17] Librarians spend more time away from their "desks." They actively engage in the governance of libraries, and they spend more time at conferences. The tasks they performed must now be performed in their absence by assistants. Although this process of reassignment has created new opportunities for library assistants, the added responsibilities too often have not been accompanied by commensurate rewards. There is growing evidence that library assistants perceive that the gap in salaries and other fringe benefits has widened between librarians and themselves rather than narrowed.

Although library assistants may not begrudge the progress librarians have achieved in salaries and other benefits, they do want a larger slice of the economic pie. Undercurrents of discontent have surfaced recently as increasing numbers of library assistants have joined employee groups. One group of library assistants, concerned about the conditions of employment, founded the Council of Library Technology (COLT). The intent of COLT is unmistakable. Its hope is to work toward an expansion of membership and a revision of its constitution in order to allow annual meetings in conjunction with ALA.[18] For a complex set of reasons, COLT probably will not succeed at organizing library assistants on a national scale. It is more likely that the aspirations can be better achieved through affiliation with local employee groups. If one accepts prevailing theories on the evolution of occupations, one must also consider prospects for a schism between professionals and library assistants. The current dissatisfactions have been exacerbated by the profession's failure to establish clearer role distinctions.

It is not my intent to suggest that the profession has not attempted to cope with this complicated issue. Several years ago the Office of Library Education of the ALA formulated a general rationale that delineated among various levels of library positions. The statement describes the kinds of activities that are appropriate to the librarian, the library assistant, the library technician, and other associated clerical support staff. The document was later adopted by the ALA Council as official ALA policy.[19]

If it were possible to transform libraries overnight so that staffing assignments and responsibilities reflected the philosophy of the ALA manpower statement, many of the current staffing ambiguities might be resolved. Of course, this is unlikely to happen. Complex organizations seldom change rapidly. The facts suggest that many library professionals will continue to perform work that clearly could be performed equally well by library assistants. In this period of prolonged personnel surplus, failure to establish a unique societal role could have far graver implications if public officials, academic administrators, and boards of trustees began to question the need to employ a library professional when the services of a person appearing to perform the same functions could easily be secured but at half the cost.

Ingredients of a Solution

There are no facile solutions to the current personnel surplus, although a variety of ideas have been suggested. Some individuals advocate various forms of certification in order to maintain professional standards, while others call for a reduction in the number of accredited library schools.[20] In the remaining sections several factors that individually or collectively could bear on the future of the professional librarian will be presented. Although many alternative factors could have been chosen, I have focused on four: (1) professional status, (2) educational reform, (3) harnessing technologies, and (4) influencing public policy formulations.

Professional Status. Academic librarians must delineate their campus role. The achievement of faculty status is viewed as one way to resolve the question of role definition because librarians who achieve faculty status are thereby expected to engage in activities normally associated with scholarship—for example, research and publication. Faculty librarians are also expected to participate actively in both library governance and professional organizations. Over a period of time, the staff that succeeds in creating such an environment will become distinguishable both in fact and on paper from that library's support staff. But even if successful, the rewards will not be reaped easily, for to succeed in academe will require an enormous amount of individual dedication and commitment. As difficult as the task may be, faculty status does represent one way to address the current role-ambiguity question.[21]

Educational Reform. Library educators will play a pivotal role in the next decade. If our schools continue to graduate students at the same rate, and if these graduates possess the same kind of education that we have become accustomed to expect, then the prospects for the new professional will be dim indeed. Library schools must redefine their educational programs and reduce the number of students they accept. Cutbacks, I believe, can be effected without damaging the educational quality of existing programs. Fortunately, the lack of job opportunities may discourage enough students so that reduced class sizes may be achieved without the initiation of any formal policy. But most important, the profession must take positive steps to upgrade the quality of its professional education programs. One action that I believe highly desirable would be to adopt a two-year masters-level degree program. (Serendipitously, a two-year program would tend to depress enrollments.) For many years, professional educators and practitioners have debated whether or not a library education should be founded in theory and principle or should emphasize practical experience. This educational pendulum has swung to and fro. In the late 1960s, due to the ferment generated by their students, some library schools reduced or even dropped core course requirements. Although understandable in the light of the upheavals that were buffeting higher education, the dropping of requirements may have been educationally questionable. Some students may have been misled into assuming that a core of knowledge did not exist. Many schools instituted programs that counseled students to take the now-elective core courses, but a program of counseling and a curriculum built around a core of professional courses are not comparable. How many medical students are given the choice as to whether or not they will take anatomy or body physiology? Doctors are expected to commit to memory parts of the skeletal and cardiovascular systems. Should not library school students be expected to learn the rules of cataloging or the characteristics of reference tools? Of course, the traditional core courses alone do not constitute an adequate program. Library school graduates must know more about organizational behavior, computer applications, and the principles of administration, communication, and group dynamics, to name but a few of the other specialized topics. Today's library school graduate must be better trained, and there is no way to provide the student with the requisite tools in a one-year library school program.

Harnessing Technologies. New technologies will produce far-reaching changes in librarianship through the remainder of the twentieth century. Although the profession must be prepared to take full advantage of these technologies, the exact nature of the changes is not clear. It is probable that some technologies will lead to a reduction in the work force of particular units, but there is little evidence on which to base a projected net decrease in the total library work force. At the same time new and exciting opportunities are possible. These could very well lead to net increases in the total library work force. In the short range, the impact of computer-based systems such as OCLC and BALLOTS will continue to alter the way library technical service departments are staffed and operated. The growing availability of bibliographic information in computerized data bases will stimulate gradual changes in the way services are offered by reference staffs. For example, as it becomes more economical to input, store, and retrieve bibliographic data, more libraries are likely to discard their card catalogs in favor of machine-readable files. Many experts predict very rapid dramatic changes in libraries, but it is more likely that the technological advances will far outstrip society's ability or willingness to absorb the changes. Consequently, the diffusion of new innovations will take longer than most current predictions imply. The library professional should be ready to seize every opportunity to use each new tool as it develops. The ability to control and influence the relevant emerging technologies may become a major factor in determining the role of librarianship in society.

Public Policy. Another unknown on the horizon revolves around the vagaries of federal and state educational policies. Shifts of policy could produce a great change in the projected demand patterns for professional librarians. The enactment of the GI Bill following World War II transformed higher education for years to come. In the long run it changed the whole structure of our society.[22] It is possible that analogous future public policy shifts could once again produce a transformation of higher education. Due to the current complexity of society and the growing dependence on information to remedy societal problems, it is conceivable that public policy could lead to a demand for information professionals that is unprecedented in the twentieth century. One fact seems clear: all professions have become increasingly dependent on public policy. Therefore, it is imperative that the library profession make every effort to develop its capacity to influence those individuals who formulate public policies.

SUMMARY AND CONCLUSIONS

The Bureau of Labor Statistics, in a recent report, projected that employment of librarians would increase from 115,000 in 1970 to 162,000 in 1985—a 2.7 percent increase per year, as compared to a 5.2 percent increase that occurred between 1960 and 1970.[23] Michael Cooper, in a recent analysis of demand, concluded that because of declining fund availability at the local government level, full funding of public libraries would be difficult to achieve. Consequently, he concluded that employment opportunities in public libraries would be limited. He predicted that the number of college and university librarian positions would probably grow, although at a slower rate than in recent years. Cooper also predicted that because the median age of librarians is high when compared to other professions, the replacement demand for librarians is likely to be higher. More librarians will be retiring than in the "age-normal occupations."[24]

Based on available data the current demand outlook for librarians cannot be interpreted optimistically. There are actions that the library profession can take that may enhance professional opportunities in the coming years. Individual librarians can emphasize the pursuit of scholarly activities as one means of creating a distinguishable role. Library managers can continue to improve the utilization of library staff and make full use of technologies as they become available. Library educators can take steps to upgrade professional programs by introducing policies that will reduce student enrollment. Faculty should be encouraged to broaden their scope of teaching specializations. Finally, library associations and professional leaders can work to influence current and future public policy formulations related to library information systems.

It is possible that the library profession might be inundated by the uncertainties and complexities of the next year, but it is exactly because of the uncertain future that the profession should establish its goals and marshal its professional resources. Several years ago, Harold Lancour succinctly summed up the elements that in the end might sway society's verdict on the profession of librarianship. Lancour observed: "by strengthening the educational requirements for those under the profession; by strengthening our professional associations; by emphasizing the intellectual character of the librarian's work; by ourselves placing an higher value upon our abilities and our work commensurate with what it deserves; by taking pride in our work, in our positions, and in our name. By doing so, the time will soon be at hand when the librarian's search for status can come to an end."[25] The search may never end, for it never has ended for any profession; but if Lancour's ideal could be approached, the hunt would open more opportunities for all librarians.

NOTES

1. American Library Association, *National Inventory of Library Needs* (Chicago: American Library Association, 1965), pp. 2–3.
2. Academic librarians were excluded from the *National Inventory* because at the time of the study no ALA standards for college libraries existed. However, the tone of the general recommendations presented the prevailing attitudes toward the manpower situation.
3. American Library Association, *National Inventory of Library Needs*, p. 1.
4. Mary V. Gaver, "Manpower for Library Occupations—1967," in *The Bowker Annual of Library and Book Trade Information, 1968* (New York: R. R. Bowker, 1967), p. 318.
5. Ibid., p. 319.
6. Statistics for the number of accredited library schools and their graduates were taken from the following sources: Sarah R. Reed, "Library Education Report," in *The Bowker Annual of Library and Book Trade Information, 1967*, p. 272; Frank L. Schick, "Library Manpower and Education for Librarianship," in *The Bowker Annual of Library and Book Trade Information, 1968*, pp. 314–315; and Carlyle J. Frarey and Carol L. Learmont, "Placement and Salaries in 1974: Promise or Illusion," *Library Journal* 100 (October 1, 1975): 1767.
7. Allan M. Cartter, *The Aftereffects of Putting the Blind Eye to the Telescope* (paper delivered at the Twenty-fifth National Conference of the American Association of Higher Education, Chicago, Ill., March 3, 1970).
8. Carlyle J. Frarey, "Placement and Salaries: The 1969 Plateau," *Library Journal* 95 (June 1, 1970): 2099.
9. Frarey and Learmont, "Placement and Salaries in 1974," p. 1767.
10. *The Chronicle of Higher Education* 11 (February 9, 1976): 11.

11. Carnegie Foundation for the Advancement of Teaching, *More Than Survival: Prospects for Higher Education in a Period of Uncertainty* (San Francisco: Jossey-Bass, 1975).
12. Ibid., p. 36.
13. Ibid., p. 48.
14. Ibid., p. 93.
15. Lester Asheim, ed., *Library Manpower Needs and Utilization*, conference co-sponsored by the Office for Library Education and the Library Administration Division of the American Library Association with the cooperation of the National Book Committee, March 9–11, 1967 (Chicago: American Library Association, 1967), p. 7.
16. Pierce Butler, *An Introduction to Library Science* (Chicago: University of Chicago Press, 1933), pp. 110–111.
17. Wilensky, in discussing the characteristics frequently identified with the evolutionary process of a profession, cites as one characteristic the behavior of a group to redefine its core tasks so as to transfer the "dirty work" to subordinates. Harold Wilensky, "The Professionalization of Everyone?" *American Journal of Sociology* 70 (September 1964): 242–246.
18. "COLT Solicits All Non-Pros: Plans a Reorganization," *Library Journal* 100 (November 15, 1975): 2100.
19. "Library Education and Manpower: ALA Policy Proposal," *American Libraries* 1 (April 1970): 341–344.
20. The M.L.S. degree itself has come under criticism recently as some affirmative-action advocates question the necessity of the M.L.S. degree as a requirement for entry into the professional ranks. It is likely that the courts will be asked to decide the future of the M.L.S. If the courts were not to uphold the M.L.S. requirement, the personnel prospects will become even more murky.
21. William H. Axford, "The Three Faces of Eve: Or the Identity of Academic Librarianship, A Symposium," *Journal of Academic Librarianship* 2 (January 1977): 276–285.
22. Carnegie Foundation for the Advancement of Teaching, *More Than Survival*, p. 48.
23. U.S. Department of Labor, Bureau of Labor Statistics, *Library Manpower: A Study of Demand and Supply* (Washington, D.C.: Superintendent of Documents, 1975).
24. Michael D. Cooper, "An Analysis of the Demand for Librarians," *Library Quarterly* 45 (October 1975): 401.
25. Harold Lancour, "The Librarian's Search for Status," in *Seven Questions about the Profession of Librarianship*, ed. by Philip H. Ennis and Howard W. Winger, Twenty-sixth Annual Conference of the Graduate Library School (Chicago: University of Chicago Press, 1961), p. 81.

ABOUT THE AUTHOR

Richard M. Dougherty is University Librarian at the University of California at Berkeley. He holds several degrees, including the Ph.D. from Rutgers Graduate

School of Library Service. He has served in a variety of administrative positions and held a number of teaching appointments. He has been active for many years in the American Library Association, and he has also fulfilled numerous editorial responsibilities with distinction. These include Assistant Editor of *Library Resources and Technical Services* and Editor of *College and Research Libraries* and of the *Journal of Academic Librarianship*. He has co-authored numerous articles and editorials and has authored or co-authored several monographs, including *The Scientific Management of Library Operations* and *Improving Access to Library Research*.

WOMEN AND EMPLOYMENT
IN ACADEMIC LIBRARIANSHIP

by Beverly P. Lynch

Whether women librarians are discriminated against in terms of hiring, promotion, and compensation remains the subject of considerable discussion among academic librarians. Together with women in other academic departments, female librarians have benefited from the efforts of the government to reduce the effects of alleged discrimination toward women. Executive Order 11247 of 1968, Title VII of the 1974 Civil Rights Act as amended in 1972, the Equal Pay Act of 1963, which was amended to apply to higher education in 1972, and Title IX of the Education Amendments of 1972, as enforced by a number of federal agencies, have led to some promotions for female librarians and across-the-board salary increases to women faculty.

Passage and enforcement of equal employment opportunity and affirmative-action laws have enhanced the status of women in academic librarianship and women in academe as a whole, although in actual numbers only a few women benefit and many who do are already in the upper end of the distribution of income in the United States. Librarians comprise just over 1 percent of the total professional work force in the United States. Of this 1 percent, academic librarians comprise 17 percent.[1] The 23,000 academic librarians in the United States[2] thus make up just 0.17 percent of the total professional work force. Of this work force approximately 60 percent, or 13,800, are women.

FACULTY STATUS

Because academic librarians form a very small occupational group within the higher education community, librarians in colleges and universities have allied themselves with the teaching faculty rather than attempt to establish a separate and distinct occupational identity for themselves. The early efforts to gain faculty rank and status for librarians were supported by the rationale that the work performed by academic librarians was similar to the work performed by the teaching faculty in terms of its intellectual content and its value:

> Librarians perform a teaching and research role inasmuch as they instruct students formally and informally and advise and assist faculty in their scholarly pursuits. Librarians are also themselves involved in the research function; many conduct research in their own professional interests and in the discharge of their duties.
>
> Where the role of college and university librarians . . . requires them to function essentially as part of the faculty, this functional identity should be recognized by granting of faculty status.[3]

In small colleges it has not been uncommon for the head librarian to be appointed from the faculty. Because the librarian was a colleague, perhaps already tenured, the concept of faculty status, at least for the head librarian, was not questioned. The movement grew within libraries as faculty status was extended to other librarians. The "Joint Statement on Faculty Status of College and University Librarians,"[4] drafted by representatives of the Association of American Colleges, the American Association of University Professors, and the Association of College and Research Libraries, now has been endorsed by forty-nine national, regional, and state associations.[5] Some disagreement remains within the profession at large as to whether librarians, as a matter of course, should be appointed to the faculty. The disagreement comes primarily from librarians working in the established, prestigious universities and from the technicians within the ranks of librarians. The disagreement is not strong enough nor persuasive enough to change the basic position of the profession.

Writing and Research as Promotion and Tenure Criteria

Now that faculty status for librarians generally has been accepted, the concerns center upon the development and implementation of criteria and procedures for the appointment, promotion, and tenure of librarians. Publishing, never a central concern of the majority of academic librarians, now is the chief criterion for promotion in many college and university libraries. To be an excellent librarian is not good enough to gain promotion or to achieve tenure. Difficulties are encountered in implementing the criteria for promotion and tenure because few librarians with the master's degree in librarianship (the terminal degree for academic librarians) are trained to do research or to write for publication. Yet these skills are necessary now in order to advance in the profession, even in those libraries where faculty status for librarians is not established. At the same time, few libraries have the money or the flexibility to grant time off to give their librarians the opportunity to undertake research projects. It is a rare promotion and tenure committee that is able to realize what the librarian's work year—one month vacation and twelve holidays being fairly common—means in terms of time for research or for writing.

Just at the time when academic librarians need to reduce their "library load" (comparable to the "teaching load") in order to write, conduct research, or train themselves to do so, the economy in higher education has slowed. For many librarians faculty status will mean a forced trade-off of library service for publishing and research. The impact of this trade-off on the future of academic librarianship is not clear. It is clear that few, if any, new professional positions will be available to academic libraries, particularly if the rationale for new positions is based upon the need of the librarians to have time for research and writing. Whether academic librarianship will be able to make the philosophical shift from its primary and traditional objective of service to the users to the objective of service to the profession through writing and publishing is not clear. Whether it can convince colleges and universities that the shift is an important one to support remains to be seen. Despite these difficulties of implementation, the movement in the profession for full faculty status will not be reversed. The status of the academic librarian as a member of the faculty will shape the character of academic librarianship over the next two decades and will influence the employment opportunities of women and minorities within the profession.

ADVANCEMENT AND EARNING DIFFERENTIAL BETWEEN MEN AND WOMEN

The projections of future employment opportunities are pessimistic for all of higher education. The number of college-age youth will decline until the end of the century and there is little expectation that adult learners will reverse the trend of declining enrollments. The inevitable tightening of the job market will mean much keener competition and a greater need than ever for objective hiring criteria.

The tightening of the labor market may be more critical for women than for men, for, in general, the choices of jobs for women are more limited, and job choices are constrained by life-styles and occupational growth rates. Although society has tried to foster equal access to jobs in higher education and to ensure the same rewards for women as well as men, women in academic librarianship will have to expand their professional objectives in order to qualify for promotions and for tenure as well as for appointment. Women will have to decide upon career strategies fairly early and obtain the necessary credentials to meet their career designs. Within the working environment of faculty status, it will mean that women will have to train themselves to do research. They will have to be willing to spend time on research, writing, professional activities, and service on university committees in order to obtain advancement. These activities represent a change in the working environment from what many women have expected of academic libraries. In the past, the college or university library has offered a pleasant place in which to work and a job that could be left for a time and then picked up again at will.

Nearly 10 percent of the total work force represented in Anita Schiller's 1966 survey of academic librarians[6] had left work for marriage or family reasons at some point during their academic library careers, returning later to jobs in college and university libraries. Nearly 6 percent of those surveyed were faculty wives. Many women in the survey entered the academic library profession after their children were grown. These work patterns are bound to result in some obsolescence of the academic librarian's skills. Women who have interrupted their library careers may find that their opportunities for professional development and advancement have narrowed.

The employment opportunities and projected lifetime earnings of women in academic libraries probably will be influenced by differences in acquired skills and demonstrated productivity. It has been argued that research and publication are vastly overrated and that the practice of librarianship itself should be rewarded. Most criteria for promotion and tenure in academic libraries attempt to reward excellence in librarianship. Like excellence in teaching, the measures are difficult to design. Measures of research and publication, being easier to identify, are usually emphasized. The future working environment in academic libraries, in which promotion and tenure decisions are made in the context of the faculty status for librarians, will present difficulties for those women who drop in and out of librarianship but expect to advance in rank and achieve tenure.

The differences in salaries between men and women librarians often are attributed to discrimination. An alternative explanation, suggested above, is that college and university library administrators respond to the choices made by women regarding their participation in the labor force and their on-the-job training. In the labor force at large, a division of labor between husband and wife is characteristic of most females. Married women, including the highly educated, work less during the time when small children are present.[7] During the time period associated with childbearing and child care, when women want either not to work or to work only part-time, some obsolescence in skills is likely. Library administrators do compare the level of skills and promote and reward accordingly.

There are no data with which to compare the earning patterns of men and women academic librarians to determine the rate at which salary increases occur. Nor are there data that compare salaries of single and married women working in academic libraries. The salary data published by the Association of College and Research Libraries in 1976[8] do show that the beginning salaries for female librarians are not substantially less than for male librarians (see the following table).

Women with less than five years of experience earn on the average $372, or 3.2 percent, less than men. This is a relatively small difference. The differences remain small until one reaches the associate and assistant director and director levels. Men hold the majority of positions at these levels and command the highest salaries. Women, comprising about 60 percent of the academic library labor force, hold the majority of lower-level jobs. Those few women who are directors or associate or assistant directors do have lower salaries.

Before speculating on the future earning patterns of women working in academic libraries, a review of some of the elements of economic theory that explain

COMPARISON BETWEEN AVERAGE SALARIES OF MEN AND WOMEN, PROFESSIONAL LIBRARY STAFF 1975–1976

Category	Men	Women
Directors	$ 22,242	$ 17,062
Associate and assistant directors	20,165	16,380
Functional and subject specialists	15,633	14,216
Branch and department heads	15,979	14,387
Other professionals— 5 years experience or more	15,476	14,196
Other professionals—less than 5 years experience	11,674	11,302

Source: Association of College and Research Libraries, *Salary Structures of Librarians in Higher Education for the Academic Year 1975–76* (Chicago: Association of College and Research Libraries, 1976), p. 8.

income variation may be useful. It is generally agreed that people decide to acquire new skills or to enhance old skills in order to maximize their total, long-term income. For an academic librarian, the costs of getting a second master's degree, a specialist's degree, or a doctorate are the reduction in present income or in leisure time. The librarian who makes such an investment expects the benefits of the investment activity to come later, primarily in the form of higher salaries, better opportunities for advancement, or increased status. Because the person will want to amortize his or her investment, it is likely that younger librarians will spend more time investing in their skills than will older librarians. If the amount of time devoted to skills improvement declines with increased age, it would be expected that increases in the salaries of younger librarians would be larger than the salary increases of older librarians.

The 1975–1976 salary data collected by the Association of College and Research Libraries can only suggest that this theory may be applicable to academic librarians, because one must make the assumption that directors of libraries are older than those professionals in nonadministrative posts. The percentage increase in the average salaries of professionals with five years of experience and over, who are not holding jobs as department heads or administrators, was larger than any other category, having increased 24 percent between 1972–1973 and 1975–1976. By contrast, the average salary increase for directors during the same period was 5.7 percent.

The data do not support directly the theory as applied to academic librarians, but there are data that apply to professors. For male academics in economics, sociology, and biology, the percentage rate of salary increases declines in the years following receipt of the doctorate.[9] The decline is so rapid that the salaries of young professors catch up with, and often surpass, those of older professors. This same pattern of earnings growth is not observed consistently for women professors. On the average, a year of post-degree experience is not the same for a female professor as it is for a male, and the lower salaries of women professors reflect this.[10]

In 1966, Schiller found that 57 percent of the women working in academic libraries were over forty-five years of age, and nearly half of the academic librarians received the master's degree after they were thirty years of age. While 50 percent of the men were between the ages of thirty and forty-four, only 25 percent of the women were. We have no cumulative data on the age of doctoral students in librarianship, but we do know that in 1973–1974, of the forty-seven librarians who earned the Ph.D. degree, only seventeen, or 36 percent, were women.[11] There are data then that *suggest* that the life-cycle accumulation of professional skills differs between male and female academic librarians. These skills differences may lead to lower salary levels and rates of promotion for women. More comparative data on educational achievement, employment practices, and salaries are needed before we are able to understand more fully the employment and salary differences between men and women in academic libraries.

Occupational segregation has emerged as a key variable in many analyses of the labor market and investigations of the issues of discrimination in work. Studies show that most women are concentrated in very few types of work. Some evidence indicates that many jobs held by women are part time and that women seek these jobs and use different criteria in the search and selection of them than do men. Many women want working hours that will match their child's school day and their husband's work schedule. They want jobs that do not require Saturday or evening assignments or overtime hours. Because not all occupations meet the characteristics sought by women, those that do have a large supply of women applicants for the jobs available. Salaries thus may fall below other occupations where the supply of workers is less and the training or educational requirements more demanding. Should this evidence apply to academic libraries, then we can understand the findings that women earn less and hold more of the lower-level positions in these libraries. Should these working patterns for women in academic libraries not change, equal employment opportunity and affirmative-actions laws will have little impact upon the overall position of women in academic libraries.

JOB VERSUS CAREER

Faculty status for librarians implies that appointment and promotion policies will be based upon ability. The difficulties come in deciding exactly what constitutes ability and how ability should be measured. Because future decisions on promotion and tenure within the library will go through the college or university-wide promotion and tenure committees, it is probable that tenure appointments in the library, as in the other academic units, will be given to those people with good publication records, with less emphasis being given to abilities as librarians and to records of service in various campus and professional activities. As job opportunities narrow in academic libraries, it will become increasingly difficult to make the decisions on initial appointments when neither research nor professional competencies have been demonstrated.

For the most part, publication or research has not been the central interest of women who enter librarianship. The interest of women in the field has been an immediate and a practical interest. Being a trained librarian has meant getting a good job. For many women, it has been the job and not the career that they have sought. As long as publication and research reflect the academic institution's priorities, preference will be given to those librarians who are willing and able to undertake these activities. Unless women change their career patterns, or colleges and universities change their criteria and measures of ability, women are likely to earn less and remain in the lower-level jobs in academic libraries.

Broad questions of institutional change will be addressed as colleges and universities move toward the year 2000. Women who have moved into the key administrative posts and hold tenured positions will have an opportunity to influence policies governing change. The demands for part-time work, of great interest to many women librarians, will probably continue. Most colleges and universities hire women on a part-time basis to handle lower-level and introductory courses. Usually these women

> are not privileged to vote in faculty meetings, nor are they eligible for the full range of faculty benefits, such as leaves, support for scholarship, tenure, and opportunity to participate in decision making. Marginal appointments, even if full time, carry one-year contracts, little possibility for promotion, little security, and almost no research stability.[12]

Should changes occur in policies governing the part-time librarian, women will have a better opportunity to enhance their skills, to pursue career objectives, and to seek higher-level, higher-paying positions within the library.

Women have sought part-time work in greater numbers than men, partly to enable them to meet demands of the family. Currently more than one-fifth of all adult women workers and one-third of all working mothers work part time, and the part-time employment of women has grown twice as fast as men.[13] Part-time workers generally earn less than full-time workers and have proportionally fewer, if any, benefits. Of importance to the professional worker is the commonly held perception that the work commitment of the part-time worker is less serious than those holding full-time jobs. The effects of part-time work and the discontinuity in labor-force participation tend to lower the lifetime earnings of women. After an initial rise in the earnings of women in the twenty to twenty-nine age bracket, earnings go up little over the rest of the lifetime. Men's earnings, reflecting full-time and continuous employment, taper off after ages forty-five to fifty-four.[14]

There is no way of knowing the extent to which these factors influence the observed salary differences between men and women academic librarians. One could expect that unless the policies and attitudes toward part-time work in higher education change, women librarians who seek equal employment opportunities and similar rates of pay will have to demonstrate the same work commitments to full-time work.

SUMMARY

The best predictor of the future is the past and the present. The employment patterns of women in academic libraries during the next twenty-five years will evolve from past and present employment practices. Because it is not likely that academic librarians will abandon their policies toward faculty status for librarians and because there will be little if any expansion in the number of available jobs, appointment, promotion, and tenure practices will determine the job opportunities. The emphasis on publication and research will lead some women to invest in additional degrees, plan their career strategies early, and work full time. These women will advance along with men into the higher-level and higher-paying positions in academic libraries. The others will not.

NOTES

1. Rudolf C. Blitz, "Women in the Professions, 1870–1970," *Monthly Labor Review* 97 (May 1974): 36.
2. National Center for Education Statistics, *Library Statistics of Colleges and Universities*, Fall 1973 Summary Data (Washington, D.C.: National Center for Education Statistics, 1976), p. 9.
3. "Joint Statement on Faculty Status of College and University Librarians," *College and Research Libraries News* 35 (February 1974).
4. Ibid.
5. *College and Research Libraries News* 38 (February 1977).
6. Anita R. Schiller, *Characteristics of Professional Personnel in College and University Libraries* (Springfield, Ill.: State Library, 1969).
7. C. Russell Hill and Frank P. Stafford, "Allocation of Time to Pre-School Children and Educational Opportunity," *Journal of Human Resources* 9 (Summer 1973): 323–341.
8. Association of College and Research Libraries, *Salary Structures of Librarians in Higher Education for the Academic Year 1975–76* (Chicago: Association of College and Research Libraries, 1976).
9. George E. Johnson and Frank P. Stafford, "Women and the Academic Labor Market," in *Sex, Discrimination and the Division of Labor*, ed. by C. B. Lloyd (New York: Columbia University Press, 1975), pp. 201–219.
10. Ibid.
11. American Library Association, *Survey of Graduates and Faculty of U.S. Library Education Programs Awarding Degrees and Certificates, 1973–1974* (Chicago: American Library Association, 1974).
12. Sheila Tobias and Margaret L. Rumbarger, "Rearrangements in Faculty Schedules," in *Women in Higher Education* (Washington, D.C.: American Council on Education, 1974), p. 128.
13. Hilda Kahne, "The Women in Professional Occupations: New Complexities for Chosen Roles," *The Journal of the National Association for Women Deans, Administrators, and Counselors* 39 (Summer 1976): 183.
14. Juanita M. Kreps, *Sex in the Marketplace: American Women at Work* (Baltimore: Johns Hopkins University Press, 1970).

ABOUT THE AUTHOR

Beverly P. Lynch is University Librarian at the University of Illinois at Chicago Circle. She holds degrees from North Dakota State University, the University of Illinois at Urbana-Champaign, and the University of Wisconsin at Madison where she received the Ph.D. She has served as Executive Secretary of the Association of College and Research Libraries and has published widely in the fields of sociology and library science.

EDUCATION OF FUTURE ACADEMIC LIBRARIANS

by Lester Asheim

Every page of this volume is concerned with possibilities that could—and should—affect the education of academic librarians. The message to the educator is clear: because in the future the operation of all libraries (including academic libraries), the functions they perform, the materials with which they deal, and the audiences they serve will very likely be different from that of the present, the appropriate preparation of academic librarians should begin now to anticipate changing needs and reflect them in the curriculum.

To say that the message is clear is not to say that it is simple or easy to implement. Even the experts can only guess at what the nature of the changes will be. The educator of today who must prepare for tomorrow must do so with only the most tentative of guidelines, and with a knowledge that in the past the prognosticators have been wrong as often as they have been right, not only about the nature of the changes themselves, but even more about the social and professional impact that the changes would have.

Preparing for the future has been, and will continue to be, the great challenge to education. It is made even more difficult today by the very real likelihood that in the years ahead changes and challenges will occur even more rapidly than they do now, and that educational decisions will have to be made in an atmosphere of uncertainty, without all the data that would be desirable; with data or interpretations of data that are incorrect; and without precedents relevant enough to be taken as reliable guides. This same challenge of preparation will face practitioners as well. They too must learn to make responsible decisions in an atmosphere of uncertainty, without all of the needed relevant data. It is the task of education to prepare itself and its students to cope with the problem.

This suggests that education for the future cannot be too specific or prescriptive. It must be general and theoretical, with its emphasis on the principles that underlie the academic library's educational function rather than on the details of its present operation. Nevertheless, as in the present, graduates of library schools will be expected to *practice* and to move into libraries or other information agencies and perform needed services immediately. In one sense, then, the problem of educating for the future is not essentially different from the problem that has faced educators in the past: how to establish the proper mix of theoretical and practical—the why and the how—so as to turn out practitioners who will be flexible; who can evaluate practice and introduce needed change; who are hospitable to new approaches but sensitive to the values in tradition; who are capable of gathering, organizing, and interpreting pertinent data on which to base innovation, but who can also make responsible decisions when the hard data are not available.

Despite the present emphasis on change, tomorrow's academic librarians will undoubtedly still be charged with fulfilling the library's traditional role in the academic setting. No matter how many new approaches may be introduced, library service will still require the identification and acquisition of wanted information, the organization of a system to provide for its retrieval, and the method of preserving it for delivery to those who desire or need it. This role, however, is not identical with the agency that performs it or the means by which it is implemented, and the library function of the future may well be carried out in an environment quite different from what we now think of as a library. Already there are computers, data banks, and a variety of nonbook materials that create an atmosphere quite antithetical to the mental image many of us conjure up when the word "library" is mentioned. The changes of the future are likely to go even farther away from emphasis on the book to emphasis on information in many formats. The traditional content of education for librarians will have to reflect these changes.

Two developments have occurred in recent years that should be helpful as we plan the new library education: (1) the move toward greater centralization of many library processes aided by the adaptation of new technology to library uses; and (2) the recognition that all the tasks performed in libraries need not be performed by librarians. Both of these developments suggest that different kinds of responsibilities can be prepared for in different ways.

SEPARATION OF PROFESSIONAL FROM NONPROFESSIONAL TASKS

As any profession grows, many of the tasks that once constituted a professional challenge become codified and routinized and can be turned over to paraprofessional staff who, working side by side with the professional personnel, carry out important functions essential to support professional decision makers. This may not seem to be a profound insight, but until recently library educators assumed that the library school's program, occupying only an academic year or slightly more, had to be designed to prepare each student for every aspect of library work that might arise within a lifetime. Although we have moved from a single program for every librarian to a number of special programs designed to prepare a person for a particular type of library or type-of-library function, we have continued to assume that someone preparing to become an academic librarian, for example, must be taught to handle efficiently every operation that takes place in an academic library.

The implications of the recognition of different levels of responsibility, each with its own training, are revolutionary. As James Thompson, a British librarian, suggests:

Academic libraries do not need a great many additional professionals. If anything, they have too many librarians now: most of them spend the bulk of their time doing clerical work which non-professional personnel can perform equally well for substantially less money. What academic libraries do need is fewer but better-educated librarians who can step into the collection-development, substantial-reference, and bibliographical-consultant positions that are now largely unfilled.[1]

Jerrold Orne, some thirteen years earlier, had seen the same thing in the United States:

three-fourths of all work done in libraries requires something less than graduation from an accredited graduate library school. It will be a happy day for me when I have suitable professionals where I need them in one out of four assignments in my library, and have each one of them backed up with three or more subprofessionals on an average. I might go one step further and wish for one better trained administrative professional for each ten to 20 lesser fry.[2]

The move toward a far larger proportion of supportive to professional staff has now begun, and with it have come some important changes in the shape and content of library education. Thus, at least two tracks of preparation have already been defined to provide for improved library services: the support track and the professional track; and within each of these, a variety of specialized programs. Programs of the future will be even more varied, supplying specific training at several different levels in order to develop qualifications for particular positions. Promotion to more complex and difficult responsibilities will require additional education or experience beyond the qualification that prepares one for a position at the beginning level in a library. The nature of the "mix" that once was required for all programs leading to a qualification for library employment can now be altered to fit the needs of each track or each speciality within a track. In the provision of superior library services, the many kinds of knowledge and each of the skills needed by the staff as a whole are not necessarily needed to the same degree by each person on the staff. Special qualifications are now recognized for the part they contribute to the whole, and education and training aimed at developing these different qualifications can be designed.

This paper will focus upon the programs for the preparation of professionals* and will assume that the preparation of support staff takes place at another level in

---

*The definition of the term "professional," as used throughout this paper, is that provided in the statement of policy adopted by the Council of the American Library Association on June 30, 1970, as revised in the spring of 1976, "Library Education and Personnel Utilization": "professional tasks are those which require a special background and education on the basis of which library needs are identified, problems are analyzed, goals are set, and original and creative solutions are formulated for them, integrating theory into practice, and planning, organizing, communicating, and administering successful programs of service to the users of the library's materials and services."

the educational hierarchy and is designed to emphasize those skills and techniques that keep the library running from day to day. I will dodge an important question that arises here—whether all those who aspire to the higher qualification must first go through the technicians' training. My predilection is to say that this should not be a requirement, because I see, as a primary distinction between the support and the professional staff, an attitude and an approach as well as a proficiency in certain skills. This is, however, a moot point. I proceed on the basis of my indicated prejudice, and my recommendations should be seen in the light of that bias.

Professional education, then, should be designed to turn out persons able to see the whole picture, but it does not follow that they must, therefore, be experts in every aspect of it. Expertise rests with individuals throughout the entire staff, and at all levels of personnel classification, but the blending of all these talents into a whole that is greater than the sum of its individual parts is one of the responsibilities of those persons who qualify as "professional" within the definition.

This emphasis upon higher qualifications for those who carry the professional title suggests to many of its advocates that professional education will thereby be upgraded, and that a sharper distinction will be recognized among the several levels of responsibility. But between an original intent and its eventual implementation there are always many stumbling blocks. At the moment, the strong emphasis upon the importance of the supportive functions, many of which were once performed by those with professional titles, has resulted in a demand that all of those who perform any of these functions should be accorded the professional title. The conflict is between those who say that from now on the professional title should stand for something much more than it presently does and those who lay claim to the title, because many who presently hold it are not being called upon to demonstrate any broader or deeper competence than the nonprofessional already possesses. The problem is the familiar semantic one that mistakes the symbol (the title) for the thing (the qualification for which the title is supposed to stand). To plan the upgrading of the degree is far easier to do on paper than it is to apply to human beings.

VALUE OF A CORE CURRICULUM

There is another problem. The move toward a sharper focus on specializations and on an increasing number of specializations at all levels, each with its own set of required competencies, presents an interesting challenge to those educators of librarians who cherish the idea of a "core" or "block" or "foundations" component in the library school curriculum. I must admit to my own strong belief in the "core" concept. I am convinced that an important aim of a professional program should be to foster a sense of professional identity: one is a librarian first before he or she is a cataloger or a reference person, a college librarian or a media specialist. Such a conviction rests on the belief that there is a body of theory, of knowledge, of service concepts that characterizes our profession in whatever setting it is practiced and to whatever audience it is extended. The person who looks forward to a career in a particular profession should be introduced early to those ideas and viewpoints, those aims and objectives, that are unique to that profession and are shared by all who "profess" it.

A look at the present required courses in library schools—required, that is, of all students no matter what their specialization—should reveal what we now consider to be these unique elements. And although each school goes through considerable soul-searching to come up with its own required "core," they all turn out to be surprisingly similar. In one way or another, the basic courses are concerned with the nature of library materials, the identification of the users of those materials, and the means for bringing the users and the materials together. These three components of the librarian's field are present in every kind of library and remain constant however much the details may vary among institutions or change over time. They are rightfully identified as basic to the librarian's understanding of his or her professional role and commitment.

Unfortunately, when these broad concepts are translated into actual courses, they frequently become how-to-do-it courses: the titles and characteristics of specific titles for reference and bibliographical uses; the process for classifying and cataloging books and other materials; the source books and reviewing media to aid in selection; the basic technical skills for operating a console. On the basis of the evidence, it would appear that many library educators see librarianship much more as a skilled trade than as an art or a profession. To know how to do the things one does in a library, rather than to understand the broad purposes for which these things are done, is what is seen as the core of our calling. It is easy to see why, when such a view of librarianship prevails, the skilled workers assume that they have, indeed, reached the highest level required for professional recognition.

TEACHING OF THEORY SHOULD PRECEDE SKILLS APPLICATION

I do not quarrel with the elements that have been identified as the core of librarianship. The materials, the users, and the means for bringing them together are the stuff of library service. But I should like to suggest, as an example, that, for the student on the professional track, the emphasis in the core program should be upon the function of information in a society, rather than upon the characteristics of ten or twenty-five or fifty major reference tools. In other words, I am suggesting almost a reversal in the sequence of content with which the student is currently presented. Instead of learning the specific features of particular reference sources or how to assign classification numbers, I would suggest that the beginning student first learn something of the purposes for which these tools and devices were designed. The core of librarianship, as I see it, rests on an understanding of the role of the library as the mediator between recorded information and the user who has need of it. With that as a base, students then go on to study in detail the specific means, present and potential, for performing that role most effectively for the particular kinds of materials held and users served by the type of library in which they plan to work. In the case of the academic library, the user is a student or a scholar, and the materials are those appropriate to support the educational program of the institution and the research interests of its faculty. It is here, then, that the specialization begins, with different approaches to the basic process dictated by the nature of those users and those materials.

Most library educators would agree theoretically with this familiar premise, but not when the logical consequence leads to designating the advanced courses rather than the beginning ones as the place for teaching the practical application of skills and techniques that librarians have devised for the running of libraries. As James Thompson has suggested:

> A library school must teach the power of libraries in society, education and culture, and prepare recruits to the profession to exploit this power for the good of the community. Traditional technical training will then fall into its proper place, as a means to an end, not as an end in itself. . . . Detailed training in special aspects . . . should come later.[3]

This is, of course, contrary to our popular belief that what the student must first know is how to *do* things, and that the understanding of the theory underlying performance, or of the principles that practice illustrates or of the social objectives supported by the services we render are elements that students can get to—if there is any time left—after they have demonstrated their ability to keep things running the way they run now. There is no point in raising all of those "why" questions until the skills themselves have been mastered. In this view, the goal should be preparation for the individual's first placement, not for some abstract ideal of advancing the profession.

> In today's tight market, library school alumni need "sellable" skills and internship experience instead of intellectual cotton candy like "library history, philosophy, and theory from Ashurbanipal to Lester Asheim."[4]

This view of "hire" education, as the *New York Times* dubbed it, is not unique to librarianship. In response to the position taken by the president of New York University, that what is needed is career education as distinct from vocational training,[5] here is what the chairman of Control Data Corporation has to say:

> our schools are going to have to . . . [give] first attention to training students for available jobs and taking care of liberal arts afterwards. . . . Mastery of a productive skill, craft or profession should be given a higher priority earlier in the educational process. . . . From the standpoint of the young person and in terms of the needs of our economy we may have no other choice than to meet basic needs first.[6]

If this view prevails, we will continue to teach—at the graduate level in a university—the way elementary schools teach children to write, by presenting existing models for rote imitation. Time enough later, if ever, to learn about the use of language as a tool for the clear expression of ideas.

The parallel seems to me, however, not to be applicable. Students at the postgraduate level in a university are not preliterate children, and the performance they will be held to should not be at the level of unquestioning imitation of existing practice. If they knew why we do the things we do in libraries, their learning to master the skills would be much more interesting and challenging to them, and they would be prepared to provide the quality of constructive analysis and criticism of current practice that a changing society requires. The almost universal disenchantment that library school students express about their professional education derives—I like to think—from the fact that they are bored and even insulted by the manual-skills level of so much of the content. Yet these same students, when they get into the field, find practice to be interesting and exciting.

Why, then, should preparation for an interesting and exciting field have to be dull? It need not be, I suggest, if the student were provided with the theoretical and philosophical framework that underlies practice. The aspects of practice that are exciting are those that are not cut and dried, do not always follow the rules, and are not predictable on the basis of what we have "always" done. Students who wish to become members of a profession should be learning how to use their heads, not just their hands; and most of today's students—certainly those we most need to move our profession constantly forward—seek this intellectual challenge.

Librarianship is almost uniquely suited to this broad-gauge approach because it is not an isolated discipline sufficient unto itself. Unlike most other professional fields, librarianship applies its principles, not to its own subject matter, but to the subject matter of all the other disciplines. Of no other field is it more true to say that all knowledge is its province. In today's library schools this is recognized in the search for strong subject backgrounds among the applicants for admission. We delight in recruiting students into our field with a master's degree (or even the doctorate) in another subject, but when we bring such students into our program, we then push them back to a level of content and a manner of presentation that are more suited to the undergraduate than the postgraduate. Our students who hold master's and doctoral degrees in other subject fields and disciplines are ready for the principles and the theory underlying library service. They want to create for themselves a "philosophy" of librarianship and not just a competency in techniques. No wonder they find our courses dull and vocational. No wonder they resist our attempts to convince them that this is a profession and not just a trained skill.

SCREENING OF CANDIDATES FOR THE PROFESSION

I recognize that in this period (the mid-1970s) a great many of our students, including those from other fields, enter library school simply for vocational reasons, with an emphasis on a job more than a career. I sympathize with their practical needs, but I do not think that a professional school need cater to them. An important role of a professional school is the screening of candidates for the profession (not just for the school), and in the competition among candidates for admission, I would give my priorities to those who have the qualifications *and the desire* (insofar as we can ascertain that) to be librarians. If some of our students come in with only the vocational objective in mind, then it is up to the schools to show them the scope and the promise of the profession with courses that challenge and excite. It is not enough for a library school to be satisfied that its program meets the expectations of its students—if those expectations are low and uninformed.

It follows, then, that if screening candidates is a responsibility of the library school, we must look much more closely at the criteria upon which we base that screening. I think that library educators are going to be forced to identify desirable prerequisites for those who are expected to deliver superior library service, and that in the future it will not be enough simply to scan a transcript and note in a rough, impressionistic way whether there seem to be several courses taken somewhere along the line in the humanities, the sciences, and the social sciences. If there is a body of knowledge that is uniquely that of the librarian, if there are skills and aptitudes essential to professional performance, then surely we should be able to suggest some kinds of background and experience that are better than others as preparation for a successful career in our field. We have always done this to a limited extent. The sampling of courses in all of the disciplines itself derives from a once widely held belief that the librarian must be a generalist. In recent years, we have begun to recognize specific knowledge needed in our field, and some schools now urge a background of mathematics at least to the level of introductory calculus for those whose specialty will be information science. Once, one or two foreign languages were considered essential tool skills for the librarian; today, many schools will accept knowledge of a computer language instead. Surely we can identify other background knowledge on which librarians will have to rely heavily in the future and that might well be taken before admission to the professional program: communication skills, psychology of interpersonal relations, logic. One can think of many undergraduate courses that would provide a better grounding than the olio of courses we now permit.

If this is true for librarianship in general, it is probably even more true for the specialties within librarianship. The elementary school librarian and the research university librarian are both concerned with making needed and wanted library materials available to their users (the core). But the materials are so different, the users are so different, and the uses to be made of the materials are so different that the means for selecting, organizing, and interpreting the materials most effectively for the particular users must surely call upon quite different qualifications and approaches. Increasingly, library schools are going to have to screen not only for library work, but for the *kind* of library work. An orientation toward research, a respect for it, and an understanding of the researcher's needs and approaches may not be a requisite for appointees to the staff of a school library or a small public library. They will need skills and aptitudes of a different (not lesser) kind. For the librarian in a large academic library, however, these research-related qualifications would be essential. The kinds of courses at the college level that introduce these concepts and procedures should be identified and made a part of the pre-librarianship requirements for those who seek a professional career in an academic library.

The stumbling block is that typical library school students do not decide on their career choice early, and even when they do, they often change their specialty within librarianship after they have been exposed to library courses that open up the possibilities of the field. Moreover, in the present job market, students want to be qualified broadly rather than narrowly in order to be able to fit into whatever openings become available. Educators sympathize with this practical need and are loath to insist upon a more narrowly focused preparation. It seems abundantly clear that if the upgrading of professional responsibilities continues, the possession of a wide scattering of minimal competencies will no longer suffice for the kinds of positions that command professional status and salaries. What was once the level of the first professional appointment will be seen instead as an advanced level of *pre*professional employment. The *academic* librarian will have to be highly qualified to be an academic librarian, and not a sort of all-purpose public, school, college, or special library employee. The interchangeable skills are paraprofessional qualifications; the professional's talents are more rigorous and exacting.

CONCLUSIONS

If we do begin to insist on appropriate undergraduate grounding for the more concentrated professional education that library service of the future will demand, the need will be even stronger, in the professional program, for a concentration on principles and theory rather than on practical skills. Unfortunately, whenever one speaks or writes of theory and practice, the audience tends to assume that one really means theory *versus* practice. That is not my intent here. I have used the word "mix" to deal with the content of our learning program, and the word is deliberately chosen. The question has to do with the relative emphasis and the relation of the one to the other, not with exclusive attention to one. Professional knowledge consists of three elements:

1. An *underlying discipline* or *basic science* component upon which the practice rests or from which it developed
2. An *applied science* or *"engineering"* component from which many of the day-to-day diagnostic procedures and problem solutions are derived
3. A *skills* and *attitudinal* component that concerns the actual performance of services to the client, using the underlying basic and applied knowledge.[7]

The proper mix, as I see it, would roughly follow the sequence outlined above: first, understanding of the underlying discipline; then, introduction to the mechanisms derived from it that lead to present practices; finally, analysis of how the skills and the attitudes emerging from the discipline and the operational devices are applied in practice. The last two—the applied science and the skills—would be related to the student's specialization (academic librarianship, for example). The logic of the sequence suggests, as I have noted earlier, that the exploration of ways in which the theory is adapted to the particular materials and the particular users should come after the introduction of basic principles, and not before. What the librarians of the future will want from their professional course work is a distillation of what we have learned from practice, not at the level of repetitive performance of manual tasks, but at the level of identifying user expectations, establishing service goals, evaluating critically the implementation of goals, and planning for improvement and refinement of present practice.

The chronological sequence, of course, is not absolutely hard and fast. Illustrations of applications should accompany the presentation of principles where appropriate, but the stress would be on seeing the practical procedures, not as ends in themselves, but as means for attaining the professional ends with which the student has already been made familiar.

I am sure that many of today's library schools intend for their courses to identify the distinction between means and ends, but the evidence certainly suggests that this is not the way our students perceive their learning experience. Ask students what they learned in library school, and they will tell you that they learned how to catalog, how to do reference work, and how to run a projector. Few will mention without prodding that they learned what the social role of the library is, how the library acts as a mediator between information and the user of it, and what the library has to offer uniquely in a mass-communication society. They will see themselves as administrators or bibliographers or media specialists rather than as creative interpreters who make the record accessible intellectually as well as physically to those who need it. But if their schooling had made them see themselves first in that interpreter's and mediator's role, then I truly believe the procedures and the mechanisms that librarians have devised take on a different meaning, and the mastery of their intricacies would be seen as a fascinating and challenging study rather than as a routine acquisition of competency in handling picayune details.

That this change should occur in the self-image of librarians is important for the future, not because it will make librarians feel better, but because without it the library's educational function cannot be successfully carried out in the changing future that confronts us. Already libraries are being challenged by proponents of a variety of "new looks" that dramatize service aims, and many librarians are intimidated by them. They do not see that these aims have long been those of the traditional librarians, dressed in a new jargon. New technology has made possible a more effective delivery of traditional services and has opened up possibilities of more services than could be contemplated in the past, but it has not really changed the ideals of library service. When we look at the "why" of library service instead of the "how to," the value of the new technology becomes immediately apparent, to be welcomed rather than resisted.

To keep the record straight, many librarians and libraries are moving in these "new" directions, incorporating new knowledge, evaluating traditional approaches, and introducing new solutions to long-standing problems that, in the light of changing times and urgent demands, are suddenly being revealed as more critical than ever before. The information needs of scholars and scientists have been more thoroughly studied than those of other groups, and as a consequence academic libraries have taken the lead in many of the vanguard experiments.

The future is likely to move rapidly beyond these first steps, however, and the librarians who will be called upon to carry the movement forward will have to be better prepared and better grounded in the principles and theory of library service if they are to meet and surmount the challenge. The changes in library education suggested in this paper may point toward some of the ways in which this preparation might be accomplished, but what is suggested here should be subjected to as critical and searching an evaluation as any other present-day solution looking to the future but based upon the past. There is no easy answer, but at least we are beginning to understand the question.

NOTES

1. James Thompson, *Library Power: A New Philosophy of Librarianship* (Hamden, Conn.: Linnet Books & Clive Bingley, 1974), pp. 17–18.
2. Jerrold Orne, in a symposium on "Library Education and the Talent Shortage," *Library Journal* 91 (April 1, 1966): 1763.
3. Thompson, *Library Power*, p. 20.
4. Steven Wolf, "Wolf's Bane," *SRRT Newsletter*, no. 34 (March 1975), p. 29.
5. John C. Sawhill, "On the Problems of 'Hire Education' . . ." *New York Times, Special Educational Survey* 11, no. 35 (November 16, 1975): 1.
6. William C. Norris, ". . . And Graduates Who Can't Get Jobs," *New York Times, Special Education Survey*.
7. Edgar M. Schein and Diane W. Kommers, *Professional Education: Some New Directions* (New York: McGraw-Hill, 1972), p. 43.

ABOUT THE AUTHOR

Lester Asheim is presently a William Rand Kenan, Jr., Professor of Library Science at the University of North Carolina in Chapel Hill. He holds degrees from the University of Washington and the University of Chicago, where he received the Ph.D. Before assuming his current position in 1974, he had for several years been a professor in the Graduate Library School of the University of Chicago, where he had previously served from 1948 until· 1961 as an Assistant Professor, then as Dean of Students, and finally as Dean of the GLS from 1952 until 1961. In the intervening years between these two periods on the GLS staff, he headed the International Relations Office of the American Library Association and was Director of the Office of Library Education from 1966 until 1971.

COLLECTION DEVELOPMENT FOR THE UNIVERSITY AND LARGE RESEARCH LIBRARY: MORE AND MORE VERSUS LESS AND LESS

by William H. Webb

LIBRARIES ARE FOREVER—AT LEAST TO THE YEAR 2000

Though I am fairly certain that libraries will last at least until the year 2000, I am not quite so sure that the same can be said about the people who use those libraries. The total insanity of our headlong plunge into the cauldron of nuclear holocaust is matched only by the wantonness with which our mental and physical resources are squandered upon the global arms race. So the best hope we may have for libraries is reduced to the incredibly hopeless premise that our warped priorities probably will produce an effective neutron bomb, one that will destroy all the people but leave their artifacts standing, unbent and unbroken, waiting until the metal rusts and concrete crumbles and weeds take over the world—until some future visitor lands on this spaceship earth and discovers the progeny of Gutenberg in the libraries.

Nevertheless we must plan at least as though the nuclear reality can be staved off for as long as is possible. And so, more optimistically, library collection development, which is the subject of this chapter, will last forever. And in that long-term hope, the concept of the storage and retrieval of information will endure. That really is what collection development is all about. And, if the past is prologue to the future, we should see a gradual evolution—not revolution—in the library of the year 2000.

Collection Development Will Continue

The process of storing information may—indeed, *should*—gradually change over the next twenty years or so. If the post-World War II years in America can be characterized as a period of large-scale acquisition of materials in university libraries (Texas, and Toronto in Canada, come to mind), the next two decades will be marked by a more discriminating continuance of the same type of activity. For the simple truth is that libraries cannot continue to grow at almost exponential rates indefinitely. Libraries *will* continue to grow, as will be made clear later. And the people directly concerned with collection development in college and university libraries will be no less important in the coming years than they have been in the past. Indeed, it is not unreasonable to hypothesize that the collection developer— whether called the Librarian, University Bibliographer, Chief Collection Development Officer, Acquisitions Librarian—whoever really makes the decisions about the policies and budgets governing materials acquisitions in the library— will almost certainly enjoy an enhanced position in the university library of the near future. The necessity for selectivity in acquisitions virtually guarantees his or her position on the library roster.

Second, the collection developer will play an even more direct role in budget planning in the next quarter century. The details of matching teaching and research programs to available budgets on the contemporary campus have already become too complex for the top library administrator to absorb. Unfortunately only a fraction of ARL library directors have even recognized the need for an integrating function below that of the head librarian. Their libraries and campuses are the poorer for it.

The creativity for the collection developer will, however, lie more in the successful balancing of the tensions between politically based budget judgments and personality-based subject support. That is, the collection developer will be torn even more acutely between supporting the politically possible and the bibliothecally desirable goal of helping people. The creative resolution of such dilemmas will increasingly mark the successful—and happy—collection development officer.

MORE OF EVERYTHING

The collection development activator of the year 2000 will deal with a world in which there is *more* of everything: more books and journals, more specialization, more inflation, more use of microformats, more access to everything, more federal and state governmental involvement, and more students.

More Books and Journals

First, there will be more books. Look at the progression in the numbers of U.S. imprints alone in the past three decades: 1950—11,022; 1960—15,012 (up 36 percent); 1970—36,071 (up 140 percent); and 1975—39,372 (up 11 percent).[1]

If we apply the same relative rates of increase to the year 2000: 1980— 49,056?; 1990—68,678?; and 2000—76,232?.

Besides books, there will certainly be more serially issued publications. I have never found a comprehensive, believable total for the worldwide number of serial titles currently being published. *Ulrich's International Periodicals Directory* (16th ed.) including the volume for irregular titles, identifies some 85,000 current titles. But that listing is so subject to the vagaries of editors' caprice, foreign publishers' language incapacities, and international as well as domestic postal ineptitudes that the number must surely be significantly larger. My guess is that universities are currently struggling to cope with a worldwide pool of about 100,000 current serial titles. Not many libraries can even attempt to grapple with a tenth of what is being published. The University of California at Berkeley—long known for its aggressive attempts to acquire all major serial titles—is able to acquire only about 35,000. My own institution, the University of Colorado, received only 9,500 titles in 1976.

Every serials librarian must surely feel inundated by the sheer number of publishers' blurbs announcing yet another new title, or another old title that has just split into two (or even three!) new series. And if impressionistic feelings are not enough, a glance at the Library of Congress' list of *New Serial Titles* should dismay even the most stouthearted. A typical bimonthly issue will contain 5,800 new entries. Indeed, looking back a few years, the 1950–1970 cumulation of *New Serial Titles* shows 141,000 new titles or changes for that period. Add the new ones for that twenty-year period to the 156,000 titles in the old edition of the *Union List of Serials* (1965) and the conclusion is inescapable: We are awash in a serial paper flood.

Will the floodtide crest by 1999? Perhaps. It is easy to speculate, so each of us can sketch our favorite scenario for the millennium. Mine is based upon the observable fact that the number of countable current titles has increased from at least 54,000 in 1960 to at least 85,000 in 1975. So on the one hand it is possible seriously to project another increase of at least 51,000 additional countable serial titles by the year 2000. Fantastic as that number may seem, such an enormous increase merely carries forward the linear progression of the past fifteen years. On the other hand, the reason I do not project such growth is because my favorite scenario has as its centerpiece the full flowering of the data-based (that is, computer manipulated) indexing and abstracting services. Thus, in the year 2000 a large fraction (20–30 percent? 40–50 percent?) of what are now periodical articles will appear instead as abstracts available only on a CRT screen or on an individually ordered printout.

More Specialization

There will certainly be more specialization within the university's garden of knowledge. We have all read at one time or another, I am sure, the dictum that 90 percent of all the scientists who have ever lived are living today. Whether that suspect statement is true or false, however, in the year 2000 we can be fairly sure (barring our nuclear holocaust) that there will be *more* scientists living, working, and reading than there are today.

The principal consequence of that fact should also be obvious: Not only will there be more specialization in the taxonomy of recorded knowledge, there will also be more specialization in the modes of the storage and retrieval of information.

There will be more index services. These will in turn continue to spawn indexes to indexes. There will be more data services. BIOSIS and DIALOG, to name only two of a dozen major services, have already inspired second-level brokerage services, such as BRS (Bibliographic Retrieval Services). As state and regional consortia coalesce, we are bound to find further brokering and packaging of such services. The imagination can run wild here: The so-called "smart" terminals will not only allow on-line interaction, they will assume the preponderant, active, even *directive*, role in the reference interview that now ordinarily precedes a data-base search. The collection development officer of the year 2000 will somehow (*how? how?*) have to integrate these modes into his or her understanding and manipulation of the political and personal supporting elements of budgetary decision making.

More Inflation

It should by now be apparent to every thinking citizen that our political leaders are both unable and unwilling to do anything to end the inflationary spiral we are now experiencing. Too many people are cashing in on the short-term benefits of inflation, and elected officials are so busy making political hay out of both the evils *and* the benefits of inflation to have any time (let alone the courage) to do anything about it. The realities reflected in statistics provided annually by *Publishers Weekly* and the *Bowker Annual* are appalling. The average U.S. imprint sold for $3.70 in 1947–1949; $5.24 in 1960; $11.66 in 1970; $12.99 in 1972; $14.09 in 1974; $16.32 in 1976. That is a 441 percent increase in twenty-seven years.

If we project an almost unreasonably conservative inflation rate of 6 percent a year compounded over the next twenty-four years, the book that cost $16.32 in 1976 will cost $66.13 in the year 2000. "Impossible!" you say. But not any more "impossible" than the incredible leap from $3.70 in 1947–1949 to $16.32 in 1976. And most serials librarians would agree that serials have inflated at a higher annual rate in the same period.

The only two events that appear able to break this cycle (which is not necessarily totally vicious) are a devastating (but not annihilating) world war or a worldwide depression. Take your choice.

The consequences of such inflation are not so readily apparent. For example, at the University of Colorado in 1969, the total materials budget was $984,000. In 1976 it was $985,449. To oversimplify a bit, Colorado could theoretically have purchased 103,579 books in 1969, but only 60,383 in 1976, a net decrease of 42 percent. Yet the world did not come to an end. We coped, as did our faculty and students. So will it be in the year 2000.

More Use of Microformats

Perhaps here more than anywhere else in these speculations there will be a steady but slow growth in the use of microforms—16-mm and 35-mm roll film, microfiche and ultramicrofiche, microcards and microprint. What irritates of course is the fact that no collection development specialist wants to skew the collection in one direction or another *solely* on the basis of the format of the material available. And yet that is the conundrum: The reality of equipment and service budgets will sometimes not allow the luxury of choice between microformats.

Thus there may not be any startling change in the collection development officer's basic buying patterns in microform as long as a variety of formats continues to thrive. The real change by the year 2000 will be in the attitude of *librarians* toward microforms. Those of us in the older generation are often much more reluctant to embrace (and ask others to embrace) the paraphernalia of microforms—readers, reels, plugs, spools, lenses, and so forth—because whoever heard of taking a good microfilm reader to bed? The snicker accompanying the image, however, hides the fact that we may have missed the point, which is that for a great range of materials and purposes, microforms are casually, even willingly, accepted and adapted to by our students and younger faculty members.

The other change that I will speculate upon is in the basic presentation of microforms for use by the reader. The technology of microform viewing equipment has remained virtually unchanged since the adaptation of 35-mm motion picture film in the 1930s, right on through the ultramicrofiche marketed in the early 1970s. A radically different viewing medium is likely to emerge quite soon, one that eliminates the need for a fairly large energy input (for a light bulb and a fan to dissipate the consequent heat). The new viewing screen will probably also eliminate the lens system now in general use, which requires a relatively long focal distance between film plane and reading plane, and therefore the familiar bulk will be a thing of the past. The new microform reader will, finally, also eliminate the cumbersome frame-finding system inherent in present readers. An electronically organized and activated indexing system will provide instant imaging of the desired page/frame/information.

The new microreader will enhance the ability of the collection development officer to meet the needs of readers in the university of the year 2000. If not all books can be microformed and carried in a shirt pocket, at least the bibliographic access to the library's collection can be miniaturized and microread. A number of libraries already have their card catalogs on COM film or, as at Georgia State, on microfiche. In fact, I am certain that in the year 2000 the majority of academic libraries will *give* away microcopies of what we now call card catalogs. Every student and every faculty member will carry off what he or she wants—whether it be the entire bibliographic data base or self-selected parts of it in a variety of practical and self-chosen arrays. Think of the possibilities for collection evaluation and development!

More Access to Everything

Lest we get carried away by too fanciful speculations about bibliographic access within a campus community, let us return to the recent past. In the late 1960s, an old publishing trick was given a new twist by several enterprising publishing firms. I refer here to the new reprint houses, such as Arno Press, Greenwood, and

Gregg. What separates these and several others like them from old-line reprinters, such as Peter Smith for example, is the fact that the upstarts dared to take over some of the duties of the collection development officer. Arno, for instance, likes to package forty to fifty titles into a neat, coherent group, such as "Science Fiction Classics" (Gregg has done that subject superbly well also), or "American Sociology," "The Black Experience," or "Women's Studies." The librarian can then buy the whole lot at a relatively modest total cost to the library and achieve instantly a level of comprehensiveness and depth previously undreamed of by the collection development officer.

In spite of faults inherent in many of these packages, the more perceptive collection developers have used them to great advantage, if only as jumping-off points and time savers for more bibliographically difficult extensions of the subjects pursued.

These packages were almost certainly the response of several astute businesspersons to the enormous increase in book funds enjoyed by academic libraries in the mid- to late 1960s. We all know that the rate of money growth has slowed in the 1970s. But there has been no commensurate diminution in the numbers of reprint packages being offered. In fact, the opposite seems to be happening. Research Publications, Inc., for example, has gone a significant step further. It is packaging large groups (from 1,000 to 7,000 and more titles) of significant research materials in 35-mm microfilm, cataloging them according to AACR (Anglo-American Cataloging Rules), and providing complete sets of catalog cards for accessing the materials so purchased.

Another form of packaging has just emerged and should grow significantly in the near future. Networked data bases, such as OCLC (Ohio College Library Center) and BALLOTS (Bibliographic Automation of Large Library Operations using a Time-sharing System), although originally used for cataloging purposes, are now emerging as reference tools in their own right and will soon be widely useful as acquisition tools as well. This expansive trend will be enhanced as these data bases are brokered out to regional consortia. The collection developer, for example, will be able to call up on a terminal or printout all the books on a particular subject, by classification number, by date of imprint, whether in print or even in reprint, by location . . . the range of possibilities goes on and on.

In the field of reprints, for instance, one commercial firm has pioneered an especially imaginative use of the MARC data-base tapes. A. M. S. Press, under the direction of Roy Young, began offering in February 1977 three-by-five-inch card printouts from MARC tapes of all reprints being accessioned and cataloged in the MARC system. A subscribing library can get the cards free simply by agreeing to use A.M.S. as a jobber for at least a fraction of the reprints it does buy. The mechanics of such a spinoff are so simple and so useful to the collection development officer that other bright people are certain to pick up the ball and run with it all across the country, up and down all the networks, and in and out of all types of materials. Can't you just visualize the ultimate head trip for every collection development officer in the year 2000? Seated in front of his Hazeltine X-10,000, playing upon the keyboard like Lon Chaney at the pipe organ in "The Phantom of the Opera" totally engrossed in pounding out a bibliographic orgy of row upon row of exhaustive citations, punching out commands for printouts of these and film copies of those, until finally, exhausted but exhilarated, he whirls around to face the gathered crowd of wide-eyed patrons who spontaneously burst into frenzied applause at the performance! That would be Access with a capital *A*.

But there is a third form of access (besides the packaging of reprints and bibliographic data for acquisitions) that almost certainly will be a reality long before the year 2000: the National Periodicals Center. Modeled after (but quite different from) the British Library's Lending Division for periodicals at Boston Spa, the National Periodicals Center may both alleviate and exacerbate some of the problems facing librarians and publishers. If the center functions in any way similar to the proposal put forth in a Library of Congress Task Force report of early 1977, a large number of serials will no longer be subscribed to by a significant number of libraries. I do not share the doom-and-gloom view expressed in the library and information industry press over this development, especially the hand-wringing on behalf of the balance sheets of publishers of high-priced scientific periodicals. The truth is, some of these publishers do not make very much money on these periodicals. For example, one major American publisher of technical journals, with a list of some two dozen titles, basically operates on a cost-plus basis. With an average circulation of only 750 copies each, these journals average about $265 each. And the price escalates yearly. As editorial and production costs go up, and as the number of subscribers who can afford them goes down, the publisher simply raises the subscription price to ensure his very modest 10 percent annual yield. He is not gouging the libraries; he is simply netting about what he could get in municipal bonds.

The better-managed and more valuable journals will survive handsomely with or without the National Periodicals Center. And long before this century is out, the more creative journal publishers will have shifted their profit center from the paper journal production/distribution cycle to data-base software and sales. They will continue to sell what they always have—information—but they will do it faster, more cheaply, and certainly no less profitably.

Thus the interinstitutional cooperation facilitated by such networks as the National Periodicals Center and data-base brokers will be a positive force for the users of libraries at the end of this century.

Finally, a fourth form of access might possibly open up new vistas for the collection developer: telefacsimile transmission of text. The library literature has been predicting a breakthrough in this area for at least as long as I can remember, maybe even all the way back to A. G. Bell. There have been several interesting experiments, such as the California-Nevada test, which took a long time and which cost a lot of grant money and succeeded in proving that telefacsimile transmission costs a lot of money and takes too long.

A new type of transmitter-receiver came on the market in January 1977 for a little over $1,000. But it too shares the almost insuperable triple burden of high equipment cost (relative to library budgets), high transmission-line charges (relative to postal charges), and high personnel costs (somebody has to stand there and feed the machine). I suspect that other evolutions in library-land will cause us to turn to other matters, just as the moral sensibilities of the antivivisectionists at the turn of this century found other fields to furrow after the Great War.

More Federal and State Governmental Involvement

We may look back with fond memories to the recent years of enormous sums of federal money flowing into collection development activities (not to mention the enormous sums of LSCA dollars for buildings). There does not seem to be much basis for the belief that such extensive federal money for acquisitions will be forthcoming in the next two decades. Rather, the *direct* federal role most likely will be limited to such activities as the National Periodicals Center, its possible regional nodes (perhaps major research libraries, the RLG, and so on), and experimental, demonstration, or research activities within the field of higher education for librarianship. The era of significant direct grants for the purchase of books and journals is over.

But the enhancement of the *indirect* federal role by the year 2000 will probably be visible in the subtle support of data-base services and access. Just as MEDLINE is a product of enormous federal support—without, however, significant outflow of dollars directly to individual medical libraries—so we may expect some measure of hidden federal subsidy in other advanced modes of information transfer.

I believe that the real impact of governmental bodies will continue to grow at the state-funding level for public colleges and universities and at the local-funding level for community colleges. The involvement of state agencies—whether as commissions, boards, or legislative budget committees—is bound to increase. And the reason is more subtle than the simple explanation that "he who pays the piper calls the tune."

As the technicians working in the statewide funding agencies become more sophisticated, they will demand much more detailed budget justifications for every line in a university's annual budget request.

In Colorado, for example, we have seen a very gradual upgrading of the technical expertise of budget analysts hired by the legislature and the governor. We put together, for instance, a relatively sophisticated array of data that had at its base a linking of Library of Congress/Dewey Decimal class numbers with HEGIS codes (Higher Education General Information Survey). By using the HEGIS-LC/Dewey crossovers, manipulated by a PDP-10 computer, it became possible for the first time to measure the actual number of books, serials, and staff services supporting any given academic discipline in all libraries at all nineteen institutions of higher education in the state.

Marvelous. Except that the budget technicians at the statehouse want to use the raw printouts for a mindless and mechanistic application to formula budgeting for all state-supported libraries in Colorado. That may or may not be any worse than the old method of "by guess and by gosh." Perhaps the difference between 1976 and 1996 will really only be the difference between the flip of a coin and the flip of a switch.

More Students

We keep hearing and reading about the end of the boom in higher education because the children from the postwar baby boom have all come and gone; we are in the "new depression in higher education." At first glance, the statistics support the gloom after the boom: In 1940 there were 1.6 million college students; in 1950, 2.3 million; in 1960, 3.6 million; in 1970, 7.9 million. The most pessimistic projection for 1990 is slightly under 11 million students; the most optimistic is slightly over 14 million.[2] Even so, we are looking at 3 to 6 million *more* students by the year 2000! What has happened is not that there are or will be fewer students; the only change has been in the *rate of increase* in the number of entering college students.

It seems to me that most of us have missed the real point of what the enrollment figures mean for our libraries: We are going to be serving at least 3 million more students in the next fifteen years than we are now.

How will we get the books to serve them? And with what access resources? Wherever I look, I see the professional public service components of large academic libraries already strained to the outer limits. I wonder how these librarians are possibly going to cope with another 3 to 6 million students.

There are additional factors at work, too, that impinge directly upon the quality and range of materials we collect for those students:

1. The average age of enrolled students has gradually risen; that trend may well continue, especially as the "stop-outs" return—more mature, more purposeful in their educational goals, and more sophisticated in their understanding of their own educational processes.
2. There will almost certainly be more flexibility in degree programs and requirements. In the early 1970s there was perhaps a more than occasional lessening of academic quality in the lowered restrictions; yet the flexibility remains and will remain, partly because of the more mature student now enrolling.
3. The competition for additional students over the next few years (the bottom of the present slump) will work permanent changes into the academic fabric by encouraging both individually structured degree programs and also a whole range of continuing education activities.

I confess that I am unable to assess adequately the consequences of these changing factors in our college and university libraries. It sounds almost trite to say that more students are going to demand more books (more titles *and* more copies of selected titles) as well as more help in handling the data available to them in the year 2000. The challenge for the collection developer will lie in more precisely defining—and then meeting—the needs of the students.

LESS SUPPORT IN MAKING AND EFFECTING JUDGMENTS

At the end of this century the collection developer will be operating in a world characterized by at least four major negative factors that lead to less support in making and effecting the judgments that will be required: more information but less knowledge, more politics but less political clout, more knowledge about information but less help for the user of that information, and more analysis but less understanding of institutional roles in higher education.

More Information but Less Knowledge

Earlier I postulated "more of everything." A consequence will be the creation of still more indexing, abstracting, and citation tools. But each of these "solutions" introduces its own additional uncertainties, ambiguities, and downright distortions. To give just two examples from a single citation indexing service, *Social Sciences Citation Index* (SSCI):

1. As students and faculty expand their use of this valuable tool, the collection developer finds himself or herself in a quandary: It becomes ever more difficult to keep from purchasing a subscription to an indexed journal frequently cited in SSCI. The consequence, in a tight budget situation, is to cancel a nonindexed title. Yet too often in my experience a nonindexed title has much more substantial scholarly worth than an indexed title in the same field. How to resolve this dilemma?
2. Title nomenclature of articles is critically important to successful indexing in SSCI: The title must describe adequately the scope of the article being indexed. Fine. Except that authors (and even editors) frequently have their own individual notions about what words they want to use in *their* articles. As associate editor of *The Journal of Academic Librarianship*, I was appalled to learn from SSCI that our journal could not be indexed in SSCI unless and until we altered our title policy to conform to SSCI's indexing requirements. Our decision was, I suppose, seen as obfuscatory: We chose the libertarian solution of letting our authors determine their own titles and to heck with the indexing service. I wonder how many other journal editors have reacted similarly?

The point of all this is, of course, that such behavior—if widespread enough in a field—will seriously distort the accessibility of needed knowledge. Thirty-seven (or 137 or even 537) citations to second-rate articles in an index will not compensate for the one first-rate piece that was never indexed or purchased.

More Politics but Less Political Clout

"Politics"—the art of persuading people that they want what you want—has always been a part of library life, especially of academic library life. In the "good old days," the librarian often had direct access to the president or chief academic officer who controlled the library's budget. By the end of this century, however, the librarian will have to interface with a whole raft of technicians in the budget/ accounting office, both on the campus and, for public institutions, at the statehouse. Direct, one-on-one persuasion almost inevitably will give way to the dreadfully sterile routine of multicarboned, stiffly worded, statistically heavy interoffice memoranda (probably prepared by the poor collection development officer). And on those occasions when a poor decision is handed down from above, there is no solid target for the librarian to attack in order to get the right decision. So life in the year 2000 may well consist of sloshing forward through the mush of bureaucracy or bounding backward into the cotton-candy world of shadowy nonresponsibility. I am sure we have already experienced some of this future.

More Knowledge about Information but Less Help for the User

With the development of on-line data bases, from OCLC to public reference services, there is the real danger that we shall equate the effectiveness of the information we do provide with the efficiency with which we provide it. Sometimes it is difficult to keep from bragging about system performance. Yet it hardly helps the student to know that we can call up any one of 137,654 abstracts from the New York Times Data Bank in one-point-oh-four seconds, when all the student wants is last Memorial Day's highway death toll.

The situation is similar for the collection developer. Our knowledge about how we can acquire information may lead us into the trap of limiting our selection procedures to those that produce data about how the book or journal was acquired, for how many dollars, from which vendor, at what discount or surcharge, and on and on *ad nauseam*. If books were like paper clips, okay; but each title is unique and cries out for its unique readers. And sometimes we shall need to make end runs around the "system" in order to bring book and reader together.

More Analysis but Less Understanding

Because of greater budget visibility among technicians, along with the integration of multi-institutional budget scrutiny within state funding agencies, the public colleges and universities will find themselves increasingly forced into a "leveling" condition. For example, in Colorado in 1972, the legislature was unable to accept the demonstrated fact that the typical book for the University of Colorado at Boulder actually cost more than at Metropolitan State College (Metro) in Denver. The typical price for a book at Metro was $8.10; at Boulder it was $11.91. The difference of course is due to the fact that Boulder is a research university, and Metro hardly more than a community college; therefore, the kinds of books purchased were often quite different at the two schools. Nevertheless the legislative funding bill for the year specified that both Metro and Boulder were to buy books at an average cost of $8.10 each.

There is also a more subtle (perhaps less maliciously ignorant) leveling process at work, one that will almost certainly become more pronounced as the century wears down. Budget analysts in funding agencies may pay lip service to the "role, scope, and mission differentiation" among institutions in their state, but I submit that this will work against the research-oriented universities without, contrarily, helping the nonresearch-level colleges. In the spring of 1977, for instance, funding agency analysts in Colorado refused to acknowledge the fact that graduate-level faculty members cannot possibly have the same number of student-contact hours as undergraduate-level faculty members. So all faculty positions throughout the state were equated to the highest common denominator—that is, all faculty averages were upped to the average undergraduate student-teacher ratio of 19:1.

The same vitiating influence in the lack of role differentiation arose in determining cost effectiveness within the library. When I demonstrated that subject bibliographers at the University of Colorado spent two-thirds of their time acquiring only one-third of the materials in their subject disciplines, our local budget analyst was aghast. He finally understood that it is easy to buy the first 200 titles (selected from *Choice*) for the undergraduate curriculum in economics; but buying the next 60 titles for the Ph.D. students in that field entailed enormously greater effort due to the necessity of searching the review literature in a dozen scattered journals, O.P. dealer catalogs, bibliographies, and faculty research want lists.

Nevertheless, our friendly local budgeteer would not allow us to incorporate that undergraduate-graduate ratio into the work statistics. He felt that if the legislature ever found out we were spending two-thirds of our effort on less than 20 percent of our students, the legislators would nail all of us to the ivied walls. Consequently the reality of the difference between a research library and a college library was masked by phony figures. So much for "role, scope, and mission differentiation." I believe that such behavior is going to be typical, and that my own institution is just once again ahead of the field.

THE FUTURE WAS YESTERDAY

So much for collection development in the year 2000. This look forward (and backward) may serve to stimulate collection development officers to think ahead—if not to plan ahead (for that option is too often denied them)—and so to bring to the future a liberal imagination tempered by a healthy skepticism for all bureaucrats, statistics, and prognostications of the future.

NOTES

1. United States, Bureau of the Census, *Historical Statistics of the United States, Colonial Times to 1970*, Bicentennial Edition (Washington, D.C.: Superintendent of Documents, 1975), Pt. II, p. 808; *Publishers Weekly* (February 9, 1976): 55.
2. United States, Bureau of the Census, *Historical Statistics of the United States, Colonial Times to 1970*, Bicentennial Edition, Pt. I, p. 383.

ABOUT THE AUTHOR

William H. Webb is University Bibliographer for the University of Colorado Libraries in Boulder. He holds degrees from San Luis Rey College, Arizona State University, and Indiana University. For a number of years he was Associate Editor of *College and Research Libraries* and in 1975 served as Associate Editor of *Sources of Information in the Social Sciences* published by the American Library Association. Since 1974 he has served as Associate Editor of the *Journal of Academic Librarianship*.

CHANGES THAT WILL AFFECT COLLEGE LIBRARY COLLECTION DEVELOPMENT

by Virgil F. Massman

Ed Holley perceptively examines the prospects of, and prognostications for, the future of higher education. *More Than Survival*[1] sees retrenchment, reorganization, redefinition of purpose, stable or declining enrollments, changes in authority structures, and a variety of other factors with which academic institutions must cope to varying degrees during the remainder of this century. Chances are that some colleges will disappear, and the survivors will have to come to grips with new realities. Whatever happens to colleges obviously will have a dramatic impact on college libraries. The purpose of this paper is to outline some of the changes that will affect collection development in college libraries in the next twenty or twenty-five years.

COMPUTER APPLICATIONS OF BIBLIOGRAPHIC AND INFORMATION-SERVICE PROCESSES

Much has been written about change, and, indeed, some types of change have fundamentally affected life in the twentieth century. The single most significant development has been in the realm of communication. Reports of ideas and events can be transmitted widely and easily through newspapers, journals, books, telephones, television, and radio, and convenient modes of travel have given people virtually unlimited mobility. Because everyone has access to the mass media, the potential and likelihood of a more uniform general culture exists. Yet there is sufficient diversity and opportunity of access particularly in publishing, radio, and transportation to both allow and encourage the proliferation of numerous subcultures. However, these subcultures, too, because of easy and rapid dissemination of ideas, are bound less by geography than they have been in the past. The library's main function has been and will continue to be to provide depth and range of informational resources and to preserve access to yesterday's news and ideas rather than simply the up-to-the-minute mass-media reports. Exploitation of existing and future improvements in communication systems will be a major factor in enlarging the library's opportunity to perform its educational functions.

There will be a dramatic change in the next twenty-five years. Perhaps change is not the correct word. Rather, there will be an acceleration of current trends resulting from the application of improvements in existing technologies. The most dramatic acceleration will be related to those areas that may be conveniently categorized as bibliographic and information services and that are amenable to computer applications.

It is important to note that many of the fundamental changes in libraries will occur more in the process than in the product. Process is used here simply as the way in which things are done, and product is the end result, that which comes out of the process.

Many of the end products of college libraries will not change drastically. The goal will still be to provide resources to support the curriculum. However, the machinery whereby the products are produced will be vastly different from the configuration presently existing in most college libraries. There will still be a need for the bibliographic identification of materials. Essentially the same or very similar bibliographic and descriptive content will be present. Finding tools will still perform the same general functions, but these in the near future will be produced by computers as microform or book catalogs rather than card catalogs. Later, by or before the turn of the century, on-line catalogs will replace the traditional card catalog. Again the bibliographic content of the card will remain fundamentally the same, but it will be in a computer memory rather than on cards, and the computer will allow many times the number of access points presently possible in the manual card catalog. With the manual system, it is just not possible to produce, file, and house enough cards to give access to every part of the card that might be of interest to the user. Furthermore, although the content of the record and its purpose will remain much as they are now, the concept of the main entry, for example, will be less significant because the computer will be able to find the record regardless of whether the user asks for the main entry, the added entry, the title, or the corporate or personal author.

With the computer, it also will be much easier to alter or delete the contents of a file as new materials are added or withdrawn from the collections. Because the machine-readable bibliographic record will be produced by the Library of Congress and other large libraries in the United States and abroad for direct entry into the local computerized catalog, both the professional and supporting staff in local cataloging departments will be small by comparison with present staffing patterns. Other routines such as those related to circulation and serials control will be fully automated, and they will drastically reduce the staff time presently associated with those activities. Thus, in the future nearly all of staff time will be devoted directly to assisting users in finding information, teaching users how to evaluate sources, and explaining what is available and how it can be obtained. The library staff's function will be almost solely to educate and assist the user while the present manual routines will be handled far more accurately and expeditiously by computers.

ON-LINE ACCESS TO FACTUAL INFORMATION IN LIEU OF TRADITIONAL PUBLISHING

There will be enormous changes in certain aspects of the publishing and distribution of information. For certain kinds of information, these changes will reshape the publishing industry. This will have numerous implications for libraries. However, it is important to point out that the changes will affect mainly the factual and quantifiable aspects of the publishing industry. Separate pieces of factual content and statistical information lend themselves very nicely to computer manipulation, storage, and retrieval. The product in some cases will be in the form of video discs, microforms, or other high-reduction storage units produced by laser and other technologies with detailed indexes and instantaneous retrieval. In many instances, increases in the storage capacity of computers will make on-line access both feasible and economical. In fact, it will be faster and more economical to update factual information in computer-produced miniaturized forms and on-line systems than it will be to update and publish new editions of works printed in paper form. At the same time, the user will be able to get a broad range of information related to many subject areas more quickly through the local terminal than by searching through the index of one or many printed volumes.

The intellectual exposition or explanation of new ideas and reports of research findings will still be published in printed form because the printed page is and will remain an efficient carrier of knowledge, because the reader will want to examine the arguments in the lab or study, and because the process of rational development of ideas with supporting arguments does not lend itself to computer manipulation. Indeed, rearranging the intrinsic arguments would eviscerate the whole for educational or intellectual purposes because the reader needs the methodology and rationale related to the discovery of new ideas and principles. Also, assuming that the presentation is well organized, rearranging or manipulating the arguments into a different sequence by computer would serve no purpose because it would destroy the logical development of an idea. Although this applies to many areas of human endeavor, poetry will serve as a good illustration here. Changing the sequence of words destroys the poem.

For factual information, then, the searcher will sit at the terminal rather than paging through a book or many books. The computer memory and miniaturized storage units will contain a wide variety of cross-discipline information, and the user will not need to go from the business to the history to the education to the science section of the stacks. The sources will have wide use and, therefore, will be inexpensive, and they will all be available from one terminal. An important corollary is that all students, regardless of the size or location of the library, will have access to a vast store of information. This equality of access to the factual information will mean great benefits to many users.

In the long term, this also will be both more efficient and productive for society. It will be unnecessary to reprint all the old factual content as is done now when an updated edition of a book is published. With the computer, it will be necessary only to add the new information and leave the old as is. At the same time, the user will have much more comprehensive and expeditious access.

Furthermore, these new forms of access will eliminate the need for the substantial amounts of shelf space now occupied by traditional types of publications. Consequently, there will be significant savings in capital expenditures for physical plants and in the equally expensive related areas of heating, lighting, cooling, and maintenance. Although the terminals can be made available in many places other than the library, the librarian's task will be to know and to teach the means of fully exploiting the data bases.

Short- and long-term cooperative, coordinated planning to expedite the development of the factual data bases would be advantageous to all of society, and the sooner this planning and implementation begins the better. Such planning should involve academia, business, government, and all other levels of society. Because such a system will be of value to large segments of society, the federal government should underwrite a large part of the cost.

The extent and range of available data bases both with factual and bibliographic content will depend upon volume of use and ability to pay. For many years, chemistry has had excellent bibliographic control of its literature. This relates directly to the economic value of chemistry to industry, medicine, and the military. Other data bases have been and will be developed for similar reasons. However, those subject areas that pertain only to very specialized areas of the humanities (for example, minor poets, painters, philosophers, and so on) will develop slowly. On the other hand, those that are of interest to college libraries will develop fairly rapidly because these will have a broad base of interest within universities and among the general public in addition to colleges.

It is important to note too that the data bases will become similar to public utilities. They will provide services at fixed costs that will become as necessary as heat and light, and there will be no escaping the cost.

LIMITATIONS OF THE NO-GROWTH CONCEPT

What will the college library of the future need to serve the educational functions of the college? Although some of the content of the library will be different, its place in the educational process will still be crucial.

The "no-growth" approach to librarianship will remain popular for the short-term future, but it is a complex issue with many ramifications. When intelligently applied, the concept has a measure of validity for undergraduate institutions. However, the possibility, or perhaps the threat, exists that it will have far more adherents than it deserves especially on the administrative level because it holds the prospect of saving money, which is always dear to an administrator's heart.

But the savings in capital investment in buildings, which is much of the motivation for espousing the no-growth concept, will be made possible and affected more dramatically by factors outside the library than by internal ones.

Actually, the no-growth concept has been applied for many years in small public libraries and in branches of major, public, metropolitan library systems; and it works well. The branch libraries maintain a collection of high-current-interest and high-use titles. For more specialized materials, the user can go to the central library, or the materials can be sent to the branch library. With the increase in availability and the decrease in cost of computer-produced microform and book catalogs, which can be reproduced easily and inexpensively for distribution to other libraries, the no-growth concept will have greater validity because users will be able to locate resources in other libraries easily. This is especially true for less frequently used materials if there are several libraries within ten or twenty minutes' commuting time. Access diminishes drastically, however, as the time factor increases. (Studies of public libraries have shown that in-person usage is inversely related to distance. The same principle applies to academic institutions.) It is unrealistic to expect people to spend a great deal of time in transit to obtain information they need. The greater the distance and the greater the inconvenience, the fewer the people who will avail themselves of other resources. And society will be the loser.

The poor will also suffer. Those with means can obtain the resources they need, but others are limited to what is conveniently available at the local level or through interlibrary loan, which will be discussed later.

The no-growth concept misses, or at least fails to address, the point in one very important respect, and that is the need for keeping abreast of current book production. Either a library continues to buy the important new books, or it will soon become more of an archive than a library. There is no infallible way of acquiring those books that will be most needed, or to put it in a more emphatic way, those books that will contribute most to the education of the reader, be he or she the president, dean, faculty member, or student. There is no way of assessing the loss if a fertile mind is deprived of or inadvertently misses an important idea because the library failed to acquire a particular book. No statistical or mathematical methodology has been or is likely to be developed that will give an answer to that problem.

While no one has ever empirically proved the point, it has always been evident that a close and fairly consistent relationship exists between the size and quality of the library and the quality of the college. Some of the obvious reasons for the relationship between size and quality of collection and the quality of the institution should be readily apparent. The better colleges tend to have faculty members who are more active in their profession, and they are better informed and are more actively engaged in keeping up with developments in their fields. Consequently, they place a greater demand on the library and have higher expectations. Hence, the library needs a greater range of resources. Colleges that have high expectations for their faculty members are likely to have high expectations for their students. This again has implications for the library. There are, of course, bright students and students with high motivation in any college, and in colleges with lower expectations for either faculty or students, the exceptional student is even more dependent upon the library for her or his education.

That current materials are used more heavily than older materials is obvious, and there are fairly simple explanations for this. The old saying that every generation writes its own history is a good example; the new history makes the old less relevant and less often read. Also, important concepts in any discipline gradually are incorporated into newly published studies. In chemistry, for example, basic formulae and principles can be found in various handbooks, encyclopedias, and textbooks, making it unnecessary for the student to consult the voluminous research whereby these formulae were developed. Thus, in many instances the student needs only the conclusions, which can be summarized in a fairly small space, rather than the entire and often lengthy reports of research that led to the conclusion. However, the student will need some access to the reports of research in order to learn research methods. In literature and history, too, the student will not need every detailed treatise but will need a substantial number of current and retrospective sources.

A college that is interested only in teaching the most widely accepted and most widely available facts will be able to get along mainly with the automated, factual data bases and very limited printed resources. In that case, the size of the library building can be even smaller than that envisioned by the no-growth proponents. Students who learn only those facts will be able to enter into the world of business and do well as long as those facts apply. However, a college that endeavors to teach its students to participate in the advancement of knowledge will need much more than that.

COPING WITH NOISE

Because capital funds for new buildings will be limited, there will be continuing efforts to limit the size of libraries. If properly planned, computerized systems can help in this endeavor.

In the future, one of the major tasks of the undergraduate library will be to keep out noise. ("Noise" used in the sense of static on the radio that interferes with the program the listener wants to hear and "noise" used in the group-dynamics sense of extraneous, irrelevant comments made in meetings when important problems are being discussed. When applied to libraries, "noise" refers to extraneous materials.) Keeping out noise is a complex problem that has not been solved in the past and is not likely to be totally solved in the future. The problem will become more acute with ready access to a staggering range of references via on-line data bases.

No undergraduate library needs all the books ever published. However, it does need adequate resources to support the curriculum and, most importantly, to support those who are engaged in the process of self-education, regardless of the quality of the institution itself. To guarantee the possibility of allowing quality education, it is better for the library to err on the side of inclusion rather than exclusion.

The information explosion will become an increasing, more imminent problem when the local library gets convenient, inexpensive access to on-line data bases with massive files of bibliographic information and large numbers of references on specific subjects. Extensive access to data bases will be a boon, but just as critical will be the noise; that is, references that are too esoteric or too advanced for the user.

Data bases will provide information in two broad areas. One, and the easiest to cope with, will be factual and statistical information, which has already been discussed above. This data base will include information in many areas—population figures, production statistics, the highest mountain in the world, mathematical formulae, chemical compounds, and so on. It is unlikely that this data base will ever incorporate too much of this factual, statistical type of information. The more basic factual information that can be found through the computerized systems the better. This information will be useful to all academic levels, to business and industry, and to the general public. Consequently, data bases in this area will become very extensive and economical because they will have utility to a wide range of users. Furthermore, it will be easy to define the question so as to obtain precisely the information wanted (for example, the population of St. Paul in 1970 or the chemical makeup of vermiculite or the formula for calculating the area of a triangle or the king of England in 1485).

The second area, that of bibliographic data bases, will present a problem. Because these will be extensive in coverage, the problem will be to utilize them effectively for the undergraduate who does not want all the references, only the most pertinent ones.

If the references are not controlled, there will be a very broad and virtually unmanageable range of requests for all kinds of esoteric materials. Although this will present problems and great expense in locating and acquiring materials, it also will result in inordinate waste because users will get a lot of material for which they have little use.

At present, the range of undergraduate requests is limited by the journal indexes available in the local library. The use of recent materials is also heavily influenced by the way periodical indexes are used and by teaching methods. The user begins with the most recent index volume and goes back until satisfactory references are found. However, if a teacher or librarian encourages the use of older volumes when appropriate, the use pattern as it relates to date of publication can be very different.

The standard indexes, such as the *Readers' Guide, Social Sciences Index, Humanities Index, Art Index, Education Index*, encompass groups of major journals in the respective subject areas and at a limited (or defined) scholarly level. They represent coverage of useful information collected in published works that are readily found in many college libraries. Furthermore, if a college does not have courses and the index to journals in a discipline, chances are that it also will have comparatively few journals in that subject area and few requests for items from those journals. This reflects a simple but important point. At present, requests are limited to those titles that the user can readily locate through local indexes and bibliographies. With access through on-line data bases, the tendency will be to include a much broader range of materials. This will broaden the reach of many, but it will also create the problem of generating requests for advanced and esoteric materials that are beyond the needs of users.

Thus, on-line data bases will have to be organized for the intellectual level and interests of the user. As the range, content, and availability of the data bases grow, this will become increasingly important. The user who wants the *Readers' Guide* type of information on energy conservation must be able to find what he or she wants without being encumbered by the technical references that would be of greater interest to the engineer who would prefer to consult the *Engineering Index*. In the future too, the intellectual and technical level of books will be indicated on the MARC records created by the Library of Congress and other libraries, and this information will be essential if college libraries are to build the type of collections needed. More consideration needs to be given to this point than has been the case thus far in the development of data bases.

ECONOMIES IN COLLECTION DEVELOPMENT AND SERVICES

Given a choice between achieving significant economies either in technical services or in reducing the quality and range of books purchased, one would hope and expect that most librarians would vote to maintain the best possible quality and range of books. That choice will indeed be more feasible in the future without sacrificing quality in technical processing.

The major periodical indexes make an effort, which is generally quite successful, to provide access to the major journals in particular disciplines. College libraries in turn tend to purchase those journals that are indexed. Thus, the journal indexes provide a significant recommendation for purchase, an inducement that represents in effect an outside selector. Of course, indexes generally reflect professional opinion in one way or another as to which are the most important journals in a discipline and which are, therefore, the most important ones to index. The point to be made here is that the journal indexes are an outside force that in large measure influences, if not actually determines, the selection of a major portion of the journals in many college libraries.

Book Selection

There are similar influences in the area of book selection. Book publishers and the editors of reviewing journals together determine which books will be reviewed in which journals; the publishers by deciding where to send books for review and the journal editors by selecting the reviewer and determining, in addition, whether the book will be reviewed at all. Thus, there is already considerable influence on which books will be purchased by those college libraries that select books based on reviews. (One might even go back one step further to point out that publishers decide which books to publish; that, too, obviously has an impact on which books a library will purchase. Everyone is familiar with stories of books that were rejected by several publishers and then became best sellers when one publisher recognized the merit, or sometimes the sensationalism, of the manuscript.)

Other influences in selection for libraries are the special lists for college libraries or the lists of best books in particular subject areas. (There have been many of these, and it is unnecessary to identify specific titles by name.) These are lists compiled by subject specialists, and they are used to evaluate collections for accreditation purposes as well as by the local library staff to discover weaknesses and to strengthen collections in some or all disciplines.

General and special subject lists have undoubtedly contributed greatly to improving collections in many libraries. By listing deletions from older editions, they can also be used and probably will be used more heavily in the future to withdraw outdated materials from the library. In spite of their value, there will always be shortcomings in these lists, and there obviously is room for improvement. Reviewers and subject specialists can readily point out shortcomings. Nevertheless, the various editions of books in the general series of books for college libraries have been valuable in upgrading the quality of college libraries.

The logic of using subject specialists for compiling lists of books for college libraries and special subject lists themselves can and will be carried one step further. In the future, a group of subject specialists will select important new books appropriate for college libraries in pertinent subject areas and send them to the libraries ready for shelving and circulating. This system will provide a number of major benefits. Each library will receive important new books within a week or two of publication. Because these will be purchased in hundreds of copies of each title, discounts will cover the cost of operating the system at a central site. All processing will be done with automated systems at pennies per copy. Each library will receive a machine-readable record for the new books every week or two to add to its local automated catalog. Accounting procedures will be very simple, with one monthly bill for the total service, and budgeting will be predictable within fairly clearly defined limits.

Concomitant with the new titles selected, deselection lists also will be compiled. Titles that have been superseded or are outdated will appear as separate files as recommendations for withdrawals. With machine-readable catalogs, it will be easy to purge the catalog of withdrawn titles. Physically removing the volumes from the library will require somewhat more time, but it will not be a major task. The entire process will be simple and inexpensive in comparison with present manual methods, and it will provide a convenient means of limiting growth by eliminating outdated materials. Large regional storage centers for preserving one copy will ensure access in case of future need.

Through this acquisitions process, college libraries will receive the most important books quickly and economically, and the general quality of academic libraries will be improved. However, some institutions will want to purchase in greater depth than is possible with the general selection plan. Furthermore, the system will not satisfy all needs. The local library still will need to monitor publishing in areas where the college has special curricular emphases as well as in those areas of special interest.

Centralized systems will achieve major savings in selection, acquisition, cataloging, and processing of major portions of new additions to college library collections. At the same time, they will drastically reduce the need for professional and supporting staff.

To maintain credibility, the system will have to be operated by a national library association and staffed by librarians with subject expertise. A commercial firm would be suspect. Even with librarians in charge, some libraries will want more and others less, and everyone will question the selection by certain titles, but that is no different from the reservations held today by reviewers and users of the various editions of recommended books for college libraries. The system should and will be under constant scrutiny by large numbers of librarians, and it will ensure better collection quality than has been the case in the past.

Although some will resist such a system initially, the logic of its use will gradually become apparent; and if the cost benefits of the system are examined, either librarians or (by default) central administrators of colleges will adopt the system. Initiating the system will require a long-range view and a commitment to devising a plan that will guarantee the best possible service at the least cost, even if this means the elimination of existing procedures and the subordination of short-term personal interests.

The centralized system of the future will do much to guarantee some minimum level of coverage of current materials, processing costs will be low, and outdated materials will be recommended for withdrawal. Although this will not achieve zero growth, it will help to control growth by making withdrawals an easy and regular process.

COOPERATION AND THE LOCAL COLLECTION

The need for cooperation in the future will be determined in large measure by forces external to the library. This is not to say that the attitudes and aspirations of librarians will not be strong determining forces, but computers and institutional policies will have at least as much impact as any internal factor.

Computers will have a substantial impact because they will make access to, and sharing of, materials easier. As noted earlier, both factual and bibliographic data bases will be common. Computerized catalogs of separate libraries as well as union catalogs of local, regional (within state), state, multistate, national, and international libraries will become the norm rather than the exception. By the end of the century, all academic libraries will have in-house computers that will serve as replacements for the present card catalog. Small neighboring libraries may share a computer for a local union catalog, and once the user exhausts local resources he or she will be able to query the other libraries until the item is found.

Obviously, the ease with which resources may be located in other libraries will have enormous implications for cooperation, and the cost of sharing will be far less than it is with the present manual system. Computerized systems also will have a major impact on the pattern of sharing. At present, major libraries complain about the drain on their resources. However, with computerized local union catalogs, most of the sharing will take place on the local level, and large libraries can gain as much or nearly as much from other sources as they give. Indeed, such general patterns have already been demonstrated in Minnesota.

Because of the financial problems that declining enrollment will create for colleges, these institutions are likely to reduce and define more narrowly the scope of their programs rather than try to serve everyone. This will lead neighboring institutions to make it easier for students to take courses in either institution. Thus, teaching staff can be shared and local library requirements can be reduced. Interinstitutional cooperation will become as necessary as interlibrary cooperation.

As with colleges themselves, it will be imperative for librarians to look at the total network of libraries. If interests are purely local, if librarians or colleges use only the selfish approach of "what can my institution gain," effective cooperation will be impossible. Only with visions that transcend the purely parochial will it be possible to establish viable, efficient, and effective cooperation.

The basic communication systems for the types of cooperation envisioned here are already available. They include telephone, teletype, automobiles, buses, facsimile transmission, cathode-ray tubes, high-speed on-line printers, transmission of print materials via telephone lines, and other such devices. Satellite communication systems will become more common. Electronic innovations will continue, but these are not likely to be radically different from present communication systems in purpose or in the products they provide.

In many places, interinstitutional management structures will become necessary to coordinate activities, to encourage the adoption of compatible equipment, to guarantee equal access for all institutions to plan new programs and applications, and to keep abreast of new developments in technology. Sharing in the planning, development, and implementation of new applications will be the accepted practice rather than the exception. Central management can improve communications and save money by locating expertise in a central office and sharing the cost among the institutions served. To ensure optimum configurations for effective cooperation, coordinated management will be necessary at local, regional, state, multistate, and national levels. Configurations will, of course, vary considerably from place to place and from time to time as situations dictate.

Money will be a major concern, but decisions regarding the best use of funds will be no more difficult in the future than in the past. When money is short, there will be temptation to lop off first the "extras" such as travel funds, special leaves and assistance for study or attending seminars, attendance at meetings, and similar moves. Cutting book budgets and staff will follow, but hopefully the necessity for this will be avoided or at least short-lived. Saving money in such a fashion can be money ill saved rather than well spent.

The college that attempts to teach the students to understand and appreciate the human condition will always need a wide range of resources for the various academic programs offered by the college. Interlibrary loan cannot serve as a substitute for the local collection under such teaching conditions. Although it is unnecessary to keep all books and journals forever, teaching methods will influence what can and should be kept or withdrawn. And this can be applied to virtually any discipline. Students in science can learn a great deal about the scientific community and about the process of reporting scientific discoveries by examining journal reports contemporaneous with the event. Students of literature can learn a great deal about an author by looking at contemporary reviews and criticism. Although few colleges have complete sets, and although they would receive comparatively little use unless teaching methods encourage their use, series such as the *Philosophical Transactions* of the Royal Society of London (1665–), *Scientific American* (1854–), the *Annual Register* (1758–), and many others in the right hands can be enormously useful educational resources. It all depends on the approaches used by the teacher and the objectives of the particular courses, department, and college.

To place limits on the size of many special libraries in business and industry and in small public libraries is feasible. Many businesses and industries are interested primarily in current applications, current processes, current products, current needs; they want information on the best formula and method available right now. With certain exceptions, businesses do not care about the research or thought processes involved in developing the machine or product or formula. Small public libraries too tend to provide mainly current-interest type of information. Consequently the size of those collections can be curtailed within prescribed limits with comparative ease so long as the user population remains static in numbers and interests. But with colleges, it is not so easy because of the institution. Although there are always new important books on both old and new subjects, it probably is easier to establish a minimal growth (but not no-growth) rate in the size of the book collection than it is to control the size of the journal collection, unless the college decides that it, too, like business and industry, is interested in teaching only currently accepted facts without regard to the explanation of those facts, in which case the library can be very small indeed.

The local college library, then, will need to continue to supply the frequently used important interpretive, theoretical, and descriptive printed works to support the curriculum. In the case of lesser-used materials, it will be easy to locate the items wanted through computerized library catalogs and other data bases. A significant type of cooperation will and should be in the encouragement, development, expansion, support, and use of the large factual and bibliographic data bases. Because these will be of value to a large portion of society, there also will be significant government support for these data bases.

The factual, statistical, and bibliographical sources essentially will be outside the library and, despite their continuing growth, will require comparatively little space inside the building. Beyond that, however, there is no way of setting an absolute size limit for a library at a quality institution unless the college, society, and knowledge themselves become static. The library must keep up with current materials. Furthermore, many areas of knowledge do not lend themselves to being indexed well enough to make it possible for the reader to find the idea or the wisdom that is sought. There often is no way of identifying the precise book or article needed. The reader must have personal, direct access to a substantial range of sources, and interlibrary loan is no substitute in those instances. If the college library does not provide them or if no other library is nearby, the user must go without. For a mediocre college, this may be acceptable, but not for a good one.

NOTE

1. Carnegie Foundation for the Advancement of Teaching, *More Than Survival: Prospects for Higher Education in a Period of Uncertainty* (San Francisco; Jossey-Bass, 1975).

ABOUT THE AUTHOR

Virgil F. Massman is Director of the James Jerome Hill Reference Library in St. Paul, Minnesota. He holds degrees from the University of Minnesota and the University of Michigan, where he received the Ph.D. He has served as President of the South Dakota Library Association and published both books and articles in the literature of librarianship. His doctoral dissertation, *Faculty Status for Librarians*, was published by Scarecrow Press in 1972.

BIBLIOGRAPHIC STANDARDS AND THE EVOLVING NATIONAL LIBRARY NETWORK

by Lawrence G. Livingston

My colleagues in this tribute to the life and works of Jerrold Orne will have taken due notice of the importance to, and impact on, academic libraries of his various careers and expertise—as professor of library science, as director of a large research library, in the theory of librarianship and in library construction—and given them the praise they so richly deserve. This brief paper will predict that the future historian of library science, assessing the impact of individual librarians on academic libraries as these will exist in the year 2000, will attribute more lasting importance to what might be termed Dr. Orne's fifth career, that of the development, promulgation, and implementation of standards in the fields of libraries, documentation, and related publishing practices. There is no doubt that, as local, state, regional, and national library networks based on computers develop, the trend will be away from the traditional local autonomy heretofore always enjoyed in academic libraries and toward standard formats, codes, and the content of bibliographic records. That future chronicler of things bibliographic will note that Jerrold Orne was chairman of Standards Committee Z39 of the American National Standards Institute (ANSI) during the period of transition from the traditional and labor-intensive methods of librarianship to the age of library systems and networks; that this period imposed the most stringent and far-reaching requirements on standardization in academic libraries, among others; and that Jerrold Orne, truly a man for his season, was equal to the challenge.

SERIALS CONTROL

My association with Jerrold Orne goes back to 1969, a year or so after I had joined the Council on Library Resources to be responsible for what evolved into a grants program in Library Automation, Networks, and National Library Service. Early on, I decided for myself that the two areas in academic libraries and in national library service generally that might be amenable to whatever influence I might be able to provide were the automation of national name-authority files and the cataloging, checking, and control of serials. Just why it is so difficult to convince some designers of library networks and systems that authority systems are at least as important in automated bibliographic processing as they are in manual catalogs eludes me yet, but there has been some success in developing serials systems, and much of the credit for it is due Jerrold Orne. Dr. Orne was appointed to the Advisory Group to the National Serials Data Pilot Project funded by the National Agricultural Library and managed by the Association of Research Libraries. The project, however many times it has been maligned, laid the groundwork for the National Serials Data Program, now an integral part of the serials processing at the Library of Congress; it also paved the way for the Conversion of Serials (CONSER) project,[1] wherein a dozen major academic libraries are cooperating with the national libraries of the United States and Canada to build a national serials data base.

In the pilot project, the difficulty of matching identical serials by main entry and/or title when cataloged by infinitely varied interpretations of several sets of cataloging rules gave ample evidence of the imperative and immediate requirement for a unique and unambiguous identification code for serial titles. This experience gave impetus to a standards project Jerrold Orne already had underway in the Z39 subcommittee. He and Fred Croxton, chairman of that subcommittee, quickly pushed for and got acceptance of the Standard Serial Number as the standard identifier for each serial title. Anyone familiar with the workings of that subcommittee and its interplay with the interests already vested in de facto standards competing for acceptance as the national standard gained good insight into Jerrold Orne's mastery of parliamentary debate—and of his staying power. Some participants in these activities used somewhat stronger terms.

In the event, the Standard Serial Number won the nod. Dr. Orne, not one to let momentum die, quickly entered the U.S. national standard as a candidate for the International Standard Serial Number (ISSN). His perseverance again prevailed. Quite understanding, before many did, the absolute requirement for a bibliographic data element (out of deference to tradition, I won't write bibliographic entry—just yet) that would have a one-for-one correlation with the ISSN, Dr. Orne worked diligently, here and in European councils, for the acceptance of the Key Title concept. The Key Title, each permanently associated with the corresponding ISSN, is formed by simple and relatively unambiguous rules from title information appearing in specific locations in the piece. Very importantly, when a serials publisher makes a title change of a specified degree, the Key Title is changed by the national center responsible for the area in which the serial was published, and this triggers the issuance of a new ISSN.

This tying of what is to be the principal identifier of serial titles to virtually all changes in each title forced some different procedures onto serials catalogers and induced changes, some yet in progress, in the rules for cataloging serials. The results are not all in, but I will cautiously predict that when all serial titles in current use in libraries have been permanently and uniquely identified with ISSN and Key Title, the concept of main entry in serials cataloging will undergo substantial revision at least. This will have enormous impact on the ways serials are handled in academic libraries, for the push for standardization on these new norms will dilute the autonomy in cataloging methods they have traditionally enjoyed. The relationship between the Cataloging Title and Key Title will also require study, because they are often identical, and maintaining both in full form in the same record is expensive. The lineage of all of this to the standards activity that created ISSN is direct; that future historian of ours will credit Jerrold Orne to a significant degree, and to his honor, I have no doubt whatsoever.

DEVELOPING A NATIONAL LIBRARY SYSTEM

In order to gain a proper perspective on the various interrelations between the development, promulgation, and implementation of standards and the proper role of academic libraries in the evolving national library/bibliographic system, it would be useful first to describe the recent past, current status, and future prospects of the evolution of that system. In that way it may be possible to see where certain standards are required and possible. At least as important is a proper understanding of those areas in which standardization is not possible and, therefore, should not be attempted.

One of the basic assumptions that underlies the development of information handling systems (to include library systems) in the United States is that each of these sytems has, and will retain, a high degree of internal autonomy. This means, among other things, that the managers of each system are free to choose for each system, and without by-your-leave from anyone at all, such things as internal formats, processes and procedures, file and index organization, and so on. The managers are also quite free to design the products and services each system will provide, given only the requirement to satisfy constituents. It is easily seen that this degree of systems autonomy, inevitable in a democratic country, almost automatically rules out any formal standardization within the bounds of individual systems. If diverse bibliographic systems are to exchange records and conduct other business (for example, interlibrary loan) with others, some degree of standardization is required if chaos is to be avoided. Because internal standardization across systems boundaries is not possible, the effort must bear on those codes, formats, and messages that flow between and among systems, and on the communications media that handle them.

NCLIS

First, a bird's-eye view of how the national library system is developing is in order. The National Commission on Libraries and Information Science (NCLIS), under statutory mandate[2] "to promote research and development activities that will extend and improve the nation's library and information-handling capability as essential links in the national communications networks" has developed and published a plan[3] for the overall development of library and information-handling services in the United States. The NCLIS plan naturally includes other aspects of information handling besides libraries. This, coupled with the fact that there exists no operating agency at the national level capable of either development or setting priorities, posed a dilemma: where to start?

LC on Network Development

Happily, the Library of Congress, under the aggressive leadership of the newly appointed Librarian, Daniel Boorstin, took the necessary initiative. Dr. Boorstin appointed Henriette Avram[4] to be his Assistant for Network Development and provided her with a small staff to push for a national library network. This was a timely event, because such systems as the Ohio College Library Center (OCLC), the Washington Library Network, and the BALLOTS system at Stanford were developing quite dynamically and totally without meaningful coordination among them. The internal autonomy enjoyed by each of these systems and others, in this era of very rapid growth, threatened to overflow to the point that some standardization *must* take place if anything like a truly national system ever were to evolve.

With financial support and other help from the Council on Library Resources, Mrs. Avram quickly began two series of meetings. The first of these called together the policy makers of the most active and dynamic components of what would logically be a national library network. In the interest of keeping the meetings to manageable size and within available resources, several persons had to be excluded who had legitimate desires to participate. This was unfortunate, but unavoidable. In addition to the managers of the major systems, the National Commission, the Council on Library Resources, and the National Endowment for the Humanities participated.

Accord on some major points was reasonably swift:[5]

1. This planning group would concentrate on the National Library/Bibliographic Component of the overall information-handling network. Other components (national bibliographic resources centers, systems including publishers, abstracting and indexing services, and so on) although directly or indirectly related to the tasks at hand would not be dealt with by this group as a matter of first priority. Some would remain outside the province of this planning group; this would all be sorted out later.
2. Among first priority items:
   a. Determine the hardware-software resource requirements of the Library of Congress as the national network node.
   b. Define the national bibliographic data base as to its composition, distribution, creation, maintenance, etc.
3. The library/bibliographic component of the overall network would evolve from existing components, to include libraries, networks, bibliographic utilities, brokers of bibliographic products and services, and so on. These would continue to exist at regional, state, and local levels. The functional relationships of these network components needed to be studied at once.

As the work of the policy and planning group went forward, it became evident that parallel work was needed at a greater level of technical expertise and detail. Mrs. Avram quickly began the second series of meetings; with the cooperation and support of the Research Library Group, she called the first meeting of the technical directors of the various active systems. Once again, there was a surprising unanimity of thought. Even in the first meeting, a diagram showing the possible functional relationships of library components in a distributive and cooperative network system began to take shape. It would be premature to consider in this paper the deliberations of either of these two groups; suffice it to say that the methodology of network development is shaping up nicely, and as it does, opportunities and requirements for standards activity become evident.

Cataloging in Machine-Readable Form

Perhaps the most important basis for the future library/bibliographic component of the national information network lies in the bibliographic products and services that the Library of Congress will provide to the other network components and libraries generally in fulfilling its role as the national node in that network. In a recent statement[6] William Welsh, Henriette Avram, and others, speaking for the Library predicted that, approximately by the end of this decade, almost all of LC's current cataloging would be going into machine-readable form and available in the MARC distribution system.

The Library also promised that its name and subject authorities will be available in machine-readable form, and outside access to its automated in-process file is planned. Reflection on what this centralized availability of authoritative cataloging and other products will mean indicates that the year 1980 presents a logical focal point around which the thinking about the design and implementation of the national library networks should logically focus. Each putative component in that network, be it an individual library, systems such as OCLC, the BALLOTS system at Stanford, Washington Library Network, New England Library Network, a cooperative processing center, a broker of services from others, or whatever, should begin now to study the implications of 1980. Certainly the availability of so much LC catalog, in-process, and authority copy in machine-readable form so early in the progression of the book or serial through the library processes will have enormous impact on how libraries and library networks do business.

COMMITTEE FOR COORDINATION OF NATIONAL BIBLIOGRAPHIC CONTROL

Even before the national library network component began the more visible part of its evolution, work had begun to coordinate the thinking and plans of the various communities of interest and to ensure that standards activities kept pace. In 1974, the Council on Library Resources and the National Science Foundation (later joined by the National Commission on Libraries and Information Science) convened a meeting in Rosslyn, Virginia.[7]

Participants in that meeting included eminent representation from the fields of libraries, standards, abstracting and indexing services, publishers, the Copyright Office, and many others. A background paper on the problems and opportunities of national bibliographic control was discussed, and the meeting resulted in one general and seven specific recommendations; the principal recommendation was for the establishment of an ongoing mechanism or body to pursue the goals of national bibliographic control. Pursuant to this, the Committee for the Coordination of National Bibliographic Control was created.[8] Dr. Orne became a charter member.

The committee meets quarterly and participation affords Dr. Orne excellent opportunity to promote new standards as the requirement for them comes up in work undertaken by the committee. When this occurs, Dr. Orne appoints a subcommittee, with chairman, of Standards Committee Z39. That subcommittee initiates the formal process in ANSI to get the standard developed, voted upon, and promulgated. Close coordination continues between the standards working party and the Committee for the Coordination of National Bibliographic Control. This permits the committee to coordinate its other projects with the standard under development as appropriate and to promote the use of the new standard when developed.

This paper will not describe all the standards activities of Z39 that are pertinent to national bibliographic control; that information is published regularly.[9] Nor will it go into detail on the work of the Committee for the Coordination of National Bibliographic Control.[10] Suffice it to say that, in addition to turning requirements for standards over to Z39 for action, the committee pursues its objectives in several other modes. For example, it may commission studies by individuals, as it did in the case of the use and potential of the International Standard Book Number (ISBN) in libraries. It may convene a working party of experts to pursue a specific objective, as it did when Margaret Park of the University of Georgia was appointed chairman of a group to draft bibliographic formats for journal articles and technical reports. In another case, one too complicated for definitive action in the near term, first a small group was given the task of developing a background paper on the use, potential, and problems of machine-sensible optical and magnetic codes in bibliographic control. When the paper was ready, a larger group, representing manufacturers and vendors of the technology and physical media (bar codes, readers, labels, and so on), users, and potential users of these coding schemes was convened. The potential for use of these codes in the manufacture, vending, shipping, receiving, processing, circulation, and inventory control of books is almost infinitely complex, as the meeting just described amply demonstrated. The problems break down into three generic areas: the label that carries the code, the code symbology, and the number or other identification that is to be coded. Each of these areas has its own complex parts; there are, obviously, many areas to be examined for the need for standardization. Some of these will be described shortly.

CONSER Project

But first, one case will be described briefly to exemplify the close interaction among the Committee for the Coordination of Bibliographic Control, the previously mentioned CONSER project, and standards. The CONSER project to date has been managed by the Council on Library Resources. In this project, OCLC has served as the host system on which the Library of Congress and the other participating libraries are building a comprehensive data base containing the bibliographic records of serial publications. As the project got under way, pressure began to build for the inclusion of statements, to be attached to each record, showing which library holds the title. This is an obvious need if the CONSER file is to support union list and interlibrary loan activity. Accordingly, the CONSER group started work on a holding-statement format for serials. When progress on the work was reported to the Committee for the Coordination of National Bibliographic Control, the requirement for formal standards activity was quite evident. The Committee asked Dr. Orne to take over, and he at once set up a subcommittee (Z39.40) with Glyn Evans of SUNY at Albany as chairman. At this writing, this standard is nearly ready for a vote in Z39.

Formally proclaiming a standard is not the end goal, of course; it must be proved useful if it is to be used. In parallel with the development of the draft standard for serials holding statements, a machine-readable union list of serials projects was being designed that obviously could serve as a test bed for the standard. The planning phase of this was funded by the Council on Library Resources.[11] The proponents of the project are Alice Wilcox of the Minnesota Interlibrary Teletype Exchange (MINITEX) and Barbara Markuson of the Indiana Cooperative Library Services Authority (INCOLSA). Their intent, briefly, is to use a mini-computer system to store the holding statements and permit their update on-line by libraries of the two systems. These holding records will be linked to the bibliographic record from the CONSER file on control numbers common to both files.

This illustrates how closely the standards work of Jerrold Orne and Z39 is related to national network developments, for CONSER is only the first of the cooperative activities operating in a mode including decentralized work and centralized authority and responsibility; the COMARC project is another.[12] Because of his experience, effectiveness, and intimate involvement in so many of these projects, Dr. Orne has significant influence upon the whole.

OTHER STANDARDS IN THE DEVELOPMENT STAGE

This paper will conclude with a brief description of several embryonic standards; the reader can expect formal action on most of them over the coming months, with Dr. Orne leading the way. Not all of them originated with Dr. Orne alone, of course. They have been discussed in various committees of ALA, in the Committee for the Coordination of National Bibliographic Control, and elsewhere. They are described here to remind the reader that action on each will at least have begun while Dr. Orne was at the helm and to underscore the importance of Z39 standards to national bibliographic control. The descriptions that follow do not necessarily represent the views of the Council on Library Resources, nor has Dr. Orne any direct part in them; responsibility for them rests solely with me.

Piece Identification Number

A glance at almost any item from a supermarket shelf will reveal that such items are marked with a machine-readable bar code.[13] These numeric codes indicate to the sensing machine certain information about the manufacturer and the product. The coded numbers are used in the manufacturing, storing, shipping, receiving, and inventory-control processes. Some supermarket chains have code-sensing devices at the checkout counter. In stores so equipped, the item is passed by the scanner, the number is decoded and sent to the computer where it calls up the item record with the unit price, stock on hand, reorder point, and so on. Numerous transactions occur automatically. Some book items sold in supermarkets are coded in this national system.

In libraries, some automated systems control circulation of books by putting bar codes on them. Other libraries are planning to control items in process by the use of bar codes. It is reasonable to expect interlibrary loan in the future to be managed using bar-coded numbers. To date none of these bar-coded numbers are the same. Some publishers control all their transactions by using the ISBN, even to include controlling the records of payments to the authors. Library circulation control systems often assign numbers arbitrarily to be bar coded. Some systems control books or catalog records on LC card numbers, and almost all systems use local control numbers on bibliographic records. It is not difficult to visualize a future wherein bookcovers would be plastered with several bar codes, each one unintelligible or meaningless outside the system where it originated. An absolutely unique piece identification number would obviate most, but not all, of these unnecessarily duplicative numbers.

Neither the LC card number (LCCN) nor the ISBN will serve as the unique piece identifier as presently known. The LCCN, of course, will never apply to all publications. The ISBN, as we know it, fails because it is not copy specific. I believe that the most logical approach to a completely unique identifier for books is to define a new data element to be used *in conjunction with the ISBN* when specificity to the level of single copy is desired. If this is done, the publisher could bar code the ISBN on all copies printed of a given book and use that number on all transactions and processes. The dealer would continue to list books with ISBN and use the number in his processes. The selection and acquisitions librarian could select and order the book by ISBN, using machine-readable records if appropriate. The book would be checked into the library and accounted for by

ISBN. The library would obtain the catalog record (CIP or MARC) by searching on ISBN, and the book would enter the library's process, which would be made much shorter if the CIP record in machine-readable form was available (as it is likely to be) when the book arrives.

Thus far in its progression from the author's mind to the reference collection, shelf, or checkout desk, the book has been well served by a single ISBN as a unique piece identifier. But, early in the library process, the identification must become copy specific, and ISBN cannot satisfy this requirement as it is. At this point, the librarian would bar code, in prescribed relationship to the ISBN, the additional data element to make the whole identifier item specific. It would be nice to suppose that a single coded addition to the ISBN would satisfy the requirement for piece identification for processing, for circulation control, and for interlibrary loan, or is that being too naïve?

The ISSN could be treated in much the same way for use as the unique piece identifier for serials. This serial copy identification code could be built into the journal article piece identifier; the whole could serve as the journal article citation code.

Library (or Collection) Code

As the commerce in books and bibliographic records in machine-readable form increases, as it surely will, the pressure to replace the National Union Catalog (NUC) code with a code better suited to the national network environment will become virtually irresistible. A standard code for library and related fund accounts has already been devised.[14] There has been discussion in standards committees of ALA on a draft code for the libraries themselves. John Kountz, Richard Godwin, and others have suggested in these meetings that the library or collection code could and should be embedded in the Standard Account Number (SAN) code. Because only four character positions are available for a SAN for this purpose, the suggestion is to use the letters A–Z in each position. This radix of 26 would yield sufficient numbers for all libraries.

Embedding the library or collection code in the SAN has several attractions. That approach holds down the number of codes to be affixed to the book, and there is no doubt that, in the interlibrary loan work, the account number and the code for the lending library will often need to be used together.

Library Patron Identifier

A unique code for each patron is needed too. Happily, this one won't have to be pasted onto the book cover. Common sense dictates that the assignment and application of patron-identification codes is a matter for the local library to handle. But I feel that the method of constructing the number and perhaps the methodology for coding it should be standardized nationally for the long-term benefit of interlibrary loan.

An Abbreviated Bibliographic Record

This is perhaps the most intriguing and challenging idea for a standard. Almost from the first distribution of MARC records, people have been trying to devise subsets of the MARC records. Perhaps the largest of these efforts was the series of meetings sponsored by the Council on Library Resources that came to be known as the Conference to Explore Machine-Readable Bibliographic Interchange (CEMBI).[15]

In CEMBI, the try for a brief MARC record failed for what, seen in hindsight, is a very obvious reason. The purpose or purposes for which the abbreviated record was to be used were not clearly specified in advance. Each participant, it seemed, had his or her own purpose, and each required a given subset of MARC data elements to satisfy that purpose. The discussants in CEMBI tended to think of all these data elements in a single matrix; the result always was a complete MARC record. Still, CEMBI had some positive results; it certainly taught how not to approach the definition of a brief MARC record, and it served as a forum for discussing the exchange of machine-readable bibliographic records.

After the CEMBI meetings, Henriette Avram took the right approach. She hired Dave Weisbrod of Yale, a CEMBI participant, to define a brief MARC record for the single purpose of reporting holdings to LC's Register of Additional Locations, an adjunct to the National Union Catalog. So narrowed, the proper record for the purpose was quickly defined. Now, Dr. Orne is suggesting that the approach can be used to define other brief records, all different and each tailored to satisfy a single, specific requirement. What follows is my extension and expansion of that idea; an attempt to show that it embodies an absolutely critical application of standards to national network library service.

At the beginning, it was pointed out that, in a library network of essentially autonomous equals, standardization in bibliographic exchange can be applied only to the messages that flow between these diverse components and to the communication means associated with these messages. Let us examine where standards may be applied in the network communications process.[16] First, standard communication lines of the desired capacities may be easily acquired from the common carriers. Standard or at least compatible communications hardware is also widely available. That leaves the messages themselves.

The layperson can visualize library network messages as a series of coded bits of information moving down the communication channel in either direction between two network components. For simplification, these library network messages may be seen to transmit three kinds of information, only two of which are pertinent to this discussion. First, there are the purely technical protocols that permit the sending and receiving devices to handle the messages. These are already largely standardized and need not concern us here. Next down the wire comes a set of instructions as to what the message is, to whom it is addressed, where the response should go, and so on. These instructions will need to be standardized also, but they are not the point of this narrative. Each message will end, as it began, with purely technical communications protocols. Somewhere in the message there must be bibliographic data, and it is here that the brief bibliographic record for identification comes into play.

One need only think about the transactions he or she would want to see conducted over a library network to begin to array the brief bibliographic records for identification he or she would need. A very obvious requirement would be for a message that would trigger a search in a distant data base for a bibliographic record. In a simple version, the bibliographic identifier might be an LCCN number. So we have already defined one brief bibliographic record to support a single function. All we need do now is standardize its coding and placement in the overall message, and we're in business. Derived search keys, such as those condensed from title, author/title, and so on, will all require similar treatment. The underlying philosophy is that, given the standard set of messages, any network component would need only to program his or her system to be capable of accepting the standard search messages and reading them in. How the component's system uses the message internally is entirely that component's business, provided only that it can output a standard network message containing the result of the search. In a simple example, the search might result in a full MARC record for a monograph, suitably formated, tagged and embedded in the response message, and addressed to the proper place.

One can see that different library transactions will require different bibliographic content in the message. The next order of business is to examine all of these requirements and standardize the brief bibliographic record for identification that will satisfy them. So defined, these brief records will undoubtedly serve other purposes besides message traffic; for example, it would be nice if the brief bibliographic record used in an interlibrary loan request could be automatically translated into a record that would support local circulation control, or am I dreaming again? In any case, the standardization of the different abbreviated records to carry the bibliographic and related information to be embedded in network messages is one of the most important requirements of a coherent national library network component. If the future can be inferred from the past, Jerrold Orne and Z39 will be equal to the challenge.

NOTES

1. Lawrence G. Livingston, "The CONSER Project: Current Status and Plans," *Library of Congress Information Bulletin* 34, no. 7 (February 17, 1975), pp. A38–42. ISSN 0041-7904.
2. Public Law 91–345.
3. The National Commission on Libraries and Information Science, "Toward a National Program for Library and Information Services; Goals for Action" (1975).
4. Mrs. Avram is another iconoclast of whom that historian of the future will take due notice for the endless effect the system of MARC formats, of which she is principal architect, is having on librarianship worldwide. See Henriette

Avram, "MARC, Its History and Implications" (Library of Congress, 1975) for a good bibliography on related subjects.

5. For a fuller exposition on the results of these meetings, see Library of Congress, "Toward the Library/Bibliographic Component of the National Library and Information Service Network." In preparation.
6. The Association of Research Libraries, "The Library of Congress as the National Bibliographic Center," February 1976.
7. Lawrence G. Livingston, "National Bibliographic Control: A Challenge," *Library of Congress Information Bulletin* 33, no. 25 (June 21, 1974), pp. A108–113. ISSN 0041–7904.
8. Council on Library Resources, "CLR, NSF, and NCLIS Establish Advisory Group on National Bibliographic Control," *CLR Recent Developments*, April 16, 1975. *Note:* The name was subsequently changed to the Committee for the Coordination of National Bibliographic Control.
9. American National Standards Institute, "ANSI News about Z39." January 1977. ISSN 0028–8942.
10. As committee projects are completed, reports on them are prepared and held for distribution. The availability of these documents will be widely announced; requests for them should be addressed to: Secretariat, Committee for the Coordination of National Bibliographic Control, Suite 620, One Dupont Circle, N.W., Washington, D.C. 20036.
11. Council on Library Resources, "CLR Supports Planning for Prototype National Serial Location System," *CLR Recent Developments*, March 11, 1977. ISSN 0034–1169.
12. Library of Congress, "Council on Library Resources Grant to Library of Congress Will Fund Expansion of MARC Studies," *Library of Congress Information Bulletin* 33, no. 51 (December 20, 1974).
13. See International Business Machines Corporation, *IBM Systems Journal* 14, no. 1 (1975).
14. For a recent report on the progress of this draft standard, see American National Standards Institute, "ANSI News about Z39."
15. Henriette Avram, "Sharing Machine-Readable Bibliographic Data: A Progress Report on a Series of Meetings Sponsored by the Council on Library Resources, Inc.," *Journal of Library Automation* 7, no. 1 (March 1974), pp. 47–60.
16. For my perception of how the national network will develop, see Lawrence G. Livingston, "The Near Future of the National Library Network," in *Proceedings of the Fall 1976 EDUCOM Conference*. In press.

ABOUT THE AUTHOR

Lawrence G. Livingston is Program Officer for the Council on Library Resources in Washington, D.C. He is an honors graduate of the University of Maryland and a translator of Russian and French. He has been active in bibliographic standards work for a number of years on both the national and international levels. He is primary Council on Library Resources member on the American National Standards Institute Standards Committee Z39.

LIBRARIES AND THE NEW TECHNOLOGY: TOWARD A NATIONAL BIBLIOGRAPHIC DATA BASE

by William J. Welsh

> If one accepts the conviction that what is past is prologue, one may be willing to accept my views of the future place of technology in libraries and the imperative need for swift development of the standards that will be needed. It is evident that the rapid advances in standards development over the past ten years have grown out of the concurrent rapid evolution of library applications of new technological devices. Increased population, increased available information, and natural demand for improved access have all led to insistent pressures to establish standards . . . technological developments make it imperative that one reviews carefully everything done in order to set new patterns for the work of the next half of the century.[1]

These words of Jerrold Orne summarize concisely some of the important concerns facing us in the 1970s, as we move forward in our attempts to improve library services. At a time when economic pressures are forcing libraries to rethink the very bases for their existence, when resource sharing begins to seem inevitable and welcome, when the concept of networking seems to offer at least a partial, if not simple, solution to our growing economic constraints, Jerrold Orne has presented us with one of the key elements to our problems. It is fitting that we honor him with essays on academic libraries at the close of the twentieth century: he has looked toward that point, and beyond.

The future of the academic library depends on our ability to direct the technology we have in hand, and that we foresee having, toward our common goal of national and international bibliographic control on a scale that will provide access to the ever-enlarging body of information now contained inside and outside libraries. Around 1960, when the possibilities offered by the computer were being seriously considered in a concrete fashion for the first time by librarians, the prophets among us had already begun to see the impact that technology could have on libraries. Jesse Shera, then dean of the Western Reserve University School of Library Science, wrote:

Note: My special appreciation to Ann Lee Hallstein, who aided me immensely by assembling material and working closely with me in the preparation of this article, and to many other Library of Congress staff who aided both Ann and me, especially Peter De La Garza, who did the editing.

The important problem that confronts the librarian today is not one of accumulation but of access to that which is accumulated. What will it profit a scholar if the entire Library of Congress sits on his desk [in miniaturized form] if he cannot select from it that which is living, vital and relevant to his needs.[2]

Jerrold Orne was among the first to predict the effects of technology on libraries. He watched the helter-skelter growth of automation in libraries. He saw the need for standardization to bring it under control and put it to use to expedite the work of the librarian. Our improved technology invites us to provide selective access to information for the greatest number of people. In the face of budget stringencies, librarians will increasingly be called upon to perform feats beyond those of handing *a* book to *a* patron. They will have to perform an increasingly active role as educators (Webster's defines education as "the act or process of providing with knowledge") at the same time that they are compelled to conserve. Like Jerrold Orne, I believe it can be done with the help of technology, but only through mutual effort can technology help us to progress. There are real problems to face in moving ahead in cooperative endeavors and the sharing of resources. Some of these problems were outlined in *Annual Report to the President and Congress, '74/'75* of the National Commission on Libraries and Information Science (NCLIS), among them the fact that our "information agencies" (libraries, commercial services, government agencies, and educational institutions) have had little experience in working together toward any common goal; the instability of funding; the lack of guidelines to ensure the development of compatible network services; and the absence of an official central agency for the processing and distribution of standardized bibliographic records. These problems must be resolved; with technology serving us, a great deal is possible. I foresee a library where librarians have the time and resources to serve truly the needs of their clients. Technology can help us toward that goal. What effects can we expect technology to have on the academic library of the future? What have we accomplished thus far? And what may be possible in the future?

BUILDING A NATIONAL BIBLIOGRAPHIC DATA BASE

If we are to better provide academic library users with the information they seek, we must first provide better access to that information. We have come a long way toward that goal, but still have a long way to go. At the Library of Congress, we have made a good beginning toward better bibliographic control, and we foresee a network that will extend such control to libraries throughout the country and eventually around the world. The creation of a national bibliographic data base will be the first step. This, of course, requires the standardization of bibliographic data to ensure compatible input from multiple sources. Assuming for the moment that LC will be a central node of the library bibliographic component of the national network, I can see such a data base evolving and growing through the mechanism of decentralized input. As I have said before, LC is eager to accept bibliographic data from other sources: we know that we cannot move forward on our resources alone. We want to, we must benefit from the cataloging expertise of other academic and research institutions, as we do currently with the National Library of Canada, whose Canadian corporate name headings we accept.

LC Machine-Readable Cataloging

To create a national bibliographic data base, we will need to have the cataloging operation at LC on-line. To serve our own needs, LC began automating its cataloging operations more than a decade ago. An automated core bibliographic system was designed to serve internal needs, with an automated national bibliographic service to serve the needs of the national library community. The system is improving our control over our processing activities and is bringing us closer to a more effective production of bibliographic information in a variety of forms.

A conference in which academic libraries participated was held at LC in 1965. The conference concluded that a machine-readable record should be developed to include at least all data available on LC's printed cards. The conferees decided that the records should be created at LC, then made available to libraries with automated systems. This was the beginning of a program to provide a standardized machine-readable record for inclusion in various data bases. The MARC (Machine-Readable Cataloging) pilot project, begun in 1966, was our first attempt at cooperative automation planning. Sixteen institutions cooperated to develop together the early procedures and programs for conversion, maintenance, and distribution of MARC data; the data were used by the cooperating libraries, and they helped us in evaluating the project. Nine of the sixteen were academic libraries. The pilot project, which ended in 1968, had been enthusiastically received, and plans were made to create a MARC Distribution Service within LC. Next came the MARC II format designed to contain bibliographic information for all forms of materials, not just books. We limited our first conversions to English-language monographs; the distribution service was subsequently expanded to include all roman alphabet cataloging. Academic libraries were among the first subscribers, and their participation in the service continues to increase. By the end of 1976, MARC distribution service covered, in addition to books in roman alphabet languages, films, serials, and maps in all languages and subject authorities. About 175,000 titles are being input annually. It is hoped that by 1980, MARC will cover all current cataloging, about 250,000 titles annually. We are presently studying the problems of nonroman alphabets. We have entered into agreement with the National Library of Canada, the Bibliothèque Nationale of France, and the National Library of Australia for the exchange of records in machine-readable form for imprints of our respective countries. Similar agreements are being negotiated with other national bibliographic agencies. Using machine-readable records from other national bibliographies will enable LC to serve more effectively the cataloging needs of academic libraries by providing better coverage and more rapid access to the published output of the rest of the world.

Henriette Avram has observed:

The availability of cataloging data in machine-readable form supplied by LC, the need to input cataloging data locally . . . the possibility of sharing these locally generated records, the potential for using computer programs across organizations to reduce the high cost of designing and writing software and the need for hardware capable of handling large character sets were all factors that put increased emphasis on the establishment and conformity to standards.[3]

Without standardization, MARC could never have been implemented. Without further standardization, it cannot move forward.

We are now seeing the development and adoption of the International Standard Bibliographic Description (ISBD), which provides, for various forms of material, a standard set of descriptive elements for each form in a standard order using standard punctuation to separate the elements. In the United States, the ISBD simplified the automatic machine recognition of descriptive elements in the cataloging record, thus reducing the complexity and cost of machine input and conversion.

In considering the feasibility of international exchange, we are immediately faced with the problem of processing nonroman languages, and the input, manipulation, and display of their character sets. The Library's Working Group on Nonroman Languages is exploring the problems related to the handling of nonroman languages by the MARC system. The general feeling is that the expansion of coverage by MARC can proceed systematically, even though some languages may have to be romanized *in toto* or in part initially. We are aware of the disadvantages of such a course, and the group has addressed itself to specific problems of how much and what kind of romanization for particular languages would be possible and acceptable.

Meanwhile, ALA and many national bibliographic agencies have adopted as a first step LC's expanded roman alphabet character set—certainly a major achievement! We are confident that as International MARC expands, academic as well as other types of libraries will have automated access to the world's literature.

While the MARC service has expanded in terms of materials converted, a further significant advance has occurred with the automation of LC's Process Information File. Implemented in late 1976, the Automated Process Information File (APIF) could eventually control all items selected for our collections (and APIF will eventually include records of items from the foreign bibliographies *not* selected or cataloged) that enter LC for processing and that are destined to be represented by LC catalog records. These preliminary records can be used by academic libraries for selection and acquisition purposes as well as to alert them to the future availability of full records for all titles within the scope of MARC.

In building toward a national bibliographic data base, with data input from various institutions, the on-line name authority file has great importance. Name authority information is now being provided, in part, by LC's book catalogs and by *Library of Congress Name Headings with References*, but these tools are not comprehensive and are not yet in machine-readable form. A system for converting our name authority list has been devised, with complete authority records for all name headings used in current MARC records along with all new and changed records for non-MARC headings. The authority records will be used to produce an enlarged version of *Name Headings* in book and microform. In due course, these records will be available through the MARC Distribution Service and eventually in an on-line mode. Gradually, a record will be provided for each name heading in the retrospective MARC data base.

When name records are on-line, LC will provide not only the established form of heading and its associated "see" and "see also" references, but also the citations of sources and the information used to determine these forms. If the work of cataloging is to be shared, the national file must include the form of entry of other institutions, and they must have access to our name authority file. There must be standard rules to follow. The problem of deciding upon and following a set of standards is especially pressing for catalogers. What we have had is, in Orne's words, a "confused and confusing maelstrom of frequently ephemeral, inept, or unqualified standards . . . the natural result of the conviction of almost every human animal that his way is best."[4]

In a cooperative system everyone must have access to the authority file. It seems probable that LC will be the final authority on names for a national bibliographic data base. Subject information is currently provided through *Library of Congress Subject Headings* in microfiche, book, and machine-readable form, and coverage has been expanded to include categories of headings previously excluded. A pilot project is being considered to determine how we can standardize subject headings for more effective sharing of cataloging chores. This entails the use of a basically identical subject heading list by the United States and Canada. The National Library of Canada was instrumental in developing LC's law schedule for Canada, and now Canada has its own classification (compatible with LC's system) for Canadian literature and history. We shall not use these assigned classes, but shall integrate rather than duplicate what they have done, and may adopt their FC and P classes for Canadian materials. If such cooperation becomes a reality, we shall be that much closer to the shared development and maintenance of a national data base that, when perfected, will ensure that a book is cataloged only once. We feel that a comprehensive study of the subject headings system is needed to pave the way for possible restructuring of the system. Sooner or later, LC will add this project to its list of priorities.

To standardize cataloging data for machine exchange even further, LC will extend the application of Dewey Decimal Classification numbers to all MARC records; there will be a substantial increase in the output of decimal numbers as MARC encompasses more languages and forms of materials. It is unlikely, however, that LC will ever be able to provide Universal Decimal Classification numbers or develop a new classification system.

Projects to Develop Decentralized Input Systems

As part of the evolution of a national bibliographic data base, LC is currently engaged in four significant cooperative projects aimed at the development of systems for decentralized input, as an attempt to avoid duplication of effort. Many libraries are cooperating and/or benefiting from these projects. If these endeavors continue as successfully as they have begun, we are confident that our projected ideas will be more than abstractions by the end of the century.

The first of these programs is the Conversion of Serials (CONSER) project. This effort involves the Council on Library Resources (CLR) as the funding and management agent, the Ohio College Library Center (OCLC) as the machine facility, and fourteen participating academic and research libraries, including the National Library of Canada and LC, cooperatively building a national serials data base. Records for serials are input on-line to the OCLC data base. The National Library of Canada and LC authenticate the records, which are then distributed by the MARC Distribution Service to subscribing libraries that are not members of OCLC.

Another file-building effort in which academic and other libraries are participating is the Cooperative MARC (COMARC) pilot study, also funded by CLR. Because LC cannot possibly undertake alone the retrospective conversion of all cataloging data, it must avail itself of machine input by other institutions, provided the records conform to the standards LC has set for the quality of its data base. Institutions participating in COMARC convert records for their own automated bibliographic systems using LC catalog copy from printed cards, proofsheets, or National Union Catalog (NUC) pages. These records, sent to LC on tape in the MARC communications format, are processed at LC to remove duplicate titles. The remaining titles are compared with the Official Catalog, and the access points are updated. The records are then distributed on tape without charge to COMARC participants, and on paid subscription to other organizations. Eventually LC expects to make these records part of the national data base.

Grant funds from CLR were also used to develop a format for machine-readable reports to the NUC. The study explored the level of MARC encoding necessary for a record, assuming format recognition at the central source would enhance the record to a full MARC record. This report is awaiting analysis by LC staff prior to release. If such a format is defined, more libraries could furnish machine-readable records, because not all can now afford to furnish records with full coding. This will be another step toward the evolution of a national data base for gathering both cataloging data and location information.

In a third project, the *Register of Additional Locations* (RAL) file for NUC is being expanded to include reports received in machine-readable form from selected outside libraries. These libraries had previously sent location reports on printed cards, which LC had to keyboard into the RAL file. New York Public Library (NYPL) was the first library to send its location reports on tape. The RAL file is now available for searching on-line internal to LC. The machine system has also made it possible to publish RAL in microform.

Four major research libraries (Harvard, Yale, Columbia, and NYPL) are participating in a fourth project that is a major step toward data-base access in a network situation. It involves the Research Libraries Group (RLG) and LC. RLG members, using the NYPL computer, will directly access the MARC file at LC for the purpose of using MARC records to build machine-readable files. When a record is needed for cataloging purposes at one of the RLG libraries, the staff will search the files of the RLG institutions through the use of a CRT on-line to the NYPL system. If the record is available, it is taken for use. If not, the search query is sent on to LC, where the LC MARC file is searched, and if the record is in the LC data base, it is transferred computer to computer from LC to NYPL.

Multiple Access to the Catalog File

These four projects show progress toward the cooperative building and use of a national data base. A further point to consider in building the national data base is the need to change our way of thinking about catalog use itself. The advent of an on-line national data base points the way to an entirely new way of approaching a "catalog." The possibilities of access to the file are expanded far beyond our present limitations by the provision of multiple access points to the machine file.

Presently, under CONSER, records are input from various locations to the OCLC system and verified on-line by LC. This is a step toward using the full potential of current technology, but it can be carried even further. We have accepted bibliographic description from certain foreign national bibliographies without change because of the economic imperative to do so. When various regional networks are interfacing, there will still be a problem because rules for choice and form of entry can be variously interpreted. For a cooperative system to function effectively, the cataloging rules must be interpreted in the same way by anyone who uses them.

In the CONSER experiment, we agreed to accept bibliographic description from other U.S. libraries, and the choice and form of entry for Canadian corporate bodies from the National Library of Canada. But to achieve common interpretability of "rules," we may move to accept the idea of the unit entry based on description. Under this system, the full bibliographic record is "entered" under title, rather than author, with added entries as "access" points in the machine-readable file. When the name authority file is interactive on-line with the bibliographic file, it will be possible to approach a work from any access point, and the "unit" entry will be given. Simplified cataloging rules would result, because there would no longer be the problem of choice of entry, although there would be guiding rules for determining the access points. A priority order for access points could be established, leaving rules only for description and form of entry. The unit-entry approach, in short, allows one file for any one author. Translated into print, unit entry makes possible a book catalog in register form; that is, entries are in no particular order, but uniquely numbered. The index entry, which is a brief record, references the unique number and gives access to the base record, which shows all access points.

Assuming that these projects are successful and that we continue to move in these directions, we can envisage a national network in which authority informa- tion and current cataloging records are on-line, and retrospective conversion is being carried out incrementally. The Library of Congress, which has provided bibliographic services to academic and other libraries for three-quarters of a cen- tury, will continue to provide traditional sources of cataloging data as long as such services are needed. Users at LC will consult the Library's catalog by CRT, while also having access to the "historical" card catalog for older titles. Books or mi- croform catalogs in a register/index format will be used for backup to the system. At the same time, we shall be cooperating with regional consortia acting as secon- dary distributors of LC data on-line or off-line.

A fully developed network could relieve regional subsystems of the necessity of maintaining their own copies of the master data base. Individual records could be available on demand; long searches could be done off-line, if necessary, in a batched mode. Bibliographic information would flow in both directions, and LC would also cooperate with major abstracting and indexing services toward the creation of an ever more comprehensive data base.

Network Development Office at LC

This structure will not be simple to construct. A nationwide network, according to the NCLIS *1974–1975 Annual Report*, should provide: (1) encouragement and promulgation of standards, (2) inducement to make major resource collections available nationwide, (3) promulgation of application of new forms of technology, (4) support of research and development, and (5) the fostering of cooperation with national and international programs. Toward these goals, LC in 1976 established a Network Development Office. The office has several objectives to assure that LC meets its responsibility in regard to networking. These objectives include: (1) to develop LC's overall plan with other units in LC for networking for the national library community relating to bibliographic services that result from technical processing activities within LC; (2) to recommend short- and long-range programs and priorities; (3) to design and develop a computer-based national library net- work and its configuration in coordination with other network-related organiza- tions; (4) to serve as liaison with national and international groups concerned with automating and sharing bibliographic resources. The role of LC in the evolving network was the subject of a study conducted by a contractor for the Network Development Office with a grant from NCLIS.

We believe the national network will develop from existing library systems and networks; we know that this will take many years and much effort. Because no identical internal systems for handling information now exist or are expected to be developed in the near future, standardization for exchange of records must be achieved to develop compatibility between these systems. We also feel that the bibliographic apparatus of LC constitutes an essential building block in a national program, but we know that LC cannot perform all the tasks or provide all the products and services required by the national network. Academic libraries are playing, and will continue to play, an important role individually and through cooperative projects such as those described earlier in helping us to achieve bibliographic control in the United States. Today we are concerned with bibliographic control, not only from a single institution's point of view, but from a national and international point of view. The problem becomes the creation and maintenance of a union catalog where each record is represented only once and stored in some meaningful way in relation to the other records. The Library of Congress stands ready to work with other centers of excellence existing in our academic and research libraries to build this file cooperatively as a first step toward resource sharing. Thus, our efforts will be concentrated on the implementation of an integrated, meaningful system for all. As NCLIS has stated: "Ready access to information and knowledge is essential to individual advancement as well as to national growth. . . . The need for information is felt at all levels of society, regardless of an individual's location, social condition, or intellectual achievement."[5]

IMPACT OF A NATIONAL BIBLIOGRAPHIC DATA BASE

Once we achieve effective bibliographic control, we can look seriously at the possibilities it offers in terms of identification, location, and distribution of information. A national network would free academic and other librarians from many of the routine chores of processing and locating material. They would be able to turn their attention to the actual transfer of information to the student, scholar, and researcher. As Shera has said, "Increasing the capacity of the Library-refrigerator does not solve the intellectual problem of the effective utilization of knowledge. How do we know what man will profit most when choosing his reading and how will we know where to find it? These are the fundamental questions to which librarians of the future must seek the answers."[6]

The academic or public librarian of the future would be called on to interpret the many points of access for the patron. These are some of the results of applying technology to technical processing as it has been accomplished so far and as I foresee it happening in the future. But I can only echo Shera in saying that I foresee the eventual impact of these applications as primarily affecting the reference functions of the library.

The on-line catalog discussed earlier would allow greater access to information than ever before. The points of access provided by machine in an indexlike approach would expand the fields of access. A patron would be more likely to find precisely the material he or she wants, with less irrelevant information, because on-line queries could be qualified more readily. Of course, having a national machine-readable data base would not automatically eliminate the problems of library catalogs if we use the file only to produce more cards. Cards should be eliminated. We cannot indefinitely afford to maintain two systems of catalog control, especially when a machine-readable catalog would offer better access to the accumulation of stored data than does the manual catalog.

Although existing MARC searching mechanisms offer limited access at this time, the system will be continuously improved as we expand our search capability. We intend to perfect the on-line catalog, backed up by batched off-line searches, until the system is as perfect as we can make it. Only then will LC close its manual catalog. Of course, we anticipate keeping this tool for retrospective searches, because we see little possibility that all the records could ever be converted, although shared conversion of retrospective records will certainly lessen the frequency with which the card catalog must be consulted.

As we move further into bibliographic and technical standardization, we can hope for a standard querying language. The language would permit a librarian to query his or her system, and if the request could not be satisfied, the system would "translate" the query into a form that could then be transmitted directly to other machine systems. We should see more direct linkages with the many commercial data bases on the market. It is likely that such services as Lockheed, SDC, and the *New York Times* Information Bank would be brokered by more of the network centers and available to all in that system.

As bibliographic control expands, we shall see more, not less, emphasis put on collection building. Academic libraries would be able to concentrate on building the collections necessary to serve their students and scholars. They would be able, through technology, to survey their clientele to ascertain what is most used and most wanted. Little-used items need not be acquired, if they could be easily located elsewhere. At the same time, larger academic and research libraries would be able to concentrate more on one of their most important functions, the building of distinctive collections staffed by specialists who would need to spend less time on the routine aspects of librarianship. At LC, we look forward to the day when we, too, can better serve the scholars who use our collections. As Daniel J. Boorstin, Librarian of Congress, said during a talk in November 1976:

> We must be fertile and comprehensive, not only in our collections, but in our use of our treasures. . . . Earlier ages have been oppressed by ignorance. It would be ironic if ours should be victimized by the excess of knowledge. . . . We must not only help any willing person to survey the wilderness of knowledge, we must help him find his way.

Proposed National Lending System for Serials

One concrete proposal directed toward the concept of sharing resources and responsibilities is to develop a national lending system for serials. A subcommittee of NCLIS was commissioned to study the feasibility of a national periodicals system similar to that of the British Lending Library. Six academic librarians were selected to participate in this study. The development of such a system would take a great deal of pressure off the larger academic and research libraries, which are increasingly called upon for interlibrary loan of serials. As subscription prices rise precipitously, more serials are cut from the budgets of smaller academic libraries, which then must call on the "wealthier" academic and research libraries for assistance. Due in great part to the efforts of ANSI (American National Standards Institute) Z-39 committee (on which Orne has served for so many years), we are much closer to the control of serials. As standards become realities, and as we cooperatively build a serials file on-line through projects such as CONSER, we approach a nationwide union list of serials. However, increased access means increased demand. For that reason, the idea of a national lending library seems all the more necessary.

Various Forms of Document Delivery

Looking further into the future, we can imagine even greater effects of technology on the academic library especially in the fields of science and technology. The NCLIS Ad-Hoc Subcommittee on the Probable Impact of Economic and Technological Trends has presented us with many stimulating ideas. These include the "synoptic" journal, where full text will be delivered on demand. An eight-by-ten-inch page of text can now be transmitted in six minutes or less by telecopier on commercial, telephone-connected equipment. As band width is expanded, it would be feasible to send a page of text not only cross-country, but around the world, in fractions of seconds, and at a foreseeable cost of five to ten cents per page.

Other advances in technology would improve upon what the NCLIS subcommittee calls the "electronic mailbox," that is, personalized selective dissemination of information whereby the client of an academic library fills out an interest profile that is stored in his or her regional network. This could be matched periodically (monthly, weekly, daily) to the records in the data base, and relevant citations or full text could be delivered to the user by printout or by television display, at the office or at home. The subcommittee also puts forth the "shoe box" file concept, in which a scientist would input his findings directly into computer storage, which would then be synthesized or "written up" by technical information specialists for publication on demand. The impact on research in academic libraries would be significant.

I foresee less concern in the future with the document itself, which would be available in any of several formats. The important aspect will be the content, and the academic librarian, no longer serving as custodian, will become an intermediary, a deliverer of information to the student/scholar. The librarian may well be supplying the document through improved computer-output microforms (COM).

One of the earliest uses of microcards by librarians was to have the entire document stored with the catalog card on the back of the fiche; when the patron looked up the bibliographic information in the catalog, he or she got the document simultaneously. The COM system offers the potential for a similar sort of service. With the refinement of the technology we now have at hand, a researcher can query the system, find his or her information, and then read it via CRT or have it printed out as fiche, again at a cost of five to ten cents per fiche. (Television transmission from microformats is a commercial reality in some banks at present, used mainly for signature verification.) A more rudimentary version of this service is currently employed at the U.S. Senate Library, where government documents are available on microfiche, and a copy of the fiche can be made in a matter of seconds. This system still uses a manual index to locate the document, but soon such an index and text may be part of a stored system, with fiche being produced directly, on demand.

Microfiche documents can be stored locally or moved by satellite transmission. When such systems are available, we shall greatly lessen the problems of interlibrary loan and circulation; the researcher will be given the text at a nominal cost or free of charge. In such systems, academic libraries will better serve the needs of the student/scholar by delivering the information itself, rather than by providing only bibliographic citations.

Academic libraries will continue to contain books, I have no doubt, but they will depend more on warehousing or remote storage as technology improves. The computer allows for automatic location and, with satellite transmission and computer-output microform, for automatic delivery. Or, we may read from the television screen at home, with the "broadcast" coming from a remote location. "Optical storage" is now less expensive than magnetic tape in large-scale, read-only applications, and so we may see more of such storing and broadcasting.

The question of funding innovative enterprises such as these is of course a large one; the politics of who pays for information will change as we venture further into such shared systems. As regional networks grow, we may see federal funding going to the consortia that will serve the greatest number of people. Again, economics will encourage greater cooperative efforts, and academic libraries will play an important role.

Expanded Reference and Referral Services

As possibilities become realities, and as we spend less time on processing materials, we shall have more time to devote to other responsibilities. I see LC acting as a stimulus for cooperation and devoting more time to serving its special constituencies. Special libraries and smaller public libraries will be served as adequately as are academic research libraries and large public libraries. The Library of Congress will give more attention to the intellectual needs of all its clients, as it is currently giving to Congress through the Congressional Research Service. Like schools, libraries are subsidized by tax dollars; as demand increases, libraries will be expected to produce more for the patron. National reference service at LC will become a reality. Currently, LC is experimenting with a pilot project for telephone reference service to a group of academic and research libraries and expects to expand it along the lines of the national network.

Someday there may be a national bibliographic service in which bibliographers enter citations into a data base, or possibly several bases, such as foreign affairs, the arts, economics. The citations could be from books, journals, and newspapers. Special-interest bibliographies of current materials would be available on-line. Data bases should also be developed for microform masters, government documents, and so forth, in addition to those for monographs and serials. An interlibrary loan system, based on the bibliographic data base, would be established, with automatic switching of requests until an item is located.

A national referral center for multiple disciplines should be a not-too-distant reality; LC provides services of this type in science and technology now through the National Referral Center. A patron queries the data base on the subject of his or her interest and is given names and addresses of organizations that have volunteered to answer reference questions in that field.

The opportunities for expanded reference services in academic libraries are enormous, thanks to the wonders of technology. And as information comes under bibliographic control, as access points multiply, the reference librarian of the future will become as much a translator as an advisor. The reference librarian will need to assess accurately the researcher's need, because precision will make a difference in terms of the cost of computer search time. Faced with a multiplicity of sources, both manual and automated, and with numerous options on how the text will be delivered, the librarian must steer through the maze, determine search strategy, and deliver the information itself, rather than merely send the reader to the card catalog. It is not too much to hope that the technology may well bring students and scholars back to libraries. And this is where they should be if the academic libraries are indeed to supplement the roles of the educational institutions in the years ahead.

These are a few ideas on how technology may affect the academic library of the future; it can go in any one of a number of ways. To quote Orne one last time, "the point is that librarians, publishers, information scientists, and any other concerned persons should now take a new look at the present and future, and jointly mark out the full program of work to be done as well as some considerations of priorities."[7]

We have, I believe, made a beginning—we know we must cooperate to achieve bibliographic control, improve access, and share resources. We must keep moving toward standardization where necessary to realize the potential allowed to us by present and future technology. Jerrold Orne has brought these needs to our attention; I hope that we, as librarians, can live up to the promise of the future that he has shown us.

NOTES

1. Jerrold Orne, "Standards in Library Technology," *Library Trends* 21 (October 1972): 296. A special issue entitled *Standards for Libraries*.
2. Jesse H. Shera, "The Library: Institutional Deep-Freeze or Intellectual Accelerator?" *Western Reserve University Outlook* 3 (Summer 1966): 6.
3. Henriette D. Avram, *MARC, Its History and Implications* (Washington, D.C.: Library of Congress, 1975), p. 21.
4. Orne, "Standards in Library Technology," p. 286.
5. *Annual Report to the President and Congress, '74/'75* (Washington, D.C.: National Commission on Libraries and Information Science, 1976), p. 5.
6. Shera, "The Library," p. 7.
7. Orne, "Standards in Library Technology," p. 292.

ABOUT THE AUTHOR

William J. Welsh is the Deputy Librarian of Congress. He is a graduate of the University of Notre Dame. Joining the staff of the Library of Congress in 1947, he rose through several positions until being appointed to his present post in 1976. In 1971, the American Library Association presented him with the Melvil Dewey Award.

PUBLICATIONS OF JERROLD ORNE

BOOKS AND PARTS OF BOOKS

Report on the Precautionary Measures Regarding Its Collections Adopted by the Library of Congress. . . . Washington, D.C.: Library of Congress, 1941. 25 pp.

"The Music Library in the College of the Future." In *Music and Libraries*, ed. by Richard S. Hill, pp. 37–45. Washington, D.C.: Music Library Association, 1943.

Subject Heading List for Naval Research Libraries (with Grace Swift). Washington, D.C.: U.S. Navy Department, Executive Office of the Secretary, 1945. 481 pp.

Textbook for the Yoeman Striker (with K. W. Joy and R. K. Burrell). San Diego, Calif.: U.S. Naval Training Center, 1945, 351 pp.

Subject Heading List for Naval Research Libraries, 2nd ed. (with Grace Swift). Washington, D.C.: U.S. Navy Department, Executive Office of the Secretary, 1946. 499 pp.

Subject Headings for Technical Libraries (with Grace Swift). Washington, D.C.: U.S. Department of Commerce, July 1947. 167 pp.

Language of the Foreign Book Trade. Chicago: American Library Association, 1949. 88 pp.

El Futuro de la Biblioteca en Cuba. Havana: Escuela Cubana de Bibliotecarios, 1950. 23 pp.

Report of a Survey of the Kirkwood Public Library. . . . St. Louis: Washington University, 1951. 54 pp.

"A Documents Housing Plan." In *Production and Use of Technical Reports*, ed. by B. M. Fry and Reverend J. J. Kortendick, S.S., pp. 138–147. Washington, D.C.: Catholic University of America Press, 1955.

"Storage Warehouses." In *The State of the Library Art*, ed. by R. R. Shaw, vol. 3, pt. 3, pp. 1–52. New Brunswick, N.J.: Rutgers University Press, 1960.

Report of a Survey of Library Facilities and Services at Redstone Arsenal, June 1961 (with Joseph Shipman and Robert Vosper). Huntsville, Ala.: George C. Marshall Space Flight Center, 1961. 18 pp.

Language of the Foreign Book Trade, 2nd ed. Chicago: American Library Association, 1962. 213 pp.

Education and Libraries: Selected Papers of Louis Round Wilson (editor, with Maurice Tauber). Hamden, Conn.: Shoe String Press, 1966. 344 pp.

"Librarianship Today—Crisis or Change." In *University of Tennessee Library Lectures, 1967–1969*, ed. by R. J. Bassett, pp. 1–12. Knoxville: University of Tennessee, 1969.

Research Librarianship: Essays in Honor of Robert B. Downs. New York: R. R. Bowker, 1971. 162 pp.

"Microforms and the Research Library." In *Proceedings of the National Microfilm Association, 1970 Convention*, vol. 19, pp. 56–61.

"Future Academic Library Administration—Whither or Whether." In *The Academic Library: Essays in Honor of Guy R. Lyle*, ed. by Evan Ira Farber and Ruth Walling, pp. 82–95. Metuchen, N.J.: Scarecrow Press, 1974.

Language of the Foreign Book Trade, 3rd ed. Chicago: American Library Association, 1976. 333 pp.

"Standards." In *The ALA Yearbook: A Review of Library Events 1976*. Chicago: American Library Association, 1977.

ARTICLES

"The Sources of 'I Promessi Sposi.' " *Modern Philology* 38, no. 4 (May 1941): 405–420.

"The Library of Congress Prepares for Emergencies." *A.L.A. Bulletin* 35, no. 6 (June 1941): 341–348.

Review of *The Annual Report of the Librarian of Congress for the Fiscal Year Ending June 30, 1941* (Washington, D.C.: Government Printing Office, 1942). *Library Quarterly* 12, no. 4 (October 1942): 848–850.

"The College Library." *Illinois Libraries* 25, no. 1 (January 1943): 11–14.

Review of *The Annual Reports of the Librarian of Congress* (Washington, D.C.: Government Printing Office, 1941–1944). *Library Quarterly* 14, no. 3 (July 1944): 239–245.

"Library Division of the Office of the Publications Board." *Special Libraries* 37, no. 7 (September 1946): 203–209.

"Training for Librarianship in Missouri." *Missouri Library Association Quarterly* 8, no. 2 (June 1947): 32–36.

"Training for Librarianship in Missouri." *Illinois Libraries* 29 (1947): 432–433.

"Subject Analysis—a Rising Star." *Special Libraries* 39, no. 2 (February 1948): 42–46.

"We Have Cut Our Cataloging Costs." *Library Journal* 73 (October 15, 1948): 1476–1478.

Review of *Index to Catholic Pamphlets in the English Language* (Washington, D.C.: 1949). *Library Journal* 74 (May 15, 1949): 805.

"Sampling Survey of Missouri Library Personnel." *Missouri Library Association Quarterly* 10, no. 3 (September 1949): 86–90.

Review of *Fifteenth Century Printed Books at the University of Illinois* (Urbana, Ill.: University of Illinois Press, 1949). *College and Research Libraries* 11, no. 1 (January 1950): 66–67.

Review of Georgette de Grolier, ed., *Livre et Document: Etudes sur le Livre . . .* (St. Cloud: Editions de la Revue du Livre et des Bibliothèques, 1943). *Library Quarterly* 20, no. 1 (January 1950): 66–67.

"What Binders Can Teach Us." *Library Journal* 75 (May 15, 1950): 837–841.

"El Futuro de la Biblioteca en Cuba." *Boletin de la Asociacion Cubana de Bibliotecarios* 2, no. 2 (June 1950): 35–40.

Review of *Library of Congress Subject Catalog* (Washington, D.C.: Government Printing Office, 1950). *Library of Congress Information Bulletin* 9 (June 12, 1950): 14–15.

"The Future of Libraries in Cuba." *Missouri Library Association Quarterly* 11, no. 3 (September 1950): 75–83.

"Planning a New Library School in Cuba." *Library of Congress Information Bulletin* 9, no. 38 (September 18, 1950): Appendix, pp. 1–9.

Review of *Annual Report of the Library of Congress . . . 1949* (Washington, D.C.: Government Printing Office, 1950). *Library Quarterly* 21, no. 1 (January 1951): 58–60.

"A Serials Information Clearing House." *Serials Slants* 1, no. 4 (April 1951): 10–17.

"Who Is Making Catalogers Today?" *Journal of Cataloging and Classification* 7, no. 2 (Spring 1951): 28–32.

"The Kirkwood Public Library—A Survey." *Missouri Library Association Quarterly* 12, no. 2 (June 1951): 184–187.

"Cuban Libraries" (with Josefina Mayol). *The Library Quarterly* 22, no. 2 (April 1952): 92–124.

"Maintenance and Reduction of a Collection." *American Documentation* 2, no. 2 (April 1952): 101–105.

"Preserving the American Heritage in a Regimented Society." *College and Research Libraries* 14, no. 1 (January 1953): 46–51.

Review of *Eastern Caribbean Regional Library* (Port-of-Spain, Trinidad, B.W.I.: Eastern Caribbean Regional Library, 1951). *Library Quarterly* 23, no. 1 (January 1953): 60–61.

"Major Problems of Military Libraries." *Special Libraries* 44 (September 1953): 268–271.

"An Experiment in Integrated Library Service." *College and Research Libraries* 16, no. 4 (October 1955): 353–359.

"The Air University Library" (Building Study). *Library Journal* 80 (December 1, 1955): 2713–2718.

"Librarian Looks at Military Literature." *Special Libraries* 47 (October 1956): 373–377.

"The Air University Library Building." *College and Research Libraries* 18, no. 4 (July 1957): 275–280.

Review of *Bookman's Concise Dictionary* (New York: Philosophical Library, 1956). *Library Quarterly* 27 (July 1957): 218.

"New Pattern of Service." *North Carolina Libraries* 16 (February 1958): 51–54.

"Wanted: A Million Dollars." *Library Journal* 83 (March 15, 1958): 798–802.

Review of David T. Pottinger, ed., *The French Book Trade in the Ancient Regime, 1500–1791* (Cambridge, Mass.: Harvard University Press, 1958). *Library Journal* 83 (July 1958): 2027.

Review of *Library Trends: Building Library Resources through Cooperation* (Urbana, Ill.: University of Illinois Library School, January 1958). *Library Journal* 83 (November 1, 1958): 3086.

Review of W. V. Jackson, *Studies in Library Resources* (Champaign, Ill.: Illinois Union Bookstore, 1958). *Library Journal* 83 (December 15, 1958): 3500–3501.

"La Biblioteca Nacional como Centro de Reproduccion Fotografica de Documentos." *Boletin de la Asociacion Cubana de Bibliotecarios* 11, nos. 1–2 (March-June 1959): 2–6.

Review of E. E. Williams, *Serviceable Reservoir* (Washington, D.C.: U.S.B.E., 1959). *Special Libraries* 51 (January 1960): 44.

"Library Binding Standards." *The Rub-off* 11 (November 1960): 1–3.

"Storage and Deposit Libraries." *College and Research Libraries* 21 (November 1960): 446–452.

Review of R. E. Ellsworth, *Planning the College and University Library Building* (Boulder, Colo.: privately published, 1960). *Library Journal* 86 (March 1, 1961): 982–983.

Review of B. C. Brooks, ed., *Editorial Practice in Libraries* (London: Aslib, 1961). *Library Quarterly* 31 (July 1961): 284–285.

"A Preliminary Survey of Facilities Needs in Academic Libraries of the United States." A working paper prepared for a meeting of the National Science Foundation in Washington, D.C., March 8, 1961. Mimeographed. Chapel Hill: University of North Carolina Library, 1961. 10 pp.

"Library Binding Standards." *Library Journal* 86 (September 15, 1961): 2889–2892.

Review of *Development of Performance Standards for Library Binding: Phase I*, Report of the Survey Team (Chicago: American Library Association, 1961). *Library Journal* 86 (September 15, 1961): 2918.

Review of E. E. Williams, *Farmington Plan Handbook* (Ithaca, N.Y.: Cornell University Library, 1961). *Library Journal* 86 (December 15, 1961): 4269–4270.

Review of Guy R. Lyle, *Administration of the College Library* (New York: Wilson, 1961). *Southeastern Librarian* 11 (Winter 1961): 323–324.

"Profile: John W. Cronin." *Library Journal* 87 (January 15, 1962): 176–177.

Review of University of Illinois Graduate School of Library Science, *Collecting Science Literature of General Reading* (Champaign, Ill.: Illinois Bookstore, 1961). *College and Research Libraries* 23 (March 1962): 174–176.

"Shortage or Waste?" *Library Journal* 87 (April 15, 1962): 1564.

"Preconference Agenda. Library Binding Workshop" (with A. J. Richter). *Library Journal* 87 (August 1962): 2698–2699.

Review of J. P. Harthan, *Bookbinding* (New York: British Information Services, 1961). *Library Journal* 87 (August 1962): 2725–2726.

"Signs of the Times." *Library Journal* 87 (November 15, 1962): 4154.

"Newspapers: A Regional Resource." *Library Journal* 88 (April 15, 1963): 1612–1614.

"Cold Meet." *Library Journal* 88 (May 15, 1963): 1960.

"Resources of Foreign Scientific Literature: Acquisition on a National Scale." *American Documentation* 14 (July 1963): 229–233.

"New Generation, Talkers or Doers?" *Library Journal* 88 (August 1963): 2852.

"Transliteration of Modern Russian." *Library Journal* 88 (November 1, 1963): 4157–4160.

Review of *Convegno di studi sulle biblioteche universitarie, 16–17 Maggio 1960* (Napoli, 1962). *College and Research Libraries* 24 (November 1963): 524–525.

"Considerations on the Conversion of One Written Language to Another with Particular Reference to Cyrillic Letters." UNESCO/NS/Doc/WP1.3. Published as a working paper in English and French. Paris, 1963. 10 pp.

"The USBE Story." *Library Journal* 89 (February 5, 1964): 803–806.

"Transliteration of Modern Russian." *Library Resources and Technical Services* 8 (Winter 1964): 51–53.

"Library Education—What's Missing?" *Education for Librarianship* 5, no. 2 (Fall 1964): 90–91.

"Libraries in Vietnam: An Underdeveloped Country." *Southeastern Librarian* 15 (Winter 1965): 203–207.

"A Survey of Facilities for the Sciences and Social Sciences in Academic Libraries of the United States." March 1965. Mimeographed. 11 pp.

Review of J. G. Cox, *Optimum Storage of Library Material. College and Research Libraries* 26 (May 1965): 250.

"Extending the Carolina Cooperation." *Southeastern Librarian* 15 (Spring 1965): 12–14.

"The Libraries of Vietnam." *South Carolina Librarian* 10 (March 1966): 7–10.

"Library Education and the Talent Shortage." *Library Journal* 91 (April 1, 1966): 1763–1764.

"Title 11-C, A Little Revolution." *Southeastern Librarian* 16 (Fall 1966): 164–167.

"Current Trends in Collection Development in University Libraries" (editor, with B. E. Powell). *Library Trends* 15, no. 2 (October 1966): 197–334.

"The Libraries of the University of North Carolina and of Duke University" (with B. E. Powell). *Library Trends* 15, no. 2 (October 1966): 222–247.

"Biographical Sketch: William A. Pease." *College and Research Libraries: News* 3 (March 1967): pp. 30–31.

"A Future for Humanism." *Library Journal* 92, no. 10 (May 15, 1967): 1893–1895.

"A Time for Standards." *Library Binder* 15, no. 1 (May 1967): 3–6, 24.

"Standards and the New Technology of Information Science." *Magazine of Standards* 38, no. 6 (June 1967): 173–175.

"The Place of Standards in the New Technology of Information Science." *Special Libraries* 58, no. 10 (December 1967): 703–706.

"Academic Library Building in 1967." *Library Journal* 92, no. 21 (December 1, 1967): 4345–4350.

"Renaissance or Oblivion." *The Rub-off* 19, no. 2 (March–April 1968): 1–4.

"Trends in North Carolina Academic Libraries." *North Carolina Libraries* 26 (Summer 1968): 101–103.

"Current Approaches to Standards for Information Science and Library Problem Areas." *California Librarian* 29 (October 1968): 256–262. Also published in *Special Librarian Association. Southern California Chapter Bulletin* 29 (Spring 1968): 90–93.

"Cronin and National Bibliographic Services." *Library Resources and Technical Services* 12, no. 4 (Fall 1968): 390–391.

"Academic Library Building in 1968." *Library Journal* 93, no. 21 (December 1, 1968): 4493–4497.

"Portents and Shibboleths." *Library Journal* 93, no. 22 (December 15, 1968): 4624–4627.

"The Place of the Library in the Evaluation of Graduate Work." *College and Research Libraries* 30 (January 1969): 25–31.

"Financing and Cost of University Library Buildings." *Library Trends* 18 (October 1969): 150–165.

Review of Ralph E. Ellsworth, *Planning the College and University Library Building*, 2nd ed. (Boulder, Colo.: Pruett, 1968). *Library Journal* 94 (October 15, 1969): 3628.

"Academic Library Building in 1969." *Library Journal* 94, no. 21 (December 1, 1969): 4364–4368. Also in *Bowker Annual of Library and Book Trade Information, 1970* (New York: R. R. Bowker, 1970), pp. 215–221.

Review of Bernard Houghton, ed., *Standardization for Documentation* (Hamden, Conn.: Archon Books, 1969). *Journal of Library Automation* 2, no. 4 (December 1969): 276.

"The Place of Standards in Libraries of the Future." *Kentucky Library Association Bulletin* 34, no. 1 (January 1970): 5–10.

Review of Ralph E. Ellsworth, *The Economics of Book Storage in College and University Libraries* (Metuchen, N.J.: Scarecrow, 1969). *Library Journal* 95 (April 1, 1970): 1299.

Review of Irene A. Braden, *The Undergraduate Library* (Chicago: American Library Association, 1970). *Library Journal* 95 (June 1, 1970): 2105.

Review of Michael Brawne, *Libraries: Architecture and Equipment* (New York: Praeger, 1970). *Library Journal* 95 (June 1, 1970): 2106.

"The Undergraduate Library." *Library Journal* 95 (June 15, 1970): 2230–2233.

"Library Standards." *Law Library Journal* 63 (November 1970): 532–537, 550.

"Academic Library Building in 1970." *Library Journal* 95 (December 1, 1970): 4107–4112. Also in *Bowker Annual of Library and Book Trade Information, 1970* (New York: R. R. Bowker, 1971), pp. 231–239.

"Architects' Fees: Their Place in Library Planning." *Library Journal* 95 (December 1, 1970): 4099–4106.

"College and Research Libraries." *North Carolina Libraries* 29 (Spring 1971): C4–C6.

"Time for Reflection, and a Program for Action." *Southeastern Librarian* 21 (Spring 1971): 36–44.

Review of *Problems in University Library Management* (Booz, Allen, and Hamilton, Inc.). *College and Research Libraries* 32 (May 1971): 229–230.

Review of S. Langmead and M. Beckman, *New Library Design: Guidelines to Planning Academic Library Buildings* (Toronto: Wiley, 1970). *Library Journal* 96 (June 15, 1971): 2063.

Review of Keyes D. Metcalf and Ralph E. Ellsworth, *Planning the Academic Library*. *Library Journal* 96 (October 1, 1971): 3101.

"Newspaper Resources of the Southeastern Region: An Experiment in Coordinated Development." *Southeastern Librarian* 21 (Winter 1971): 226–235.

"Renaissance of Academic Library Building, 1967–1971." *Library Journal* 96 (December 1, 1971): 3947–3967. Also in *Bowker Annual of Library and Book Trade Information, 1972* (New York: R. R. Bowker, 1972), pp. 320–356.

Review of Charles H. Baumann, *The Influence of Angus Snead MacDonald and the Snead Bookstack on Library Architecture* (Metuchen, N.J.: Scarecrow, 1972). *Library Journal* 97 (June 15, 1972): 2163.

Review of *Proceedings of the Second Conference on Federal Information Resources*, Washington, D.C., March 30–31, 1971. *College and Research Libraries* 33 (May 1972): 244–245.

"Standards in Library Technology." *Library Trends* 21 (October 1972): 286–297.

"Academic Library Building in 1972." *Library Journal* 97 (December 1, 1972): 3849–3855. Also in *Bowker Annual of Library and Book Trade Information, 1973* (New York: R. R. Bowker, 1973), pp. 454–462.

Review of Alphonse F. Trezza, ed., *Library Buildings: Innovation for Changing Needs*. Proceedings of The Library Buildings Institute. . . 1967 (Chicago: American Library Association, 1972). *Library Journal* 97 (December 1, 1972): 3878.

Review of *Advances in Librarianship*, vol. 3. *Library Journal* 98 (May 1, 1973): 1454.

Review of Ralph E. Ellsworth, *Academic Library Buildings*. *Library Journal* 98 (June 15, 1973): 1895.

"Academic Library Building in 1973." *Library Journal* 98 (December 1, 1973): 3511–3516. Also in *Bowker Annual of Library and Book Trade Information, 1974* (New York: R. R. Bowker, 1974), pp. 276–281.

"Great Academic Libraries of the Military Establishment." *Library Journal* 99 (February 15, 1974): 458–463.

Review of Ralph E. Ellsworth, *Planning Manual for Academic Library Buildings*. *Library Journal* 99 (April 1, 1974): 968.

Review of James Thompson, *Introduction to University Library Administration*. *Library Journal* 99 (November 1, 1974): 2822.

Review of *Library and Information Services for Special Groups*. *Library Journal* 99 (November 1, 1974): 2822.

"Academic Library Building in 1974." *Library Journal* 99 (December 1, 1974): 3099–3104. Also in *Bowker Annual of Library and Book Trade Information, 1975* (New York: R. R. Bowker, 1975), pp. 251–259.

Review of Godfrey Thompson, *Planning and Design of Library Buildings*. *Library Journal* 100 (May 15, 1975): 928.

Review of Herbert Ward, ed., *New Library Buildings*. *Library Journal* 100 (June 15, 1975): 1196.

Review of G. R. Lyle, *Administration of the College Library*, 4th ed. *Journal of Academic Librarianship* 1 (July 1975): 24.

"Academic Library Building in 1975." *Library Journal* 100 (December 1, 1975): 2207.

"Academic Library Buildings: A Century in Review." *College and Research Libraries* 37 (July 1976): 316–331.

Review of H. B. Schell, ed., *Reader on the Library Building*. *Journal of Academic Librarianship* 2 (July 1976): 140.

"Academic Library Building in 1976" (with J. O. Gosling). *Library Journal* 101 (December 1, 1976): 2435–2439.

Review of *Libraries and Library Services in the Southeast: A Report of the Southeastern Cooperative Library Survey 1972–74*. *Journal of Academic Librarianship* 3 (May 1977): 122.

Review of J. A. Urquhart and N. C. Urquhart, *Relegation and Stock Control in Libraries*. *Library Journal* 102 (May 1, 1977): 995.

Review of Herbert Ward, *New Library Buildings: 1976 Issue, Years 1973–74*. *Library Journal* 102 (May 15, 1977): 1161

JOURNALS EDITED

Editor, *Missouri Library Association Quarterly*, 1947–1951.
Editor, *Washington University Library Studies*, 1949–1951.

Associate Editor, *American Documentation*, 1953–1957.
Editorial Consultant, *Library Journal*, 1962–1964.
Editor, *Southeastern Librarian*, 1966–1972.
Issue Editor, *Library Trends* 15, no. 2 (October 1966).

INDEX